A DALES
NATURALIST

Roger Nelson

DALESMAN

First Published in Great Britain 1993 by
Dalesman Publishing Company Limited,
Stable Courtyard, Broughton Hall,
Skipton, North Yorkshire, BD23 3AE.
Text and drawings © 1993 **Roger Nelson**
Photographs by **Norman Duerden** and by **Roger Nelson**
© 1993

Dedicated to the memory of my father and mother

NORMAN AND PHYLLIS NELSON

of

STORITHS

ISBN **1 85568 058 0**
Typeset by **Lands Services, East Molesey, Surrey.**
Printed and bound by **Redwood Press Ltd.**

Contents

1 *January*

Over the years there have probably been more letters to *The Times* about the arrival of the first cuckoo than about any other great momentous issue. It is little wonder that something so evocative should arouse our perennial interest. Many of us have our roots in rural smallholdings, and our daydreams tend to wander towards quaint cottages with honeysuckle round the door.

In my part of the Dales the first cuckoo is heard within three days either side of the 27th April. However, that is only one of hundreds of events in the natural cycle which recur within a few days of any particular date each year. I have records of these things going back many years, from thousands of rambles around my home above Bolton Abbey. My aim in this book will be to give a week-by-week account of what to look out for as a naturalist in the Dales, so that you may increase your awareness and enjoyment of nature.

In writing a book to this sort, the first difficulty is knowing where to begin. A case has been made for starting a country diary in October, when hill sheep are being flushed in preparation for tupping and arable land is being prepared for seed. Dales farmers are more likely to assert that the year begins with lambing time, or with dairy cow turning-out time a few weeks later. An ornithologist might choose the first day of Spring on 21st March, when the main nesting season is just about to start and the first overseas migrants are expected any day.

It may seem as odd that Winter officially starts on 21st December, but that from then onwards the days are actually growing longer. The bleakest winter weather normally falls within the forty days from 8th January to 16th February. Thus there could be justification for starting the year about the 28th January, on the basis that on average it is likely to get warmer thereafter. There seems little logic in starting a New Year 1½ weeks after the shortest day and 4 weeks before the coldest, except that the 1st January falls then. To start there is likely to irritate most people least.

Our ancient forebears pondered less. In times of uncertain life expectancy they knew that the shortest day heralded a period of privation, and that they could best prepare mind and body for it with a celebratory feast. They drank and ate the surfeits of Autumn, nuts and fruit, berry wine and ale, fatted geese and wild game. To bolster their optimism they decorated their huts or halls with bright fresh evergreens and other symbols of renewal and fertility. Their pagan revels still show through in our Christmas festivities.

Unfortunately, by New Year's morning our balding Christmas trees, wrinkled holly berries and flabby mistletoe are most likely to remind us of our own fragile mortality. Now is the time, then, to draw deep breaths of new hope, and to demonstrate our resolve with a brisk long walk in the countryside. Let us see what we shall see, and determine to look afresh at it.

January 1st – 7th

In choosing a route at this time of year, our first consideration must be the weather. It is likely to be cold and windy, with rain or snow showers never far away. The wild birds and animals know this too, and shelter in open woodlands on the lower shopes. In planning a nature walk you should leave the bare tops to those who hike for hiking's sake and those who make a living there. Choose instead a path by becksides and hedgerows, and through mixed woodland. Allow time to stand awhile along the way. Wrap up well, put on your wellies and a waterproof top coat, and remember to take your binoculars.

My first call is to the bank of gorse below the house. True to form there are some bushes in bloom. The golden-yellow flowers have the structure of miniature sweet peas, but are borne on branches as defensively spiny as any desert cactus. Were it not for these spines, gorse would be a valuable livestock browse. Green gorse was milled for winter cattle feed until recent times. The old saying that gorse is in flower when kissing's in fashion is not entirely true, for on its steep stony banks it does not like drought. It therefore flowers least when kissing is most in fashion, in the hottest part of Summer. But even then there will be odd flowers for those who look hard enough, just as there will in the depths of Winter, even if they are coated with ice.

Other flowers which you may find so early in the year include the odd bright daisy or dandelion, if the day is sunny, and perhaps a stunted buttercup or shepherd's purse. However, these are the remnants of last year's flowers, and do not hold any promise of Spring. For that you must wait until you enter the woods, where honeysuckle winds its shreddy-barked stems up the trunks of saplings to reach the light. There you will see that near the end of each vine the side buds are swelling, and at the very tip is a pair of bright new green leaves, first-born twins of the New Year.

And there is bird song to be heard even now, particularly if the day is bright. The starling warm upon the chimney pot momentarily startles me with a clear curlew's call mixed in a brief series of clicks and whistles. Robins and wrens issue bursts of song at rivals, though at this time of year they only sing long enough to resolve the dispute. Rooks tossed on swaying treetops clamour and caw, often squatting in old nests to stake their claims for later.

Perhaps the most consistent singer in this first week of January is the mistle thrush, aptly named the stormcock. In December he establishes himself on a bank well stocked with berry trees, and sings with gradually increasing complexity right through to Spring. He is a greedy pirate, and will defend his chosen haws and hollies against all comers, churring and rattling. But his song, suddenly bursting through the stillness as a snow flurry dies away, ensures his pardon. At present it is no more than a repeated "toodle-teeoo" and variations, but it can be heard a quarter of a mile away, a joyous sound in these dark days.

Not all mistle thrushes establish fixed territories in Winter. Others join in with the mixed flocks which fly low over the pastures and scatter ahead as we walk. Viking fieldfares abound in such flocks, their silvery underwings flashing in the weak sun as they rise. Less noticeable are the redwings, often gathered in holly bushes and crab-apple trees round the field edges. Their smaller size and boldly striped faces readily distinguish redwings from other thrushes, even if the day is too dull to pick out their tawny red flanks.

Following a beck towards the river, I pass below a rough hillside of scattered oak and ash trees undergrown with hawthorn. Here, as expected, there is a pair of bullfinches, so secretive that I might have missed them had it not been for their softly called "teu". Bullfinches are a pest in the orchards of southern counties, but here their soft pinks and greys, picked out by black and white, make their infrequent sightings always welcome.

Along the riverside the dipper hunches on a rock, his chips and churs and warbles mingling with the water's babble as he proclaims his territory. Any venturesome neigh-

Mistle Thrush
(Turdus viscivorus)

Fieldfare
(Turdus pilaris)

Redwing
(Turdus iliacus)

Fieldfares and redwings come to Britain for winter, and often move in mixed flocks. The fieldfare is the larger and noisier of the two, and has a noticeably grey head and rump patch.

Nelson 92

bour which flies by must expect a chase to the boundary already won by this one. There, as the chaser becomes less certain and the neighbour moreso, the boundary is disputed. The two will pose a few feet or just a few inches apart and sing at one another until honour is satisfied, white chests puffed out, white eyelids blinking, and beaks pointing skyward. Meanwhile, under the rippling surface, the ancient crayfish folds her bundle of eggs under her tail and backs further into her watery cave.

In the woods there are still pheasants aplenty, but they are stupid hand-reared birds, as likely to run towards you as away. For me their tinsel colours are no match for the rich brown tapestry of another gamebird which shares their habitat, the lovely long-billed woodcock. One of these latter springs up in front of me from amongst the dead bracken near the wood's edge, and slaloms away effortlessly through the trees on powerful wings.

On the rather bare floor of winter woods it is worth looking out for well-worn badger highways, especially near setts. Over half of all badger setts are on steep banks near to a stream and within 80 yards of the outer wood wall. Latrine pits partly filled with fresh faeces indicate that the sett is occupied. Badger faeces are rather like those of a dog, but usually darker coloured and of a looser consistency. If you find a sett near a public footpath do not linger around or tamper with it, but bear it in mind for later in the year.

If the wood appears quiet and lifeless, make for a point where the deciduous and coniferous trees grow side by side, and then listen. Mixed parties of small birds frequent these areas, and can be located by their tiny squeaking contact calls. Being at the centre of a mixed flock is an exciting experience, and binoculars swivel hither and thither almost as fast as the beaks of the feeding birds. A typical party contains the four common tits (blue, great, coal and long-tailed) with treecreepers and goldcrests. Travelling in flocks gives each individual the advantage of many pairs of eyes keeping watch for danger. In monospecific flocks this advantage has to be balanced against the increased competition from many birds using the same method to look for the same scarce food. The mixed flock provides a solution. Each species has its own special technique and preferred food item, and no individual suffers from undue competition.

Rare visiting species often latch on to these mixed flocks, and today I am lucky enough to see a lesser spotted woodpecker. This tiny gem often passes through the Dales, but is only visible when the trees are leafless. It is about the size of a nuthatch, but with colours, call and flight similar to its greater spotted relative. Unlike either of these commoner species, however, it looks for food mostly on the smallest branches an inch or less in diameter in the tops of tall trees, and so is lost in the leaf canopy for half the year.

And finally, as I approach the wood wall on my way home there is a movement on the ground away to my left. I freeze by a tree, and squeak through tightly pursed lips. A weasel pops its head from the wall. I squeak again and the head pops out 20 feet nearer. How on earth did it cover that distance inside the wall in so little time? Another series of squeaks from me, and the inquisitive little tiger leaves the wall and ripples across the ground towards me. Then it disappears, but pops up again only a few feet away, having travelled among a mole run under the litter. It studies me, moving its head to left and right, bright eyes twinkling. It stands up on its back legs for a better view, dashes back a yard, and does it again. Unlike the larger stoat, it has no black tip to its tail, and the undersides are pure white, not creamy yellow. Now it is so close that I can see the white patches in the pale red at its mouth corners. Then it catches my scent and is gone.

Marvellous little beast! Why do we dull humans use 'weaselly' as a derogatory term? It is a terrific hunter of all small mammals up to the size of a young rabbit, several times its own weight. True, it occasionally raids birds' nests, but then so do the much more common wood mice upon which it preys. True, it probably relishes pheasant chicks. Who can blame it when they are so unfitted for survival that they will later have to be chased to make them fly for gentlemen to shoot? The weasels of the wild woods deserve a better press.

January 8th – 15th

Winter has begun to bite. In the mornings there is thick ice on water in the troughs. Clouds of breath float behind the sheep as they run towards me, their feet clattering on the frozen ground. But frosty nights usually mean cloudless nights, with cloudless days to follow. Never mind if the white frost lingers all day in the shadows of dry stone walls, so long as the sun is bright and the air is still. In this season such days are precious gifts, to farmer and naturalist alike.

We naturalists need look no further than our own gardens for the first delights, since most of us put out some food for the birds in Winter. There are many types of bird food and of bird table which can be made or bought, and different birds have different requirements. I do not like to unbalance natural things too much, and stick to a single nut hopper and a daily handful of mixed leftovers and bread crusts, crumbed in the kitchen blender.

Blue, great and even coal tits will readily hang from nut hoppers, whereas wrens will only take finely grated cheese or peanuts thrown into wall bottoms or other hidden places. Starlings, house sparrows, chaffinches, robins and blackbirds will squabble together on an exposed platform, whilst hedge sparrows mostly creep about below picking up fallen crumbs. Nuthatches will join in the throng on the table, but they specialize in carrying away beakfuls to cache in tree-bark crevices. More splendid visitors such as jays and great spotted woodpeckers can be enticed into gardens near low-land woods, though they are ever cautious. Winter siskins will also visit gardens near woods, and are particularly attracted to orange-stringed nut hoppers. Greenfinches, which are greedy nut feeders in Spring, are much less common just now.

Many birds learn new behaviour from copying others at feeding stations. The classic example is pecking open milk bottle tops, which spread throughout the country within a few years of it first being recorded. I have noticed that hedge sparrows are becoming less timid at bird tables, and they will doubtless evolve a more aggressive strain in the coming years. And blue tits have learnt that if I forget to put out food, they need only peck at the window to remind me.

It has to be seen, however, that excessive tameness or boldness is aberrant behaviour, and Nature does not tolerate this lightly. The hunter, whether it be the stalking lioness or the hovering kestrel, is always on the look-out for anything that is not quite right. So it is, then, that we may be alerted by a sudden silence and panicky flight, and get to the

a. Greenfinch b. Chaffinch c. House Sparrow d. Hedge Sparrow
e. Great Tit f. Blue Tit g. Robin h. Song Thrush i. Blackbird.
j. Starling.

window just in time to see the hawk crouch over a captured bird on the lawn, peck out the top of its head, and flash away with it over the hedge. A feeding robin has itself become food, its only epitaph a few tiny feathers still drifting down.

Kestrels will sometimes learn to take birds from bare gardens with little cover, stooping swiftly to the kill from a half-hidden vantage point. However, they prefer to take prey from the ground in wide open spaces, and concentrate on voles at this time of year. The raptor which accounts for most bird table losses is the yellow-eyed sparrowhawk, swift, powerful and agile. He flies in low, skims over the garden wall, picks out a victim in an instant, and closes in. Sometimes the intended prey gains refuge in a thick bush, where it can lose the hawk in a tangle of branches. Sometimes it finds sanctuary inside a dry stone wall, perhaps leaving the hawk with a tail feather or two. But sometimes again the frantically fleeing bird is hit in mid-air with lethal grace, and is carried away to be plucked and eaten on some favourite rock or stump.

It follows from this that we must site our bird table near to a clump of bushes into which small birds can dive for cover, though not so near that they become prey to hidden cats. If you have no suitable bushes, a loose pile of cut branches is even better.

The sparrowhawk will take birds up to the size of a mistle thrush, but there is another raptor even more potent and deadly. It does not bother our bird tables, unless we keep pigeons round the house. I first saw one in this area in August 1962, when a visiting Scottish keeper made a determined attempt to shoot it. Fortunately these are more enlightened times, and the keepers on our local estate now have written instructions from their employer not to kill this or other raptors. I refer, of course, to the peregrine falcon, which now regularly nests on rocky hilltops in the Craven area, notably around Kilnsey Crag. One has even nested near Leeds city centre in recent years.

In Winter the peregrine roams widely on its peregrinations, often following the main valleys to prey on lapwings and gulls as they cross from coast to coast. It may be seen harrying mallard along the river in the early mornings, or we may simply find a scattered bunch of feathers in an upland pasture as evidence of its passing. Grouse, partridge, lapwing, pigeon and black-headed gull seem to be its favourite victims, though any bird of open spaces in that size range may fall prey. Luckily summer peregrines defend a large territory, and are never likely to be so common as to seriously deplete the population of any of their food species.

The presence of lapwings and gulls up here in Winter is interesting. As a boy I used to believe that lapwings went to Africa for Winter and that gulls were only seen inland when there were storms at sea. Now that we travel more easily ourselves, it has become plain that many lapwings go no further than the nearest muddy estuaries on the Lune and Humber. Since these two are separated by only a few hours steady flight we may see lapwings on arable land just to the east of us on any day of the year, and flocks fly over the Dales in the hardest of weather. These passing flocks often roost on selected holmes, and it is interesting that the overnight roosting fields chosen year after year by the lapwings are those on which the snow thaws first after a heavy fall.

I still believe that herring and black-backed gulls only pass through in Winter if there is bad weather following within 48 hours, though in an English Winter that is a fairly safe bet anyway. Many other sea birds cross from coast to coast in this way, often by night. I have seen a cormorant on the river near Ilkley and found a dead guillemot on the moors above Bolton Abbey. Even more surprisingly, little auks have been found dead or exhausted on Beamsley Beacon and Rombalds Moor, especially after a few days of fog and low cloud.

However, the black-headed gull is now a permanent resident, having adapted its seaside scavenging habits to the increasingly common landfill sites of our consumerist society. Some will go to the estuaries, sewage farms and city parks in times of prolonged hard weather, though frost alone is no deterrent. This is because the hard ground allows farmers to spread large quantities of stored manure with less risk of their tractors damaging the sward or becoming bogged. The gulls, together with rooks and jackdaws, find many tasty scraps in this muck, and will home in on a muck-spreader from miles away.

This second week of January is a time of fine balance. On the one hand the worst of Winter is imminent, as signalled by the departure of the last remaining meadow pipits and pied wagtails. Most of their kin left long ago to distant places but a hardy few hung on until now, and will be back in late February. On the other hand the sycamore and horse chestnut buds have swollen slightly, there are small, shiny leaves at the tips of sheltered elder branches, and bluebell bulbs have pushed green points above the woodland floor. In mild winters the hazel catkins may be open and shedding pollen even now, and at very least both they and the male alder catkins along the riverside should be swelling and lengthening with promise. On any bright day gnats will emerge and congregate to dance in the sunlight in damp places. The winter thrushes and wood pigeons are anticipating lean times by cramming themselves with berries, the squirrels are so fat they almost waddle, but deep in her burrow the doe rabbit has new life stirring in her belly.

January 16th – 23rd

For a few days there is a mild spell. Tree branches drip, and there is a thin paddle of mud in gate bottoms. The frost is drawn up from deep in the soil to make mini-glaciers on damp hillsides. Ice on the local fish-ponds floats loose but does not melt away. Robins sing more consistently during the brighter spells, the starling adds a blackbird imitation to its repertoire, and the stormcock's clarion call becomes more prolonged and variable. Townsfolk begin to comment that Spring is just around the corner.

Then late one afternoon a sparse powdery snow begins to fall, scuttling away in eddies as it meets the ground. Imperceptibly but inexorably it floats on down, so that we are surprised to find the ground white over at dusk. When I step out to bring in some logs after dark there is an inch of snow in the yard. The children run out in their night-clothes and wellies to dance in the cold softness under the outside light, and go to bed excited.

Next morning there is just enough snow for tracking across fields and open spaces, but not enough to follow a trace through bracken and bramble in the woods. Snow presents the naturalist with a rare opportunity to study the behaviour of our mainly nocturnal mammals, and it is surprising what we can learn. My first revelation comes as I leave the house and find the croft criss-crossed with dozens of rabbit tracks. I have not seen a rabbit near the house since last Summer, but it seems that there are plenty about. The same is true in the fields: rabbit tracks everywhere, in places so many that for dozens of yards it is impossible to walk without each step falling on rabbit footprints. Here and there a beer-coloured stain with a couple of black dots shows where a rabbit has stopped to pass urine and dung pellets. On a minor prominence the snow has been scratted away and there is an accumulation of rabbit droppings and urine. The tracks show that several have visited and marked this place in the night to leave scent messages, challenges, assertions of masculinity, or genteel hints of impending oestrus.

To the novice an animal's footprints seem to point the wrong way. The prints may fall clearly in groups of four as the animal canters along, but surely the larger prints should belong to the hind feet and therefore fall at the back? It is true that in most mammals the hind feet are larger, though the mole and the badger are exceptions which spring to mind. If you want to know why the hind feet fall in front of the forefeet when tracking, my best advice is to watch carefully how the feet fall next time you see a slow motion chase on a televised nature programme.

The larger tracks of hare cut through the jumble of rabbit tracks. I love to see a hare at any time, but particularly now that they have become scarce. In the early 1960s, after myxomatosis had almost wiped out the main opposition, hares became such a pest that the moorside farmers organised a hare drive. As I recall, over 200 were seen and 80 shot in one evening. Now that so many rabbits are resistant to the Myxoma virus and that a series of mild winters has allowed their population to explode, the noble hare has a harder time. Poisoning from thistle sprays in Spring, and possibly the future effects of EBHS (European Brown Hare Syndrome) virus, mean that each hare sighting is to be treasured at present. I therefore change direction to track the hare, following his familiar spoor with ease.

Despite the snow it is foggy, and the white silence is broken only by the crunch of my feet through the snow's crust and the occasional muffled cawing of a distant rook. In this sort of snow last night's tracks are easily distinguished from this morning's by the small fragments of broken crust disturbed around the latter, and I note where the hare has laid up for some hours in a bob of rushes and set off as he heard me coming. His track suddenly disappears fifty yards further on, but can be seen re-starting in a different direction five yards away. It is an old trick of the hare's to baffle pursuit by a sudden prodigious leap, twisting in the air and setting off again at a sharp angle. I smile to myself in admiration of his worthiness, and follow the trace with renewed interest.

Finally I see him through the mist about 100 yards ahead, unhurried, almost playful. Hares always seem longer legged at this time of year, with their bellies tucked up and their bodies held well clear of the snow. He leans forward on tiptoes and swivels his ears to listen ahead through the obscurity, whilst his eyes watch me behind. He settles back on his haunches, flicks the snow from his forefeet, and grooms his face. Then he sets off with his nose to the ground as if following a scent trail, though when I reach that point there is no other track apparent. Was he possibly following a scent left by a doe before last night's snow, was he sniffing for preferred food items beneath the snow, or was he not smelling much at all but keeping his nose close to the ground on the off-chance?

At my father's cottage nearby a fox has entered the garden, pausing awhile on top of the stone gatepost to test the wind before crossing to the compost heap in hope of scraps. I come from a long line of gamekeepers and hill farmers, and cannot resist trying to track the fox to his earth even though I no longer shoot. A fox is not especially difficult to track in an inch of snow across open country, and I make good progress at first.

Here the tracks show where he has pounced through the snow into the tussocky grass to catch what must have been a field vole, and there he has dug up the rotting remains of a pheasant. A fox likes his meat gamey as well as fresh, and will bury a half-eaten carcase or even an egg in the same way that a dog buries a bone, to return to it later. Despite his doggy ways, however, the fox's spoor has much in common with that of the cat. When trotting, both species place each forefoot directly in line ahead of the other and each hind foot exactly in the print vacated by the fore. When moving steadily ahead, therefore, both species leave a straight line of apparently single prints evenly spaced. The fox's are terrier-sized and fall about 18 inches apart, whilst the cat's are smaller, fall about 10 inches apart, and are typically devoid of claw marks.

Now our fox's tracks enter the open door of an empty barn, but there seems to be little to attract him. Hay has largely been replaced by silage, and bedding muck is better shifted with tractors than gripes. Stone barns now often contain neither feed nor stock, and therefore attract neither rodents nor their predators. Perhaps he once found a rabbit that had crawled in here and died, or a summer rat's nest, so that it is always worth a visit. So is a waste-bin, even here in the hills, and the tracks show where he has stood on his hind legs to reach into a litter bin on a roadside picnic site. Then the tracks disappear on the bare tarmac, and it takes patience to find where he leaves the road again, 300 yards along and on the same side. Back up onto a moorland ridge, he has paused to squirt urine onto a small rock. I note the place with interest, to be sniffed in Summer if I need to know whether there are foxes about, and then follow the spoor down into the wood. Along the wood wall there are the prints of another fox, and the two run side by side over a gap into the trees. Here I lose them, for what little snow has fallen in the wood is broken up by the undergrowth.

Foxes start to become intensely territorial in December, and some may mate then, producing cubs in February. Around here, however, the peak of the mating season is reached in the second half of January, and early risers may be lucky enough to see a dog and a vixen playing together around wood edges at first light. Keepers will sometimes set several fox snares near together at this time of year, knowing that if a vixen is caught her smell may attract several dog foxes to the same fate. Most people will be hesitant about walking through woods at night, in case they are mistaken for poachers, but if you know where the public road passes near a hilly wood it is worth parking up there late one night about now, and listening. The eldritch scream of the vixen, half bitch, half cat, can make hairs stand on end, but the answering 'yip, yip' of the dog as he grows ever nearer and more excited will soon have you so engrossed that you forget any primitive fears. The same nuptial cries from urban foxes can be heard in city parks at night, but such places are also used for human courtship activities, and there you will have to be sure that your intentions cannot be misunderstood.

January 24th – 31st

After the scouting fall of snow there is a menacing lull. The soft easterly breeze develops a cutting edge and the skies darken. It is bitterly cold even at mid-day. We check our pantries and our shovel handles, and the farmers look to their sheep.

The blizzard starts at dusk, and throughout the night we hear the wind buffeting the house, driving the powdery snow against the windows. By morning the countryside is immersed beneath a swirling sea of wind-driven face-stinging snow. All day we are busy digging out roads and calling on pensioners, but new drifts fill in the stone-walled lanes faster than we can clear them. Eventually even the tractors have to retreat before they are blocked in from behind. Nature reigns unchallenged, whilst her subjects peer out from entrenched positions in earths and setts, cowsheds and kitchens.

On the second morning the storm has eased, but we are too involved with human problems to make peace with Nature. It is not until the third day that we step out to find all serene, with an apologetic yellow sun struggling to break through the haze of sporadic snow showers. I have known these fields and woods in Winter ever since I used to walk through them to school in sou'-wester, clogs, and short trousers. I can therefore set off with a fair idea of where it is safe to put my feet, but I would advise you as a visitor not to venture out without a local guide. In drifted snow it is all too easy to twist an ankle or fall into the icy waters of a drift-covered beck, and I do not want to lose a reader from hypothermia before the end of the first chapter.

My first visit in this sort of weather is to the riverside and the valley bottom dams and fish-ponds. The latter are frozen over, and only the occasional waterhen remains, walking flatfoot and forlorn around the reeded edges. One surprises me by flying off from high in an alder tree, where it has taken refuge from ground predators now that the waterside vegetation is exposed to attack from all sides. The mallard which normally roost around these ponds are packed onto the river in flotillas of up to 30 birds. There are sadly too many mallard these days, as evidenced by the large numbers of colour mutants and the fact that so many continue to take food from visitors right through the Summer. This over-crowding favours the transmission of intestinal worms, which build up to a heavy burden. Now that the hard weather is here, those worst affected will succumb. The vixen knows to check the riversides on nights such as this, and the bones and flesh of dead ducks are barely cold before they become the welcome raw material to build the bones and flesh of her newly seeded embryonic cubs.

There is a shortage of good wetland habitats in the Dales, most of our tarns and reservoirs being too acid and stony-bottomed to provide much food. There are exceptions, however, at places like Gouthwaite flats and the flood pastures of the upper Aire valley. Water-fowl moving between these places often pause to rest and feed where inlet streams have made muddy corners in the numerous smaller reservoirs. Once these places are frozen the same birds follow the main valley systems instead, so that in hard weather we may see various unusual species on the rivers of the upper Dales.

Goosanders have become quite common winter visitors to the area and now regularly breed here in Spring. Canada geese and teal both nest amongst the heather near our moorland bogs, but I am surprised to see them here in January, the Canadas on the river above Barden Bridge and a flock of eight teal scattered over a snow-drift beside a hill stream not a foot across. The teal fly off at great speed, describe a circle about half a mile across, and fly back in to the same point on the same stream, paying me no further attention. As their ducks move awkwardly through the loose snow towards the stream, the drakes softly call "plip" to each other and pose in the weak sunlight for me to admire their green and chestnut head markings through the binoculars.

On the pool in the river bend below Lobwood there are half a dozen tufted duck, and a short distance away a drake goldeneye, his pied plumage being readily distinguishable from the tufted's by his white breast and the large white spot below each eye. And finally before I leave the river for

There was a marked increase in the great spotted woodpecker population in the Dales between 1960 and 1980. It is now the commonest woodpecker in the area, and is present throughout the year. Adult males are distinguished from the females by the scarlet patch on the nape

In flight the species is recognised by its heavy-headed appearance, undulating progression, and pied plumage with large white shoulder patches

Great Spotted Woodpecker
(Dendrocopus major)

nelson 92

the woods there is a pair of pochard, looking strangely ill at ease on the running water. These are diving duck which favour shallow lakes, and their presence here indicates that even the major reservoirs are frozen. Later I will hear that this week three great crested grebe have been separately handed in to the RSPCA at Skipton, having been found by roadsides exhausted and dying.

In the woods the tracking is not good. The prints are blurred by snow showers that are still falling, though tracks of the all-too-numerous feral cats are recognizable. I find fresh roe deer tracks made within the last half hour, and follow them where the animals have moved at speed along regular paths and squeezed their way through surprisingly small holes in tangles of briar. Finally they break from cover, three does, and with a few white rump flashes they are at the wood wall and then effortlessly over it and away. Roe deer have been trying to colonize these woods since the early 1960s, when I saw my first one here, but it is only during the last decade that they have really gained a foothold. Now each wood has several, and with a quiet approach you should be able to find them quite easily about now, when the undergrowth is sparse and they are less able to hide and creep back behind you.

The snow crumps beneath my feet as I walk, and I stop to listen to the wood. The silence is so intense that I can hear the snow particles of a light shower striking against my hat. Then there is the clear "pik" of a greater spotted woodpecker, and I move off to look for it. The "pik" is repeated every few seconds as the bird works its way through the treetops, and it is not long before I see the movement and focus on the crimson nape which identifies it as a male. At first the bird is on a dead ash, ripping out beakfuls of soft, dead wood and throwing them over its shoulder to fall onto the snow below. Then, having pulled out some luckless grub with its long, sticky tongue, it flies onto a sycamore and moves rapidly up one of the main limbs, breaking off flakes of bark to search for invertebrates beneath. A patchy brown path against the dull green of the untouched bark shows where it has followed a similar path several times before. At one point it moves underneath a horizontal branch and hangs upside down, its feet wide apart and its stiff tail counterbalancing the thrusts of the neck as it hammers at a soft spot. Then there is another "pik" from a few hundred yards away, and our woodpecker flies off, calling as it goes.

Most of the small birds seem to have either flown away down the valley or perished in the blizzard, but in the bare larch branches I find a mixed flock, mostly consisting of long-tailed tits and goldcrests. The other tits can find a living round bird tables in this sort of weather, but there is a couple of great tits nevertheless. Great tits have already started to call and to form pairs by late January, and although they do not become strictly territorial for another fortnight there are rarely more than two in mixed flocks from now on. There are also two treecreepers with this flock, creeping up the main trunks and probing with their finely curved beaks into the thinnest of cracks, reaching the parts that other birds cannot reach. They seem too fragile and exotic to survive our northern winters, but their specialist feeding techniques and their ability to roost deep within hollow trunks means that they will survive cold snaps that kill more robust looking species.

There is a churring alarm call, the birds scatter for cover, and a kestrel flies low over the young larch trees. Kestrels do not usually hunt in woodland, but the voles which they prefer are now protected by a blanket of snow. They must seek where they can, trusting only that the same weather which deprived them of voles will have dulled the vigilance of some small bird. Kestrels will hunt until late dusk in this weather, moving from the woods to roadsides and moor edges as the light fails, hoping for some nocturnal rodent to pop out early through the snow. I have even heard of them hovering over brightly lit motorways in the middle of the night, for voles love the uncultivated grass of motorway banks, and the snow thaws there before anywhere else.

A clatter of woodpigeons startles me from my thoughts as I approach a bunch of hollies where the wood opens out. The droppings on the snow suggest that the pigeons have been feeding here for several hours. Holly berries are not highly palatable, and are only eaten in quantity when all the rowan and hawthorn berries are finished. A quick inspection of nearby bushes shows that this is so, except for scattered berries at the tops of the most inaccessible twigs. Tracks on top of the snow-drifts show where rabbits have taken advantage of the unusual access, not only to eat any remaining berries which they could reach but also to eat the tips of the twigs themselves and the bittersweet bark of some of the larger branches. Tracks also show where a wandering pheasant has picked hips from a dog rose and pulled them apart, to eat the red flesh and discard the irritant seeds.

Over the next few days many wild creatures will be forced to consume items which they would have rejected a month ago, and those which do not adapt to the struggle will succumb. This is Nature's way, but nothing is wasted and every death leaves the species stronger.

2 February

February can be the grimmest of months, particularly for those of us who are old, or ill, or prone to ambush by the Black Dog. For the last three months we have been coddled in winter clothes, eating too much and getting too little fresh air and exercise. Yet at the beginning of February there are still more than two months to go before the swallows return.

No matter how stark the picture is as February opens, hold on to the thought that it is the gateway to the year, and when it closes there will be no going back to the cold land, at least for this year. Not for nothing is the month called 'Fill-dyke', for there are always heavy floods at some time during the next five weeks. And for there to be floods there has to be rain, preceded by milder weather and a thaw of any lying snow.

Think only, then, as February opens to frost and snow, that by the month-end the blackbird will be singing from the tree-tops, the plovers will be calling in upland pastures, and the bright yellow blossoms of the merry coltsfoot will be catching the sunlight under some wayside hedge.

A change is better than a rest, and a time of change lies just ahead.

February 1st – 7th

For several days the temperature remains below freezing point even when the sun tries to shine. Snow melts on the house roof but freezes again as it drips from the eaves, making rows of icicles outside the kitchen window. The local waterfalls are decked with icy chandeliers. The fallen snow develops a crust strong enough to support a walking man, and then another inch of snow falls on top of it one night. I set forth at dawn to see what has been moving.

Sunrise is preceded by an orange glow, and the snow briefly turns pink as the light breaks over the hill. From three fields away I hear the dry call notes of lekking partridge "kuwaaaait-it, kuwaaaait-it". The remnants of last back-end's family flocks gather at sparring grounds about now, and the males have noisy running quarrels at dusk and dawn and through moonlit nights. Gradually the family loyalties break down and the new year's pairs are bonded. This morning they are so busy fighting that I reach within yards of them before they scatter in confusion. Two crash together as they take off, and swear vigorously as they whirr away, leaving a few grey feathers floating down.

Birds' feathers need preening and grooming even in this cold weather, and I am intrigued to see both blackbirds and magpies separately taking 'dust' baths in the powdery snow. Is this the avian equivalent of a brisk cold shower, does it help control parasites, or does it act as a conditioner for the newly developing spring plumage? And is it significant that both species have all or part of the plumage coloured black? There is more to it than I can ken, for several corvid species, including the non-black jay, will deliberately take dust baths on ant trails and nests in Summer. They will even hold ants in their beak tips and stroke them through their feathers, in a ritual known as formication.

Blackbirds, jays and magpies are particularly noticeable in early February. Blackbirds are still in loose flocks of up to a dozen birds, including some which have flown in from Scandinavia to winter here. They move through mixed woodland, and where there is a small stream full of leaf litter they scrat about amongst the wet leaves looking for choice invertebrates to supplement their berry diet, up to their hocks in water. Jays have already formed pairs, though two pairs may still move together for added security, or congregate at selected bird tables near enough to their woodland homes. They will take scraps from a bird table to hide them where there is no snow, and after the thaw they will be seen near to banks of oak looking for the acorns they buried there in Autumn. Their close relatives the magpies are more likely to be seen on roadside verges, gathered like a group of smartly dressed undertakers, picking at the remains of rabbits hit by cars.

Rabbits seem to be attracted to roads once the drifts have been cleared and the tarmac salted. They come there partly for the salt, which most herbivores crave when feed is poor, and partly for the comparative warmth. The surface of the snow remains at freezing point no matter how valiantly the low sun tries, but the dark-coloured road absorbs what little heat there is. It makes a pleasant place to sit out when the rabbits are above ground with empty stomachs. A rabbit's food passes twice through its intestines, emerging the first time as a soft green jelly which is eaten directly from the anus before passing out a second time as the familiar pellets. This enables the animal to absorb the sugars formed when cellulose is broken down in the posterior intestine on the first passage. It also means that rabbits can manage perfectly well for a day or two without eating fresh food, but after a few days of snow they become extremely destructive. Many a fair-weather dalesman returns to his hamlet in Spring to find the climbing roses clinging dead to the cottage wall, eaten off from ground level to eighteen inches above the level of the highest drift that Winter. And many a farmer lifts up a roller bale to find a neat hole through the plastic and a warren nibbled through the silage inside.

Hares are less given to this sort of mischief, but they suffer for their gentility. In hard weather some will seek shelter in woodland, where they more easily fall prey to foxes and snares. Others range widely into unfamiliar territory, where they fail to find adequate cover. They shelter down wall-backs, their redness dangerously obvious against the snow in the afternoon sun. When the snow thaws we will find some crouched in life-like poses amongst the flattened tussocks, as cold and dead as the soil beneath them.

The badger, on the other hand, sleeps snug and safe in his sett at the wood's edge, moving around his tunnelled home for exercise or to use the underground latrine. Tracks in the snow show where the sow, now heavily pregnant, has come to the surface and pottered from one hole to another, here sitting on her rump in the snow to groom herself, there rolling over on her back. Other tracks draw me away from the sett, firstly a squirrel with its long ratty toes and the brush marks of its tail trailing here and there. Then the similar-sized but more dog-like tracks of a stoat, each group of four falling close together at intervals of about eight inches. I decide to follow these as far as I can on their meandering trace, seeing where the little hunter has paused on every prominence to look and listen and catch the scent. The little spoor follows a stream out of the wood, and then unexpectedly presents me with the most fascinating scenario. For here the tracks of the stoat suddenly lengthen and then merge with those of a mallard, whose wing tips have beaten against the snow in his struggle to take off. Almost unbelievably the tracks of stoat and mallard suddenly disappear, and about 30 yards further on there is the half-eaten carcase of the mallard with stoat tracks around it, leading off into a hedgerow where I lose them. Picture, then, what has happened: imagine the stoat gripping the throat of the flying duck, one terrified of flight and the other of death. I doubt if anyone has ever seen such a thing, but the story is written plainly in the snow and cannot be denied.

Whilst I ponder, a twittering flock of small birds alights in the alder by the stream, moving through the finer branches like tits. These are siskins, not tits but finches, with a preference for ash and birch and alder. The bright greenish-yellow breasts of the males catch the weak sun as they hang upside down to probe the dried remains of last year's female catkins. Siskins are an emergent species at present, now visiting us every Winter although I had not seen one in this area until 1986. Another ascendant finch is the crossbill, again not recorded locally by me until 1986 but now seen every Winter. Crossbills can be surprisingly tame, particularly near fresh water in the heart of coniferous woodland, but they can also be infuriatingly difficult to identify high in the evergreen canopy, when their dull reds and greens cannot be seen against the sky. The crossed beak tips are not half as obvious as illustrations show, and if anything the beaks appear unusually round-ended. If in doubt, the falling debris from pine cones pulled apart by the birds will give them away, particularly when there is snow on the ground.

The siskins on the old alder catkins remind me to check the hazel trees, but the new male catkins there are frozen half-open, the yellow anthers just peeping out from the cracks down their sides. On the pussy willow trees there are a few swollen, shiny-green buds, but these are galls, not signs of Spring. When I cut them with my pocket knife there are soft white grubs inside, protected from the frost and waiting for warmer weather to develop into adult gall wasps. Similar galls, called oak apples, can be seen in the bare branches of young oaks, whilst leaf galls lie protected in the woodland litter.

Wandering homeward with the sinking sun sparkling the snow I see a little owl in broad daylight, perched on a gatepost. It checks me nervously with bobbing head and yellow eyes, before winging off with undulating flight. Owls are normally out in daytime only when they are starving, mating, or feeding young, the foremost being applicable in this case. In northern Britain the little owl is at the limit of its range, and although numbers will build up after a series of soft winters they crash in hard ones. With snow on the ground and bitter frost each night, the owl is forced into increasingly desperate behaviour, eating carrion and hunting by day.

Normally seems squat and drumpy, but can comfort its neck into many unusual positions

Feeds on a variety of items, from carrion to insects. In Spring and Autumn worms form a large part of the diet.

Often seen at dusk perched on gate-posts, wall tops, and telephone poles. Unmistakably owlish, small and rather grey.

Little Owl

(Athene noctua)

nelson 91

Sparrowhawks also feel the pinch now, with small birds being fewer and more experienced, and the element of surprise more difficult to achieve. A hawk in hot pursuit of a chaffinch flicks over a wall into the path of an on-coming lorry, and is thrown up in a high arc to land with a thump, blood dripping from its death-dealing beak. A little owl, half-dazzled in the sunlight, flies into a wire. It is brought to me with a broken wing, and dies two days later.

Yet at sunset, amidst all this death and deprivation, a pheasant crows "coq-coq" across the valley to remind us that life goes on and that even now the sap is rising.

February 8th – 14th

The moon wanes, the wind changes, and a slow thaw begins. At first it is still possible to do some tracking, though the prints blur rapidly. Patches of green begin to re-appear, and from them the fairy footprints of small mammals lead out over the snow's surface, falling as tight little groups of four a few inches apart. In some places the fore and hind prints have melted together whilst the two sides have remained distinctly apart, so that the print appears to be that of a single cleft hoof, with hoof marks in line ahead like those of a small bi-ped. In more superstitious times this gave rise to stories of devils, but I can see where their maker has climbed hazel trees and pulled strips from honeysuckle bark. This confirms that they are the tracks of a wood mouse, the most arboreal of our northern 'mice'. In southern England the stripping of honeysuckle bark is reckoned to be the work of the common dormouse, a delightful creature which is regrettably absent from the Dales.

Wood Mouse (Apodemus sylvaticus) Field Vole (Microtus agrestis) nelson 92

In boggy places there are now some lawn-sized patches of green, and meandering furrows on the ground surface here show where moles have tunnelled along between soil and snow during the past week before rooting their way back below. One has even come up through a drift onto the snow's surface, apparently for no better reason than a bit of fresh air and a squint at the moonlight through pin-point eyes. We can also see collections of green droppings outside newly exposed mouse-holes, with piles of rush pith and bits of grass rhizome in the little 'garden' by each hole. These show where the field vole has survived quite happily out of reach of hawk and owl, sleeping underground in his nest of dried grass and emerging at intervals through well-worn tunnels to the abundance of food protected with him beneath the snow. The grey-brown, short-tailed field vole is most at home amongst the rushes and tussock grass of damp pastures, whilst the chestnut and white wood mouse likes to be near trees and bushes where it can make good use of its long tail when climbing. Half-way between them in both appearance and habitat is the bank vole, which prefers waysides and gardens and may even now be helping itself to your bulbs. I have kept all three species as pets when it was still legal to do so, and charming pets they made for a schoolboy eager to study the ways of tiny creatures normally seen only fleetingly or dead.

Another small mammal which I often kept as a pet in those days was the common shrew. Shrews are no relation to mice proper, being insectivorous and having pointed teeth instead of the chisel-shaped incisors of rodents. This feature can best be seen in owl pellets, which you can find below owl roosts in evergreen trees at this time of year. If the pellets are dried and then teased apart, the head bones of shrews will be readily identifiable by the red-tipped teeth. Live shrews secrete a special saliva which is thought to have a paralysing effect on their prey, and they use this to good effect during periods of very cold weather. Because they cannot survive on vegetable matter as mice do, or dig for food like their cousin the mole, they have to set up small stores. This they do by catching earthworms during milder spells, biting several times through their front segments, and storing them near to their nests. If you carefully look under flat stones during mid-Winter you will eventually find a shrew's nest beneath one, with a few paralysed worms knitted into a tiny ball either in the nest itself or stored nearby.

Another cousin of the shrew is the hedgehog, which solves the problem of winter food supply by laying on fat in Autumn and then hibernating in a ball of leaves just below the surface. In an average winter this works perfectly well, but if the weather is too mild the sleep is disturbed and the animal uses up its reserves too soon. If the cold is too prolonged, however, the poor urchin may die during hibernation without ever waking. Very soon afterwards a fox will pick up the scent of decay and pull the flaccid bundle from its hole, so that often as the snow thaws at this time of year we find a hollowed-out hedgehog skin on some steep, leafy bank. If you happen upon a live hedgehog wandering about in mid-Winter, give it as much tinned cat food as it will eat and return it to exactly where you found it as soon as possible afterwards.

One further mammal to which we must return this week is the irrepressible rabbit. Rabbits breed like rabbits, and in less than a week after the shortest day they are at it, heedless of Winter's wrath. The young conceived then are born in late January, and will emerge this week at twelve days old even if they have to break up through the snow's crust. There they sit, in bunches of three or four, eyes half-closed against the glare, a menace and a pest but undeniably a sight to warm our winter-tired souls.

As the thaw continues a wind builds up, and then it begins to rain, band after band lashing almost horizontally across the countryside. On the high fells around Cam and Cray the snow loses its grip, and comes gushing down the becks. As the dale widens the valley bottoms go under, and half-submerged stone walls jut out into the swirling waters. The riverside cricket pitch at Bolton Bridge is flooded, and a heron lounges elegantly on a boundary post like a bored fielder, only half-hoping for a catch.

Many of our winter herons will soon be flying away to large heronries nearer the coast, but a few will stay to nest in the Dales, mostly in coniferous plantations. These latter birds will be seen over the next week or two gathered in small groups on special standing grounds. These are usually on sheltered wet banks near to streams, where the birds can pick up the odd vole or early frog whilst indulging in their mating rituals. If you chance upon a group of herons at a standing ground at this time of year the nesting site will be less than a mile away. The birds are very sharp-sighted and difficult to stalk, but if you find the heronry there will be activity there from now until late Spring for the patient observer.

The onset of mating behaviour in birds is linked to a simple increase in daylength, almost irrespective of the weather, the indirect hormonal process from eye to gonads taking several weeks. By mid-February, therefore, those species or individuals whose physiology has not been disrupted by winter hunger have already begun to mate. Herons are one example, but rooks, jackdaws and grouse are also striving, as are smaller birds such as dippers, nuthatches, robins and wrens.

Rooks have enjoyed the muck-spreading in recent weeks and are in good condition, glossy and sleek. Now they assemble at their nest sites to clamour and caw, holding their heads out low and fanning their tails as they shout at each other. Fights break out, with birds tumbling through the branches. Under one rookery I find a dead rook with deep stab wounds in its breast and abdomen, an unusual instance of a fight which has gone too far. Jackdaws are already paired, but now form clacking flocks by ancient ruins, deserted quarries, and stands of hollow ash to vie for the best nesting holes. On moor tops the grouse are almost equally noisy, the red combs of the dark cocks swollen and almost glowing with passion. They make short flights with ostentatious landings, cackling from any low prominence, "Hoi! Ur-Ur-Ur-r-r-r-r-r, Go-back, Go-back, Go-back, back, back, back," a thrilling sound to us moorsiders.

Dippers, robins and wrens have displays similar to each other's, but that of the dipper is the earliest. Many winged insects spent Winter as larvae on the river bed, and these keep the dippers well-fed throughout the year. The bird is therefore one of the first species to respond to increasing daylight, and will start nest-building before the end of this month. Dippers are already in close, attentive pairs, hunting together from stones by the river's edge and even feeding each other. In courtship the cock assumes the upright posture of his territorial display whilst the hen curtseys prettily before him, flicking her wings and turning slightly with each dip, until either mating takes place or the pair join forces to pursue a passing interloper. Robins and wrens stage similar performances in our gardens, whilst the nuthatch poses on some lofty branch in the wooded valley. There he attracts his mate and proclaims his territory with a series of short, clear whistles regularly repeated, interspersed with an occasional surprisingly loud note like the whistle of a shepherd calling up a dog.

We must not be too optimistic at these signs of mating, for they are governed by daylength and are therefore a response to the date, not the weather. But other signs more directly linked to the warming of the soil may be seen, most obviously in tree buds. Those of the horse chestnut have swollen and become sticky on the outside, there is a golden tinge to the long narrow buds of the beech, and the tips of pussy willow buds are showing silky white tufts. Even the moss on wall tops, which we hardly notice at any time, suddenly throws up a little forest of stalked spore capsules, which look marvellously exotic when viewed across the sunlight with a hand lens.

Even invertebrates are on the move, water snails slowly and heavily across the bottom of a pond, and the odd skater light and fast across its top. Dor beetles dig down into sunny hillsides, throwing up little piles of sandy soil as they prepare their nesting quarters. And in the woods the first grey moth of the year is disturbed by my footfalls amongst a hazel stand. As I move a branch to watch it, the newly opened lamb's tail catkins shed little clouds of yellow pollen, and there is hope.

February 15th – 21st

If you have ever watched hares in March or lambs in May, you will have seen individuals suddenly run short distances, jump up in the air, and throw themselves about, bright-eyed and panting and looking for mischief. There are odd days in February that make me feel like that, when all of a sudden there is a glorious, sunny day, one's spirit bursts with joy, and there is nothing for it but to act daft a bit. True, there are rarely more than two or three such days in the month, and they hardly ever run consecutively, but it is a wonderful feeling to rub dew on your face and laugh at the sunrise.

Acting daft is not a sustainable enterprise, and I am soon distracted by bees flying into the garden. The sun has warmed up the hives a few hundred yards away, and at the same time opened up the crocuses, aconites and snow-drops in the border. By mid-morning almost every crocus has a bee or two on it, and even a lone wasp and a small tortoiseshell butterfly pass briefly by, fully one month before they are due to appear. Greenfinches zizz monotonously from the overgrown garden hedge. Cock chaffinches accurately predict "In another month will come a WHEATear" from high in sycamores behind the house, their prettily descending call notes reminiscent of bluebell woods in May. Both these finches were in flocks a week ago, the green-finches in small bands roving widely and the chaffinches under beech trees in crowds of a hundred or more.

On the hen-house roof the house sparrows chirp and squabble. Their name-mate the hedge sparrow (no relation) clears his throat with a whisper song deep in the hedge, and then climbs higher up the bush to let rip with his pleasant squeaky warble. The song, like the bird, is half-robin, half-wren. The hedge whereon he sits is a tangle of hawthorn and wild gooseberry, with the buds of both just showing green where the leaf tips are testing the air. Beneath the hedge the first small white flowers of barren strawberry and common chickweed, almost lost amongst their foliage, are there for those who will seek them. And the first fully open dandelion of the year basks in the morning sun, relishing the ministrations of early insects.

I stride out across the fields to visit beck and pond, river and wood. Four skylarks pass high overhead, flying half-sideways and issuing snatches of song. These are the first I have seen since December, and are probably robust, mature males which will grab the best territories. Half-a-dozen snipe spring up from a boggy patch as I approach, and scatter ahead with the swift, erratic flight which protects them from both raptors and gunshot. These are also new arrivals, though some snipe are present here on all but the very hardest days of Winter. The same is true of black-headed gulls, which are now gathering in large flocks on these upland pastures and beginning to show grey heads where the new season's colour is growing through. Another newly-returned species is the stock dove, a pair of which flick out of an empty barn as I pass and are away across the valley in seconds. Stock doves go to the flatlands for Winter, but return to our old stone barns to nest. I believe they earned their name from their close association with live-stock when the out-barns were better utilized, but others assert that it comes from their being the basic stock from which racing pigeons were bred.

Partridges are now paired, and I stop to watch a pair through the binoculars. The cock bird struts around in an upright posture, his bristling ear-tufts and the raised feathers on his neck, breast and back making him appear much larger and brighter than the hen. She runs busily all around him making pecking gestures at the ground, keeping all the time hunched and low, the line of her body as nearly horizontal as his is vertical. Now she turns towards him and peers closely at his sides as if about to pick a speck of dust from his immaculately barred flank. Then she passes underneath his front, stroking her upper sides across his lower breast, and walks away shaking herself with pleasure. He appears for all the world like a perky little colonel, full of pomp and bluster, and faintly embarrassed by all this foreplay stuff.

On a muck midden by one of the larger becks a welcome grey wagtail fossicks for grubs and pupae, now and again jumping into the air to snatch a passing gnat. Its first name belies its smart slate and yellow appearance, and even 'wag'

Grey Partridge
(Perdix perdix)

is a poor description of its tritty-trotty tail action. Grey wagtails are essentially waterside birds, and love to nest on the face of those moss-covered rocky outcrops which turn becks sharply sideways. This one flies to just such a bend, and begins to pick its way amongst the detritus left by last week's floods on the flat shore opposite the outcrop. I also check this little sandy drift, and find the clear prints of a mink which has passed this way during the night. Mink are now nothing like so common as they were in the early 1980s, due partly to natural checks and partly to the cage traps of angling clubs further downstream. Doubtless this one was driven up here by mating and territorial urges, but it must also have been aware that tasty frogs will soon be congregating to mate in our moorland ponds. I divert to the old fish-ponds, long since disused and partly silted-up, to see if any have arrived yet.

There are no frogs to be seen, but two pairs of tufted duck are there, where two weeks ago there was only ice. A few mallard are also there, whilst under a stand of oak trees nearby there are more mallard, together with wood-pigeons, two jays, and a squirrel. They seem to be picking from the surfeit of acorns remaining there since before the snows, and it is possible that these are especially attractive now as they soften and sweeten prior to germination.

Padding quietly through the wood I twice glimpse voles darting across the path, tying in with reports I have received this week of 'mice' seen crossing the roads at night. These unusual sightings are indicative of the mating frenzy that is calling all the timorous beasties from their cosy nests to show bold heart and win fair lady. One species which will not be ready to mate until high Summer is the roe deer, but I note that one which bounds gracefully ahead of me has stub antlers in velvet thrusting up already.

The forest floor across which it springs now has threads of green woven into its dappled brown. The first leaves of wild garlic and arum lily are visible amongst the more slender and numerous ones of the bluebell, and the flower heads of dog's mercury have begun to uncurl. Catkins are now fully extended on most hazel trees, and on the tips of green nut-buds the female flowers are beginning to show as tiny scarlet tufts. You really need to look through a good little hand lens to appreciate female hazel flowers, but anyone who takes the trouble to do so will not be disappointed.

In these valley-bottom woods the various tits are well into their courtship activities. Two coal tits are so engrossed in their nuptials that they pass within six feet of me, the one which I presume to be the male chasing his mate very closely and repeatedly trying to cover her. Then he settles on a branch a few inches in front of her with his crest raised and wings fluttering, making juvenile begging noises with his beak open. Males will often feed females during court-ship, and I begin to wonder if I have mixed up the sexes. Whilst I puzzle, my attention is drawn to a pair of blue tits on the ground a few yards away. The male repeatedly makes short, flycatcher-like sallies into the air, trying to settle on the female's back each time he descends. She in turn jumps up onto dry grass stalks and other low perches too fragile for two, to tease him and egg him on. And even as I watch these two, a third tit species calls "pee-ter, pee-ter, pee-ter" over and over again.

This last is of course the great tit, which will call every daylight hour for the next few weeks. His phrases are so variable that they often baffle even experienced bird-watchers. In the space of this week I hear great tits call "pee-ter, pee-ter...", "you-see, you-see...", "zwink-link-link", "bzoo-tit", "tsi-wit, tsi-wit...", "ti-ti-KER, ti-ti-KER,...", "chrrt, chrrt....", "peep, peep...", and a harsh churring alarm call. Many of these calls are repeated several times in succession, followed by a short pause before the whole sequence is repeated, hour after hour. And if you happen to travel for an hour or so in a car and stop in another piece of parkland, you will hear great tits calling in a different dialect or using a different set of call notes. One even fools me with an almost perfect, if *pianissimo,* rendition of a blackbird's owl alarm.

Blackbirds which were last week in flocks in the woods are now making long, high flights from wood to copse and garden, as the visitors prepare to move back north and the residents move into nesting territories. Last year's young cocks are developing bright yellow beaks and eye rings as they come into breeding condition, and are challenging the old order. There is much chuck-chucking as the light fades, and shrill alarm calls cut through the stillness at dusk.

Then, just on the edge of dark, the distant honking of geese grows nearer, and a V-shaped skein passes high overhead. At that height in fading light they may be greylags or pinkfeet heading for breeding grounds in the far north, or just Canadas moving back up onto our reservoirs. We hillfolk are unskilled at identifying flying geese, but we know that when they again start to fly northwards over us, the hardest days of Winter are past.

February 22nd – 28/29th

Just to curb our optimism, Winter turns back for another bite. There are two nights of hard frost, followed by dull days with damp, chilly winds. Then a sleety rain starts, and develops into a heavy downpour as the temperature rises.

On the day after the rain the lapwings come pouring back in. I am away at the time, but when I arrive home my wife tells me she has heard them. I cannot resist following a wallback down to the low fields after dark, to sit on a throughstone and listen. It is foggy, and they are nervous at being back in our upland pastures after so long in the estuaries and flatlands. Their voices through the night mist sound sad and tremulous, their only call a thin "pee-er, pee-er" as they fly a few yards and alight again, frightened by every passing rabbit. Tawny owls hoot in the distance, and as I walk pensively home I notice that at least two, perhaps three, are in the trees by the house. One kewicks, and one or two hoot back "hu-hu-hu, hu-hooooo", the calls becoming more excited and fluttery as the birds move towards each other.

Next morning it is still misty, but there is a light breeze and the sun it trying to break through. Under the outside light there is a splattering of copious liquid faeces on the stone flags, where one of last night's owls has left an ownership mark. On the coping stones of the barn roof a starling pips, squeaks and warbles his one-man-band of a song, throat engorged, wings flapping, and taking himself very seriously indeed. But now he has competition from the true *virtuosi,* for this week the song thrush has come back to us from softer country, our resident blackbirds are once more in full voice, and the song of the mistle thrush is nearing its peak.

Of the three songs I love the blackbird's best. The mistle thrush's is loudest, but his range is limited, with 2−7 toodle-doodle notes repeated every few seconds. The song thrush, as Browning noted, tends to repeat its notes even more: "Pure bliss, pure bliss. Quick! Quick! Wake up, wake up". By contrast the blackbird's mellifluous voice defies representation in words. It is a rolling quicksilver joy of a song, evocative of still June evenings and of love's young dream.

But June is still far off, and lapwings call me to other joys. I set myself to a long walk out over the moor, and back by wood and river. All along the fields the lapwings are now in full cry, the estuaries forgotten, their gizzards coping well with the change of food, and their attention now focused on winning territory and mates. They resent my passing through the claims they are staking, and practise for more spectacular displays later by making half-dives at a safe distance, calling "tee-ee-wit, wit, wit, tee-wit". As they swerve back upwards on pounding wings by heart lifts with them, and lifts again as I hear the lark begin to sing. As the mist clears I see him, rising vertically despite the strong breeze, and singing continuously as his fluttering wings carry him ever higher. How does he draw breath without ceasing to sing, and why do his eyes not water like mine in the bright light and cold wind?

My trip over the moor is in search of both curlew and golden plover, which normally arrive a day or two after the lapwing. Golden plover congregate on specific parts of the moor, on peaty flats where bilberry and stunted heather struggle up amongst the cotton-grass and bent. I look for the first arrivals around Shepherd's Close and Cold Moss, and soon spot a lone bird standing atop a crowberry hummock. It stretches its wings as if about to fly, and then folds them away again. I approach slowly and obliquely, stopping every few yards to admire its spangled upperparts and black breast through the glasses. When the tension becomes too great it takes off, to be joined by a mate hidden until now in the ground cover. They fly slowly around me out of harm's way, repeatedly calling a mournful "tew-pewr" at my intrusion. Then a flock of about 20 plover appears at speed over the ridge, seeming at first like racing pigeons. My two birds let out a rippling contact call, accelerate away to join the rest, and are lost from sight. Far away in the opposite direction I hear the long, bubbling trill of a gliding curlew, but do not see the bird all day.

As I come down the moorside towards the woods, I divert to check a spring-fed, weedy pond in a sheltered dell. After some searching amongst the sphagnum and rushes around its edge, I am delighted to find my first frog-spawn of the year, with still a day or two of February to go. It has only been laid in the last few hours and appears rather concentrated, the clear jelly around each egg having not yet swollen to full size. Underneath the spawn the pair are still in amplexus embrance, perhaps even still laying, and they swim away locked together as I gently move the egg mass. As these eggs are being laid, the eggs of trout which were laid last December will be just hatching. Transparent little alevins, their hearts visible between eyes and yolk, will be even now wriggling their way over a gravel bed further down the beck which starts from this pond.

Parent trout will have long since returned to the main river, though a couple may be in the bellies of a pair of goosander which I see high overhead on a nuptial flight. With their hook-tipped saw-bills and their powerful paddle-feet, goosander are adept at catching trout. I have watched goosander from above in fast-flowing rivers, effortlessly maintaining their position with lazy leg strokes, and seen one continue to do so even when it raised one orange foot from the water to preen itself. I was with my brother some 30 years ago when he shot the first goosander we had seen round here, and when it hit the ground we found four good-sized trout in its gullet and crop. Now the bird is much more common, and occasionally has to be culled under licence to protect fish stocks, though I still admire its fishing expertise and its smart plumage. At this time of year, with the green head and red beak set against an oh-so-delicate pale pink, the drake appears a regular dandy. Woe betide the old trout that would call him effeminate.

Continuing downhill along the steep-sided valley of this feeder beck, I call on the badgers at their sett. They have been spring-cleaning, and there are large mounds of sand and old bedding outside their holes. This week the cubs will be born, and like any human mother the sow wants to ensure that her young start life in a clean nursery, free from bugs and smelling of greenery.

In the riverine woodland there are long-tailed tits in attentive pairs, waiting for the hawthorn buds to decide to open before they start their nests. The loud laughing call of a green woodpecker rings across the valley, and I spot him in an oak tree, throwing back his head as he calls. A tawny owl flies in broad daylight across the river, too intent on mating to observe his normal discipline.

On the riverside alders the hard, purple catkins have begun to relax. Elder leaf buds, open in early January but almost dormant since, have suddenly started to bourgeon, making splashes of green against the pale branches. On an open bank beneath some ash and elm a lesser celandine is in bloom, the first yellow starfish on a new sea of green. I wander miles in search of a coltsfoot in flower, and eventually find one by the roadside two minutes from home. All is in order, and the month is complete.

3 March

It is traditionally claimed that March comes in like a lion and goes out like a lamb, but this is only partially correct. Certainly the weeks immediately prior to March have some savage storms, and as soon as the month is over the hill sheep begin to lamb, but March itself is characterized by the diversity of its weather. The general climatic tone of the month is dull, cold and damp, but there may be odd days when we can work outside stripped to the waist, and others when the lane is blocked with snow.

Snow or shine the year turns a corner this month, with the first day of Spring falling most appropriately on the 21st. From the vernal equinox onwards the days will be longer than the nights, and will remain thus for the next six months. Once the clocks change, we can again start to go for walks in the evening, to check the moor for wheatear and ring ouzel, and to look for bird nests in the hedgerows. The cock blackbird which started to sing in the last days of February will by the end of March have wooed and won a hen, mated her, helped build her nest, and be proudly inspecting her first mottled green eggs in their rustic cradle.

March 1st – 7th

From the first week of March there is enough light to wake me before six in the morning. There is also a dawn chorus to be heard, not yet the full glorious medley but well worth an audition. Whilst the household slumbers, I brew a mug of tea and take it with me into the garden. There are worms still out on the surface of the lawn, and fresh worm casts just visible in the first grey light. The robin begins to sing first, cutting through the cold, damp air with an exultant aria, now shrill, now wistful. What registers on our ears as a thing of beauty is to another cock robin little more than a string of foul oaths and boastful threats. Other robins are soon swearing back, and are joined by wrens, hedge sparrows, chaffinches, blackbirds and thrushes, all cursing vigorously in their own languages. But hunger is still a potent force so early in March, and as the light strengthens the singing becomes more spasmodic and the birds disperse to fill their crops.

Sunrise approaches, and mallard start whizzing down off the tops in twos and threes and small groups, gliding at high speed with wings half-closed, the dominant males sheering and sidling across the paths of others to impress prospective mates. Most have left the river now for the moorland bogs where they nest, but for the next week or two they will still be seen on nuptial flights high above the valley. A few fool-hardy, half-tame birds may have already begun nesting by lowland streams, but will later lose most of their eggs or ducklings to casual waterside predators.

After breakfast and a few essential jobs, I set off for a potter, to follow my nose with no pre-conceived route. Down the fields the cries of lapwings have merged back into the familiar background of early Spring. Three males are in close pursuit of each other, flying a few inches apart as they veer and twist, turning almost upside-down at the top of each dive and straightening out as they loop back up. Then from rivalry they switch to alliance to mob a passing pair of carrion crows, distracting those birds' atten-tion from the first muddy scrapes of lapwing nest sites. A pair of curlews, stalking long-legged and hunchety-backed through a bog in the next field, join the 'tewits' in pestering the crows, seeing them off down the fields to the edge of the wood.

On the wood wall runs a grey squirrel, undulating along the top-stones with sinuous grace now that his winter fat deposits have melted away. Soon he jumps up onto a sycamore branch which overhangs the wall, and is lost from sight amongst the trees. All along the wall-side on this mixed deciduous part of the wood, the sycamore seeds which came spinning down last Autumn have begun to germinate. Their little stalks, ending in tightly curled twin leaves, have thrust up everywhere through the warming soil, a sure sign that the grass will soon be growing in the fields. Inside the wood, however, the ground tells another story, for here it is littered with bud casings where the squirrels have been busy. As soon as sycamore buds reach about half-an-inch in length the squirrels find them irresistible, and begin to nip them off, strip away the outer casings, and eat the sweet, succulent centres. Fortunately there are millions of buds, and although I count six squirrels in as many hundred yards this morning their effect on any one tree barely amounts to what gardeners would call a little judicious pruning.

Also beneath the trees I notice how flighty the woodcock

are. Normally these birds sit tight and rely on their very
effective camouflage, but today they spring up some fifty
yards ahead of me, and in twos or threes instead of singles.
These are northern migrant birds which have wintered
here, and are now preparing to depart to Scandinavia. Some
of our resident woodcock nest very early in the year, and
as I check around each site where woodcock have taken off
I am disturbed by the sheep's-cough alarm call of herons.
This gives way to the familiar piercing squawk as three or
four flap away from a dense stand of spruce in the heart
of the wood. I examine the evergreen canopy high above
from several angles, but there are so many dark clumps
that I cannot decide whether the birds are nesting there.
Eventually I decide that they are not, and had merely congregated there after stuffing themselves with frogs at the
old fish-ponds at first light this morning.

At the fish-ponds the usual two pairs of coot are back to
their trysting place, having spent the Winter away in some
city park or reedy mere. There are also large masses of frog-
spawn varying in age from a few hours to several days,
though very few frogs are apparent. They have probably
taken refuge from the herons in the mud at the centre of the
pond, though their mating frenzy is so strong that within a
few hours they will once more be grappling in the shallows,
their baleful eyes betraying nothing of their fierce emotions.

On the boggy sheltered bank above the pond the first
pale primrose is open, and in the trickling feeder stream
little blotches of a greener yellow show where the golden
saxifrage has begun to bloom. As I sit and talk to the
primrose, a great black rook flies over carrying a spindly
black twig. My eyes follow it to the rookery a quarter of a
mile away, and I notice for the first time that the nests are
taking shape again. After loitering with intent around their
rookeries for the last two months, the rooks have finally
begun to refurbish old nests and begin new ones. For the
next fortnight the skies around English villages will be
crowded with rooks carrying twigs their own length or
more. Not for these aviators the careful stowage of cargo
amidships, for once they have chosen likely twigs they carry
them home in the tips of their beaks with no noticeable
increase in effort or disturbance of equilibrium.

If the rooks are nesting, then hares should be fighting
by daylight, and I opt to walk up the valley side and over
the moorland track back home. For a few hundred yards I
follow the river, and note with pleasure that two pairs of

oyster catchers are back from the coast. Oyster catchers are perfect bimbos, immaculately decked out in black and white with fancy trimmings, but notoriously brainless when it comes to choosing a decent nest site. Another black and white waterside bird, but this time exactly attuned to the Dales, is the dipper. By watching two ripping wet moss from exposed stones and carrying it away, I am able to see where they have started to build their nest. It is sited where water drips down a rock face overhanging the river, and is so well tucked in beneath the tree roots and trailing ivy, and so inaccessible to man or predator, that I am unable to distinguish the dome of tightly woven moss. At the top of the bank the roots merge into the trunk of an elm, the branches of which are flecked with the pinkish tufts of newly-opened flowers.

As I leave the valley bottom, a third black and white bird of damp places goes flying uphill past me, its undulating flight and cheery "chissick" immediately identifying it as a pied wagtail. This is another species which leaves the Dales in Winter, but like the other birds that have already arrived back it only moved away to milder parts of Britain. The same is true of red-legged partridge, a pair of which jump up before me a few hundred yards further up and run off at speed without needing to fly. These are introduced birds, sometimes called French partridge, their plumage being perhaps a touch too rococo for local taste.

Eventually I reach the moor gate and follow the wall up onto the ridge, stopping to examine a freshly-dead stoat in a wall-bottom tunnel trap. Stoats, like most other living things, are obsessed with bound-beating and claim-staking at this time of year, and fall easy prey to keepers' traps when running through unfamiliar territory. Interestingly, this one has a large female tick attached behind its ear, and several dark brown fleas looking to escape from its cold body onto my warm one.

Reaching the ridge top at last, I come to a high stone wall which separates the moor from a rough, benty field called an intake. Hares congregate in these intakes to stage their mating jaunts, and as soon as I peep through I see two moving across the front of me and a third approaching across the field, his nose down on their scent trail. The first, apparently a doe, stops and crouches. The buck sits boldly upright a few yards away. She moves forward a few inches with her belly pressed to the ground like a stalking cat. He jumps up and swivels in mid-air as if stung from behind.

As he lands she jumps right over him and kicks his ears with her back legs. The third hare, another buck, reaches them, and all three run round several times in a wide circle. Then two face each other for a fight, rising up on their back legs like performing dogs, and boxing with flailing forefeet. Tufts of white hair float out of the *mêlée,* until one backs down and runs off 20 yards to groom himself. For a while all three nibble the grass as a diversion, until I make a sucking squeak between finger, thumb and lips. Then they all run towards me, and stand within a few yards, their twitching nostrils plainly visible to the naked eye. I once shot three hares in circumstances such as this, but today I simply change my squeak to a sudden handclap. All three run off kicking their heels in the air, almost as if laughing at their own hare-brained temerity. The mad March hares are running, and the month is truly underway.

Brown Hare
(Lepus europaeus)

nelson91

March 8th – 15th

With the return of birds like the lapwing and curlew in late February, and the flowering of coltsfoot and primrose, the last two weeks have encouraged us to believe that Spring has now gathered an unstoppable momentum. It is therefore puzzling to note that the hawthorn buds, which showed green at the tips three weeks ago, have still not opened, and that none of the lapwing nest-scrapes is lined. There is even a new influx of winter fieldfares, though their local meanderings make it difficult to see whether they are coming or going. Sages prod mole-hills with their sticks, and forecast hard weather still to come. Since there will always be at least one more spell of frost or snow within the next month, they are bound to be right eventually.

Even during this lull, careful observation will show some advances. Those mole-hills, for instance, are not, as in November, a sign of impending wintry weather. At this time of year their sudden spread across open fields is linked to the onset of the mole mating season. Females tend to remain in a fixed territory, but the males dash about along a maze of unclaimed and disused tunnels, cleaning and scent-marking them. If you catch a mole at this time of year, you need only rub his excretions onto your trap and re-set it in another tunnel for the scent to draw in another fiercely pugnacious male to his doom. If you are lucky enough to catch a female, her urine rubbed on the trap will draw in several males. In March 1972 I caught 12 males and 2 females in 18 days using one trap repeatedly re-set at the same point, and other 'mowdy-catchers' can boast more than double this. There is a vast reserve of moles in our woods, where they are never trapped, but an excess of mole-hills in a good field is usually a sign of neglect, and mole-hills in silage can lead to listeriosis in livestock. I like and admire moles, and once kept one as a pet, but they are very successful little beasts and have to be kept under reasonable control.

Another mammal which can make an entertaining pet but which has great pest potential is the grey squirrel, sometimes condemned as a tree rat. In the early 1950s, when brass was brass, a bounty of a shilling a tail was paid on grey squirrels. Many a country lad climbed to perilous heights to take up to five bob's worth out of a nest, making sure to leave enough for next year, until the policy was abandoned. Now that nobody even bothers to shoot them any more, grey squirrels have settled down at steady numbers; they never did reach the plague proportions predicted. At this time of year they give birth to three or four young, often in bulky nursery dreys high in the branches but sometimes inside ratty little holes gnawed through the shell of hollow trunks. If you pass near a nursery nest in the early morning, you may be surprised by the harsh chatter of one or both parents as they come running out on a limb to scold you.

If the grey squirrel is the 'tree rat', the 'water rat' is actually the water vole, a chubby faced, chocolate-brown little chappie who is almost entirely vegetarian. He prefers the flatlands, where grassy banks overhang slow-moving water, but he can be found throughout the Dales where becks meander across valley bottoms to meet the river. Like the mole, our largest vole is on the move, and can be most easily seen just now before the waterside vegetation grows up to hide him away. To increase your chances, leave a few ounces of freshly-chopped apple on some little island in the beck, and sit to watch it with the sun behind you and the wind in your face.

Freshly-chopped apple has a fatal attraction for many rodents, though rabbits seem to prefer chopped carrot. It is no longer economic to shoot rabbits, since in these days of pre-packed consumerism few butchers will buy them. Gassing of the burrows with cyanide is an efficient if repugnant method of control, but cage traps baited with carrot can be surprisingly effective. At this time of year some damage limitation can also be achieved by taking the young from their nests, for rabbits are now beginning to breed in short tunnels on the surface instead of deep within the burrow. If we are too tender-hearted to kill the suckling rabbits and simmer them with bacon and onion, they will prove to be robust pets. I once released two which I had kept for a few weeks, and was thereafter embarrassed by them running up to me each time I passed that way, until they either reverted to the wild or surrendered to some bemused cat.

It needs experience to recognize a rabbit nest, for as soon as the doe has excavated about a yard of tunnel and a nest chamber, she blocks the entrance from the outside, tamps down the excess soil, and scrats fresh earth over it before leaving. The young are born in the spherical end-chamber in a nest made of dried grass and fur from the mother's belly, and are virtually helpless until their eyes open at ten days old. The doe visits each night, re-blocking the exit as she departs, though eventually she has to leave a small breathing hole. If the scent from this hole wafts past a rambling badger the litter is lost, for he will dig straight down to the nest, ignoring the entrance hole, and make short work of the coneys within.

Although we have only considered mammals so far this week, there are hopeful signs amongst other life forms, notably birds. Cock pheasants have suddenly become noticeable in woodside pastures, and their "kurruk" calls have begun to ring across the side valleys each morning. They patrol their boundaries full of pomp and circumstance, studiously ignoring the neighbouring cocks doing the same a few feet away. Where their territories include roads they will even challenge on-coming vehicles, and the sad results can be seen by roadsides for the next few weeks. Also by roadsides we begin to notice magpies constructing the protective shells of their domed nests in tall hedges. This seems to be a case of the worst burglar having the biggest guard dog, for none of the magpie's relations protects its eggs to this extent and yet the magpie is itself a notorious egg-thief.

Black-headed gulls used to regularly suffer nest raids by human egg thieves, though gull eggs are less commonly eaten now. By mid-March over half of these gulls have developed their full dark brown head plumage, and they are back in full voice in noisy flocks around the moorland bogs where they nest. Collared doves are also calling again, and have returned to their preferred nest sites amongst cypress trees in village gardens. And beside the becks that flow through these lowland gardens the townie mallard have begun to lay eggs in their downy nests.

It is not only birds that lay eggs, of course. In their chosen ponds the frogs are now mad with desire, croaking even at midday and splashing around in the shallows with gay abandon. Those which have been unable to find a female have locked themselves onto other males, and any female who arrives late may find herself loved literally to death by the over-zealous attentions of several males at once.

The crayfish in the river is another egg layer, but she mated last Autumn and is still carrying the fertilized eggs in a berry cluster beneath her tail, waiting for the water to warm before they hatch. Under the next stone, ever watchful for the crayfish's claws, the bullhead has her belly so distended with eggs that they can be seen glowing orange beneath her skin. Soon she will lay them in a hidden sandy hollow, to be fertilized and guarded by her grimly faithful mate. And if, whilst looking beneath stones for crayfish and bullhead, you chance upon some fast-moving 'worms', these are not miniature eels but yearling brook lampreys, living their mysterious primitive lives in the river-bottom mud.

As this week draws to a close there are two final things for which you should look, and for these you will need to

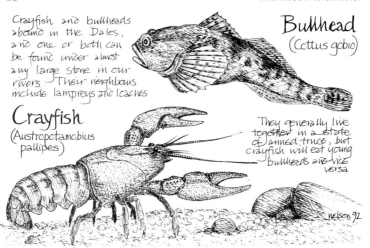

Crayfish and bullheads
abound in the Dales,
and one or both can
be found under almost
any large stone in our
rivers. Their neighbours
include lampreys and loaches

Bullhead
(Cottus gobio)

Crayfish
(Austropotamobius
pallipes)

They generally live
together in a state
of armed truce, but
crayfish will eat young
bullheads and vice
versa

nelson 92

drive out at night. They have both spent Winter sleeping in holes below stones or around the base of trees, but their similarity ends there. The one is the warty toad and the other the spiky hedgehog.

Toads have begun moving at night from their wintering quarters to their mating pools, and since they prefer lowland or even riverside pools you should look for them where roads run along wooded hillsides near to rivers. You can often identify these places in advance by walking along such roads during the day looking for squashed toads, for they may cross in large numbers and use the same crossing points for several nights year after year. They cannot leap out of danger like frogs, for they crawl quite slowly at all times, and just now the females are likely to be encumbered by the smaller males locking onto their backs even before they reach the water.

Hedgehogs you may find anywhere, though they too favour roadsides near damp woodland. They will even seek out migrating toads themselves, for they are able to cope with the toad-skin's irritant poison and are rather partial of the dainty flesh within. Hedgehogs may occasionally be seen in Winter, as already mentioned, but from now onwards you will start to see them regularly, and can trust them to have sensed that the need for hibernation is over.

March 16th – 23rd

Spring wrestles with grizzled old Winter as to who shall claim the year. Now Spring's young strength wins a round, and there is a sunny day with warm showers. Then wily Winter surges anew, assailing us with dull raw mornings, driving sleet, and a covering of wet snow. As the bout continues the clock ticks by, with the days lengthening until light and darkness hang in the balance.

Birds, being both warm-blooded and well-insulated, can afford to take some liberties with the weather, and give free rein to their mating urges as the equinox approaches. The fiery little wren throws every scrap of his being into his song, delivering it now from some exposed branch in defiance of hawk or hail. From lungs the size of split peas, through a larynx no bigger than a lentil, the hurried notes explode. "Who-can-sit-here-and-t-t-triiillll-as-I-do-as-I-do-as-I?", he claims, and with the song plainly audible to us a furlong away it is no idle boast. When he is not singing he is crafting domed nest shells of moss and fern, several in each territory, in the hope that a she-wren will fancy one of his prime locations and set up home with him. Those that she rejects may nevertheless endure, and serve as winter shelter for years to come.

The dipper's nest-shell is a larger version of the wren's, but in its base now sits the cup of dry oak leaves which constitutes the insulation and damp-proofing layer. This week four or five eggs will be laid into this cup, as the hardiest of our small birds commits itself to the future. Some larger birds have already begun to lay, notably the tawny owl and the rook. The owl nests on a simple bed of dry woodchips in the hollow end of a broken branch, in some ancient ash or alder by a stream. Rooks, of course, prefer company. As the week begins we see them carrying mouthfuls of grass and old bedding muck to complete their nest linings, and sometimes hear strangely muffled cooing noises as they pass overhead. By mid-week we notice that amongst the birds walking draggle-trousered across our pastures, there are pairs in courtship display. And a few mornings later the sentry cocks by each nest side, with the tail tips of their mates just showing over nest edges, confirm that laying has begun.

In the woods and gardens below the rookeries, the thrush family takes the initiative. The boldest of them is the storm-cock, who not only makes his nest in a high fork amongst bare branches, but draws attention to it by weaving shreds of wool, lengths of baler twine, and scraps of plastic bag into the structure. If you fail to see the nest, his churring alarm call with lead you to it, though he is quite capable of seeing off any jackdaw or magpie which approaches too close. His cousins the blackbird and song thrush site their arbours more discreetly amongst holly and ivy, laurel and yew, or hide them away in deserted outbuildings. The two species have very similar nests at first, but as they approach completion the song thrush distinguishes the inside of hers with an immaculate rendering of wood pulp and mud. When dry, this will provide a backdrop for her sky-blue eggs more perfect than any velvet for a pearl.

On the high moors all the grouse are cocks, or so it seems if we stick to the paths. They perch on rocks or way-markers, their cinnabar eye-wattles almost throbbing with colour, or stick their heads above the heath-sward to croak at rivals. A few females may have already started laying, indeed I have even heard of them laying in February, but most do not begin until the heather burning finishes in mid-April. If we leave the paths and strike out through the heather we will see that they are merely skulking out of sight, and will join their chosen cocks as they fly off low on whirring wings.

Meanwhile very different wing-tips whirr high above, as the snipe makes near-vertical display dives of a hundred feet or more. Not only do his wing-tips whirr, but the stiffly outspread lateral tail feathers vibrate, making a quivering sound illogically known as 'drumming'. We can hear several drumming at once over moorland bogs at this time of year, and when territories are won we may even have the chance to study a stationary snipe well away from cover, as he stands proudly on a wall-top, shouting "chuka-chuka-chuka" through the mist.

Another wader which will perch on wall-tops and fence posts, particularly around wet moorside pastures, is the redshank. Redshank arrive back on these upland breeding grounds this week, having wintered in southern Europe. They can be readily distinguished from snipe by their "tlu-lu-lu" calls, the white on rump and wings, and the bright orange legs which give them their name.

Reed buntings also share the snipe's predilection for moorland bogs, at least whilst they are with us for breeding. They are more commonly considered as resident lowland birds, but at this time of year there is an influx of migrant reed buntings from mainland Europe, and a few pairs come to breed on our hills. If the weather is to be harsh in late March they will linger by riversides, so that their appearance on the uplands is a welcome sign. The black head and white collar of the male make him easily seen, and if your eyesight is not too sharp you need only listen for his monotonous "psst-psst-psaw-ch-ch-cht", repeated every few seconds for hours on end. The reed bunting is an expanding species, but his cousin the yellow bunting, or yellowhammer, seems to be on the decline in this area. Yellowhammers also arrive here about this time, but there are now so few compared to 30 years ago that they may be missed at first. Look where deciduous woods meet moorland for your best chance of finding them.

The buntings flying in from the Continent travel together with two other species, the pied wagtail and the meadow pipit. Resident individuals of both species began to re-appear in the Dales a fortnight or more ago, but now there are suddenly dozens to be seen. The wagtails remain around our farmyards and stone-walled lanes, but the pipits follow streams up onto the moor and almost immediately begin to display. The display consists of a lark-like rising flight from the ground up to about 30 feet, followed by a gliding descent with neck and tail raised, singing all the while.

Wagtails and pipits are insect eaters, and their return in large numbers is one signal of the start of the flying insect season. Other hints come from the first emergence of pipistrelle bats at dusk one evening, and the rising of trout in the rivers. My children run gleefully from a pioneer bumble bee which wants to inspect their brightly coloured clothes, and later bring in a seven-spot ladybird which they have found in the croft. A small tortoiseshell butterfly suns itself on the garden gatepost, having probably wintered either deep within the stone wall itself, or in a nearby out-building. It is rather unusual for insects to over-winter as adults, and most prefer the safety of pupae. An example is the dung-fly, which begins to emerge from now onwards but which will not become really common until dairy cows are turned out in another month or so. Some insects have even spent the winter as larvae, and up the moor this week I find an unidentified woolly-bear caterpillar, probably of one of the tiger moths, taking a quick feed amongst the heather after having survived for weeks beneath the snow.

If the arrival of wagtails and pipits is linked to the re-appearance of flying insects, the insects' resurgence is in turn due to the new growth of flowering plants. Coltsfoot and celandine are now common on roadside banks, and amongst them the first watchful flowers of the moschatel are in bloom. The pink stumps of butterbur have thrust through bare sandy ground by streamsides, whilst yellow king-cups light up the boggy places. Bright-eyed daisies dot our pastures amongst the newly-growing grass, and the woodland floor has turned green with fresh leaves of arum, bluebell, wild garlic, and dog's mercury. The flower heads of this latter have now uncurled and opened, though they serve as but a setting for the lovely blushing wood anemones that have begun to shine amongst them.

Of all the flowers that bloom this week, however, pride of place must go to the insect-attracting pussy willow. The male catkins of this small tree are often affectionately known as 'palm', because whatever the weather they always manage to open by Palm Sunday. In the days before cut flowers were available all year, sprigs of pussy willow traditionally graced country cottages with their honeyed scent, scattering pollen on embroidered dresser-cloths at Easter. Individually the little rabbit's-tail flowers are perhaps nothing special, but when seen as a host on the tree in some damp old hedgerow they signal better than any calendar that Winter has fallen, and Spring has won through at last.

March 24th – 31st

The ever-cautious hawthorn finally relaxes, and its leaves burst forth from their buds. The prickly hedges flush with a soft green, beginning in some sheltered riverside lane and moving day-by-day up the valley side. The patches of black that remain are suddenly washed with white as stands of blackthorn blossom. Eventually the warmth spreads up to the hillside larches, with the green glow starting around the edges of the plantations and suffusing inwards to their hearts.

Long-tailed tits see these green signals, and throw themselves into nest-building. Their favoured building site is the downhill side of some thorny bush on a steep bank, so that we may look upon the domed nest from above and yet not reach it from below. The nest itself is the most wondrous creation, and takes both partners over two weeks to construct. Lichens, moss, cobwebs and strands of wool are woven together into a thick elastic felt, gradually assuming the size and shape of an ostrich egg. The outer layer is decorated all over with greyish lichen, whilst the inside is lined with hundreds of feathers. The entrance hole is near the top, and when the feather lining becomes visible through it you may be sure that laying is about to commence.

Our thrushes have already begun to lay before the end of March, and this week we can compare the eggs of the three common species before the birds begin to sit. For me there are no jewels so beauteous or so perfectly set as the fair speckled gems of the song thrush, though unfortunately they also attract the wrong sort of attention. Few of these early eggs, laid when cover is still sparse, will make it through to hatching, for magpie and jay, weasel and wood mouse, all must have their Easter eggs too. The blackbird's green and brown mottled clutch attracts less attention, though the parent birds, now fixed in their shrubby territories, have become more prone to the predations of sparrowhawk and cat. Only mistle thrushes have a decent chance of success, so that each pair will normally rear only one brood per year to the other thrushes' two or three. The eggs of the mistle thrush fall mid-way between those of their two relatives in colour, but are larger and have a pinkish tinge.

Meanwhile a fourth thrush arrives high on the moor, having spent Winter in the Atlas Mountains of North Africa. Alighting on some lone mountain ash, the ring ouzel surveys with triumph the rocky bracken-clad heath of his birth. Across the pastures below, scattered flocks of his cousin fieldfares and redwings work their way slowly eastwards. A cock curlew dances attendance on his mate with raised and fluttering wings, whilst she zig-zags coquettishly before him. A pair of small swift teal fly past and drop into the heather beside a rushy bog to discuss nest sites. Lesser black-backed gulls soar high overhead shouting "argh-argh-argh-keeaargh" as they assess the hills for their egg and carrion potential, and their consequent suitability as places for rearing young. Then a bold and dashing little merlin bolts into view on the sky-line, freshly returned from the marshlands and hungry for pipits. The ring ouzel drops from his tree-top perch and swerves away amongst the rocks to safety, his panicky flight alerting another newly-arrived migrant, the wheatear.

Wheatears have had a hard time of it in recent years, and are much less common now than they used to be. This decline is partly due to several long periods of drought in sub-Saharan Africa, where wheatears spend the winter months. They can, however, be surprisingly drought-resistant, and when I lived in the north-west Kalahari Desert I once saw a cock wheatear over a hundred miles from the nearest running water. A greater part of their decline seems to me to be due to the current emphasis on preservation of raptors. From having far too few raptors, due to the cumulative effects of old-fashioned pesticides, we now have rather too many. The wheatear, with its habit of perching on moor-edge wall-tops, is a perfect sucker for both sparrowhawk and merlin attacks, though the merlin may itself fall prey to the sparrowhawk where their ranges overlap. Wheatears, which were as common as titlarks 30 years ago, are now so scarce that you may miss the first arrivals. This is a pity, for they are the first of the truly African migrants to return and in a good year may be seen up here from the 18th March onwards.

Lesser black-backs are not the only species keeping an eye on the moors for eggs and carrion, for great broad-winged carrion crows know that this is the season for tewit eggs and sheep cleansings, and patrol the intakes accordingly. They cry "pawk, pawk" as they pass, but then appear incongruously light-hearted as they perform the exaggerated wing-beats and graceful glides of their nuptial flights. This week they have begun their nest-building in the tree-tops up isolated wooded valleys. The carrion is the most solitary of our three common crows, through even he will often tolerate two or three others in the same patch of woodland. His nest resembles that of a rook, but in areas where nests are regularly shot at from below the base may be unusually thick. I have even known a carrion crow incorporate many short lengths of rusty wire into the base of his nest as a sort of primitive armour plating, for all crows are clever and he is the cleverest.

His bright-eyed little cousin the jackdaw hides his nest from view, but pairs may now be seen carrying scraps of sheep's wool, sometimes collected directly from the sheep's back, into holes in hollow trees or old buildings. If the inside of the hole was originally too large it may have been filled up with hundreds of twigs, a practice which causes problems when jackdaws select one of our chimney pots as a likely-looking nest-hole.

The jackdaw's nest, high, dry and dark, could not be more different from that of the coot, which is also nest-building now. The coot drags strands of rotting waterside vegetation together to form a warm humid island of compost rising several inches from the water. Unlike the recently-returned dabchick, with which she shares her pond and her nesting habits, the coot does not even cover her eggs when she leaves them. Until the plantain and flag iris leaves grow up to hide them, the eggs are exposed to the gaze of every aerial egg thief. It is surprising how few are taken.

Part of the reason for this must be their island situation, though this would pose no barrier to the amphibious mink. When mink were at their most common, the numbers of coot, waterhen and other riparian nesters plunged. The relatively few mink that remain in the upper Dales are bloated with a surfeit of frogs and young rabbits at this time of year, and hardly bother bird nests. The mink is also one of the few animals that can cope with the poisonous skin of toads, apparently by catching and skinning them under-water. In Spring 1979 I found a cache of dead and half-dead toads amongst the roots of an alder beside the old fish-ponds, which I attributed to the ravages of a mink. Some of the live ones were horribly mutilated, with their entire hindquarters eaten away whilst their forelegs still made crawling movements and their eyes blinked. Most car-nivorous animals, and especially mustelids, will kill way beyond their food requirements when faced with a prey which cannot flee, such as housed chickens, but this was the most grisly example I have yet seen.

Common Frog
(Rana temporaria)

nelson 92

Common Toad
(Bufo bufo)

Yet despite all the common frog and the common toad remain common, largely due to the abundance of their offspring. They may remain away from their native pond for up to four years before they reach full adulthood, but once they return each pair may produce a couple of thousand fertile eggs. With that sort of family they can afford a few losses. Toads prefer lower-lying habitats than frogs, and because their eggs and tadpoles are distasteful to fish they can breed in ponds which frogs cannot use. But in these particular old fish-ponds frogs and toads breed side by side. The great wobbly masses of frogspawn, just beginning to hatch, are now overlaid by long thin strands of fresh toad-spawn as the bonded pairs weave erratically through the vegetation, laying all the while.

There is one final event to be experienced before the end of March, and that is the start of the badger watching season. In fact badgers can be seen at any time of year, and I know of enthusiasts who have sat through driving sleet at midnight to glimpse one in Winter. For me the season starts when the clocks go forward, and in the few days between then and the end of March there is usually at least one mild calm evening which is suitable.

I potter up to the badger sett long before sunset, pausing at a fox earth along the way to sniff and listen. Most fox cubs have been born during the last week or two, and by approaching an earth with the softest of footfalls and listening at the entrance you may hear the sucking and snickering noises deep within, until your scent wafts down the hole and they are silenced. The vixen's breeding earth never smells as strongly as the dog fox's lair, but there is the faintest tomcat whiff about it and the first fly of the season buzzes past my face as I listen.

At the badger sett I settle down on the opposite bank with my back against a tree, and let myself soak into the surroundings. An early speedwell on the bank beside me closes its bright blue bird's-eye as the sun fades. The blackbird's chickering alarms die away. A venturesome wood-louse emerges from beneath a stone, makes a short foray over my hand, and returns to his hole to await a safer darkness. Night steals colours from the spectrum, leaving only shades of grey. I begin to imagine black and white striped faces at every hole. An owl hoots once, and then a roding woodcock flies over going deceptively fast on steady wing-beats, head high, beak dipped. "Croak-croaky-croak-squeak," he calls repeatedly, stepping up the tempo if he meets a rival on his border patrol.

Then suddenly the badger is out, a smallish sow with a finely tapering face and short bushy tail. She goes below and emerges from another hole, pointing her nose upwards and testing the wind. Then she is gone again and I quickly check the time: 8.17 pm. A few seconds later she is back on the surface, nosing around the table of earth outside the hole and rubbing her scent glands on an elder stump. Satisfied, she settles on her rump in a slight hollow, leans backwards, and contentedly grooms her black belly fur with her clumsy forepaws. Finally she stands, shakes herself, scratches her ear with a hind foot, and trots off again below ground to give her cubs one last drink of milk before she sets out to forage. I slip softly away into the night, leaving her in peace in the home her family built a hundred or more generations ago.

4 April

April is lambing time for horned ewes, and our hill farmers take on a distracted look. Lambs skip and bleat in their picturesque way, though they are born to get snow on their backs and the hard weather is not finished yet. Snow and frost there may be, particularly if the Winter has been mild, but April's principal mood is endearingly girlish. She cannot decide whether to laugh or cry, and gives us both sunshine and showers in equal parts.

And of course these April showers bring forth wild flowers, so that from a couple of dozen species that have flowered in the year up to the beginning of the month, we surge ahead to four score by the end. Take an illustrated book of flowers and a little folding lens in your pocket, and identify the blooms where they grow. You will be continually entranced, not only by the quiet beauty of our flora but by their delightfully rustic names. Shepherd's purse, lady's mantle, milkmaid, cowslip, mouse-ear, forget-me-not, red campion and Jack-by-the-hedge are amongst those which will start to bloom in April.

We begin the month with the tree branches bare and the skies almost empty, and end it with the freshness of new leaf and the twittering of swallows.

April 1st – 7th

The change to British Summer Time means that mornings are darker again for a few days, but there is a restlessness in our blood now which takes no account of clocks. I awake before dawn and sit on the bedroom window ledge, looking out over fields where lapwings nest. As the light strengthens, I begin a methodical search through binoculars, checking the darker patches for the protruding heads and tails which reveal the tewits' nest sites. I count four, note their position carefully, and get ready to go and visit them.

I can walk straight to the first one, for it is on the edge of a small boggy patch within a couple of yards of a dead thistle, and its position was easily memorized. There in the simple saucer of fragmented straw sit the four pointed eggs, arranged with perfect neatness. The parent has only started sitting within the last few hours, and it will be another 25 days and nights before the eggs chip. The young which emerge will be already robust, able to run from the nest on long strong legs within an hour or two of hatching. To sustain this development inside the shell, the lapwing is required to lay quite a large egg for the size of her body. This is perhaps one reason for the pointed end, another being that when all four points are together the eggs fully and exactly fit the four quadrants of a circle. There is thus a minimum of wasted space, enabling all four eggs to be properly covered throughout the long incubation.

After the first nest the others are more difficult to find, especially with the parents screaming and dive-bombing to distract me. Now that I am actually in the fields instead of looking at them from above, the number of dark tussocks has increased and the original marker points are not so obvious. But the time spent looking for them is not wasted, for as I scrutinize the ground I find the first snail I have seen this year, positively racing homeward through the dew before the sun catches him out. And in the first warming rays a creeping buttercup blooms by the bog, whilst creamy anthers light up the little brown tufts of field woodrush amongst the rough grass.

By going to the sites that seem about right, and walking out from them in ever increasing circles, I am eventually able to find two of the remaining three memorized nests. Even then I walk past one within a couple of yards before spotting it on the next time round. Both have three eggs, which even in this open field are marvellously camouflaged by their blotched and speckled olive-brown.

Ground-nesting birds almost always have eggs which are dull-coloured or blotched, or both, with the obvious advantage of making them difficult for crows and gulls to find. Those which do not fit this rule include some ducks, geese and harriers, which nest in ground cover and are large enough to defend their eggs, and grebe, which cover their eggs with debris when they leave the nest. Other birds that lay white or very pale eggs have to hide them away in holes, the only exceptions amongst good-sized birds round here being the collared dove and the woodpigeon.

In another fortnight these two will lay quite large and obvious white eggs, and what is more they will lay them on a simple flat platform of twiglets in the very areas most frequented by magpies, jackdaws, jays and squirrels. Nor will they lay large clutches in anticipation of heavy losses, for two is the norm. I can postulate that they lay white eggs because they have recently evolved from an ancestor which nested in holes, like the stock dove, but I cannot understand how such tempting and visible eggs escape the attention of the egg thieves afore-mentioned.

Nevertheless the two species not only survive but abound, the collared dove in particular having dramatically extended its range over the last three decades. Woodpigeons will nest in any thicket, from hilltop larch plantations through holly and hawthorn hedges down to valley bottom gardens, but in the Dales the collared dove stays near villages. This week the two species attract our attention with the repetitive cooing that accompanies their mating rituals, and in wooded gardens we may compare their notes. The harsh "kwerrr" belongs to the collared dove, but it also has a harping three-note song "coo-COOO-kuk" compared to the sleepy "coo-HOOOR-cu, coo-coo" of the woodpigeon.

These two birds have to wait for at least some leaf cover before laying their eggs, but birds that stick to the rules have already begun to lay their white eggs in holes. Thus the little owl is even now incubating her four, deep within a gnarled old oak, whilst in a much larger hole in a riverside ash the goosander has laid about half of her down-bedded clutch of ten. The greater spotted woodpecker will not lay hers for another month, but her mate is already testing the trees in which he will excavate the nest, and proclaiming his territory by drumming. To do this he selects a solidly resonant dead branch in a wooded amphitheatre, and bangs the tip of his beak against it with great force and rapidity. This produces a vibrating *basso profondo* which carries for several hundred yards, and sets a thousand grubs a-cringeing.

The kingfisher will also lay her white eggs in a hole in late April, and as with the woodpecker the male is busy defining his realm at present. For this he needs nothing more than his vivid colours and a reedy "peep, peep". For the next few days we will see him flying up and down the river, sometimes with his mate, way beyond their usual range. Kingfishers seldom nest in the upper Dales, though we may occasionally find abandoned attempts in overgrown sandbanks, identifiable by the fish-bone pellets scattered nearby. Their usual nesting range reaches up the Wharfe to within a mile of Bolton Bridge, and up the Aire beyond Gargrave. One has successfully nested for several years on a tributary of the Aire at the bottom of my sister's garden in Skipton.

Another hole-nester is the starling, which has eggs of

such a pale blue as to almost pass for white. This week the pairs may be seen repeatedly entering holes in trees and barns carrying feathers and scraps of dead grass to complete the nest begun by the male in March. I climb a beck-side alder in the valley to check a likely-looking hole for eggs, and when I peer therein I am immediately set upon by a swarm of small black fleas. These are evidently the offspring of parasites which plagued starling nestlings in this hole last year, and they have probably been poised on bended knees for days waiting for the first meals-on-wings to arrive. They must be disappointed with me, for I manage to brush most of them off without falling from the tree, and later duck my head in the stream to make life difficult for the rest.

There is a blue tit nest-hole in this same tree, but these tits are not nesting yet. They need to see leaves on the trees and butterflies on the wing before they begin to lay, so as to be assured of a supply of caterpillars for their young. In fact some blue tits are still in small flocks, and I watch one such party moving through the branches of a wild damson. The bright new colours of their mating plumage make a pretty sight amongst the newly-opened blossom, but their half-raised crests and repeated churring notes show that this is more a loose association of pairs than a properly constituted flock.

As I watch them tearing at unopened buds in search of larvae, a slightly larger and duller bird alights on the top-most twig. For a few seconds I am in doubt, and then it resolves my problem by singing "tsip-tsap" a few times, ending on a "tsip". It is, of course, the chiff-chaff, a lowland bird which passes here about now and comes back through in September, but rarely remains.

In the Dales the chiff-chaff cannot compete with the hardier willow warbler, which it very closely resembles. Willow warblers normally arrive a week or two after chiff-chaffs, having travelled much further, but now that one has returned I cannot resist looking for the other. I start by the riverside willows which give it its name, and wander up through the woods to its favourite moorside birches, but all to no avail. The only item of interest is the large number of fox droppings strategically placed along the moor-edge track, linked to dog foxes extending their home ranges. They do this partly because they are having to help feed their families, but also because the vixens have vacated large parts of their own territories to remain near to the breeding earths.

Across the moor there seem to be grouse everywhere, supporting the old adage that they are most when they are least, and vice versa. Thus in the breeding season after the ravages of Winter they make themselves very obvious, but when the chicks are young they all hide below the heath-sward. I check amongst the bobs of heather and crowberry for eggs, but find only bare hollows with the odd tell-tale feather. The crowberry itself rewards inspection, however, for it is now showing dark red clusters of tiny male flowers. The neighbouring bilberry is also in flower, the tiny pink lampshades appearing at the same time as the first pale leaves. Bilberry flowers have a tangy-sweet nectar content which is only just discernible to adults, but I chewed hundreds on Storiths Crag as a child and the taste of the flower even now transports me back to those happy days.

April 8th – 15th

The moor is a grand place to be now, and sunrise finds me lying amongst the heather overlooking a hidden sphagnum bog. Across the hollow, plainly visible through the binoculars, a Canada goose sits on her downy nest attended by a fussy gander. Triumphant larks sing high above, and all along the ridges pipits adjust their boundaries with fluttering squabbles. On a patch of moor grass beside me, a dor beetle rolls a pellet of sheep dung into a freshly excavated nursery crypt.

Dor beetles form a surprisingly large part of the diet of kestrels and other small raptors, to say nothing of foxes, but hen kestrels are laying now, and the cocks will be searching for larger prey to take back to their mates. I see one dive into the rushes below and fly off with a field vole, then a few minutes later watch a moor owl quartering the same patch. The moor owl takes the place of the barn owl in most parts of the Dales, and hunts in a similar way. It is often seen by daylight over damp moorland fluttering like a giant brown moth a few feet above the rushes, now gliding on raised wings, now hovering, now wheeling aside or dropping like stone onto some furry little victim.

Some moor owls stay all year, and nest within a mile or two of where I am watching this one, but others come from northern Europe for Winter. These latter are now moving northwards again, at the same time as the residents are re-establishing their territories, so that for a week or two we may see moor owls amost every day. Other large raptors are also passing through from further north, including the odd harrier, goshawk, osprey and golden eagle. They sometimes stay a week or two, causing a stir amongst bird tickers, but they are not really at home here. Thus in one year an eagle is found dead after crashing into a power line, and in another a hungry osprey is driven to raiding local trout farms and even killing pigeons. It was also during this week in 1972 that I last heard of ravens on our moors, though until about 1964 they nested on Rylstone Fell whenever the keepers missed them.

Today I see none of these scarce birds of passage, and after about an hour I pick my way down across the bog, disturbing the Canadas by my approach. They fly round me on buzzing wings, bugling "get, get-over," and becoming greatly agitated as I pass by their nest and inspect its five huge eggs. A little further on, a snipe flushes from almost under my feet, and I find its nest concealed within a bob of rushes. The four eggs resemble those of the lapwing in colour, shape and arrangement. They are slightly smaller than the lapwing's, but their size relative to the hen's body is probably even greater.

The snipe's nest reminds me that woodcock must also be sitting, and I head down off the moor through rough farmland to check the woods. En route I call at one of the very few permanent ponds on this hillside, which I have not checked since last Autumn. Little white flowers of moorland crowfoot star its surface, whilst inverted backswimmers row frantically below. A shiny black whirligig floats up to change his air bubble, and jerks away back down through fronds of weed. In a muddy underwater glade a group of crusty water lice creepily squabble over a tadpole's mortal remnants. The frog tadpoles here are now almost half grown, though one is grabbed by a backswimmer even as I watch, and quickly subdued by the bug's lethal proboscis. These moorside ponds are aquatic microcosms into which we can peer like gods, but their life forms are best studied in July, when dragonflies are on the wing, and so I carry on downhill.

There are woodcock in any Dales wood that lets in enough light for bracken to grow, and they are not uncommon birds. But their camouflage is so superb that you will often walk past within a few feet without suspecting their presence, particularly when they are nesting. If you are actively searching for woodcock nests, then seek out those parts of the wood overlooking a stream or muddy patch, where the trees are not too closely packed together and where there is a good mixture of old and young, broad-leaved and coniferous. You should then zig-zag back and forth across these patches, stopping every few yards and starting again rather sharply. This will so disturb any sitting woodcock that if you happen to stop within a couple of yards of its nest it may fly off as you start moving again. I follow this procedure for almost an hour, concentrating on those areas where I have found nests in the past, and find not a single one. So much for the protocol.

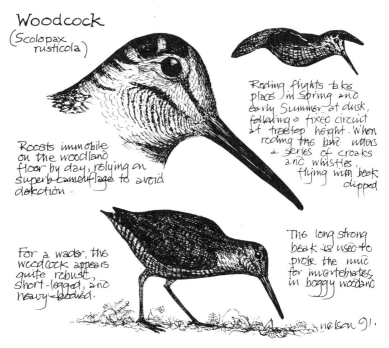

Woodcock
(Scolopax
    rusticola)

Roosts immobile on the woodland floor by day, relying on superb camouflage to avoid detection.

Roding flights take place in spring and early summer at dusk, following a fixed circuit at treetop height. When roding the bird utters a series of croaks and whistles, flying with beak dipped.

For a wader, the woodcock appears quite robust, short-legged, and heavy-bodied.

The long strong beak is used to probe the mud for invertebrates in boggy woodland.

nelson 91.

The time is not wasted, however, for my wandering disturbs a harsh-voiced jay, and I find what seems to be its nest near the top of a young larch. Jays choose inaccessible nest sites, and although they are not especially high I have only ever found one to which I could climb. Even that one taxed my agility and had no eggs when I reached it, so that my knowledge of jays' eggs comes only from books. Jays remain with us throughout the year, but they can be very secretive when it suits their purpose, and are not much seen during the leafy seasons. Magpies also become less noticeable, and if their bulky nests are highly visible they are nevertheless well protected from below. Near my home last year, two keepers at opposite sides of an ash tree both shot at a magpie nest in the topmost branches, only to see the bird fly off intact as they turned to walk away.

On the woodland floor I note that the first bluebells are opening, and lie down beside one to share its scented breath. The wood anemones, or windflowers, are now wide open and beaming at the sky, but wood sorrels are only just daring to show their pale faces. The wood sorrel would pass for a shy little sister of the wood anemone, but it is actually related neither to the windflower nor to the true sorrels. It gets its name from its three-heart leaves, which have a tangy-acid taste that was once used as a sour relish to liven up bland salads.

Green leaves are bourgeoning now on pathside hazels, and even the more impetuous of the sycamore and birch saplings are showing new leaf. The very quality of light is different, for the sun has begun to rise more steeply and the air is fresh and clear. As I leave the woods the morning sun warms by face and lightens my step. I do not exactly skip, but I feel that at any minute I might. A mistle thrush hops through the dew with her beak half-full of grey grubs, a sure sign that her eggs have hatched. When she cocks her head on one side, is she really looking at the ground, as the experts agree, or listening, as anthropomorphism suggests? I stick to the traditional idea that she is listening for movements, for how else could she find those grubs below the ground surface? I watch her pick up a larger victim, only to discard it, and on investigation I find one of our big black slugs, lying now like a miniature whale pierced by the bird's harpoon.

The re-appearance of these molluscs is a sure sign of impending rain, and indeed we may know that in April a sunny dawn heralds a wet noon. I am at my furthest point from home, and stride out along the river bank as the clouds gather. A grey wagtail escorts me some of the way, gossiping all the while to distract my attention from its nest on an ivy-covered rock face across the river. Four sand martins fly over going erratically upstream, freshly back from Africa and following the water-course up to their native sandy bank. Sand martins are always a welcome sight in Spring, not only for themselves but also because they blaze the trail for the willow warblers and swallows a few days behind. Most smaller birds, even upland species like the ring ouzel, migrate back here by following the east coast up to Humber, the Humber to the Ouse, and thence to their chosen dale and beck. A visit to Spurn Head or Blacktoft Sands at this time of year has more thrills for the ardent bird watcher than the Cup Final and the Grand National combined.

I also follow a favoured beck back up towards my roosting site, noting where nuthatches have clayed up an opening in an old oak branch to leave a hole just big enough for them to squeeze through to nest. Further on, where the valley sides begin to steepen, I visit the long-tailed tits to see how they are faring. Hawthorn leaves now partly mask their nest, but an inch of dark tail protruding through the feathered entrance shows that the laying hen is within. Also on this bank the first poor-man's pansies are in bloom. Some southern botanist christened these 'dog' violets, to distinguish them from the sweet violets of his chalky downland. To me it was the man and not the flower that was dog.

Another derogatory term is 'weed', and many of the species we call weeds would be in plant pots on our window sills if they were rare. At this time of year we might wish that some of them were more rare, particularly groundsel and ground elder. Groundsel has only begun to flower this week along the wayside, but it has been flowering in my garden for at least a fortnight, and has to be cleared before it seeds. When the lunchtime rain has passed I set myself to tackling these diligent survivors in the border.

Nature must rather resent gardeners tampering with her handiwork, and I am a reluctant spadesman. I find myself studying ladybirds and bumble bees, and following honey-bees around to check their preferences. A robin settles a few feet from me, in search of worms on the weeded bits, and I break off to look for his nest. I find what I take to be it amongst some ivy on the wall, but realise my mistake when I see a pair of hedge sparrows bringing moss to that nest. House sparrows are also nesting, busily carrying dead grass under the slates on the hen-house roof. The starling, by contrast, makes only a couple of visits to her hole in the barn wall, with her beak apparently empty, and I realise there are eggs in the nest now. Thirteen bird species nested in or immediately adjacent to my garden last year, and the tedium of weeding is pleasantly fragmented by the boyish fun of bird-nesting.

And on the 14th, as the week draws to an end, I finally hear the sound I have been anticipating all week. On an early morning walk up Strid Wood the delightfully clear and lazy cadence of the first willow warbler comes streaming down, like the sound of dappled sunlight. With my eyes closed and a bluebell to my nose, it could almost be May.

April 16th – 23rd

One swallow may not a Summer make, but one willow warbler certainly makes a Spring. Within a day of the first one being heard, we can stand anywhere in open woodland and listen to half-a-dozen at once. From riverside beeches to moorside birches the flood of little songsters spreads out. They work their way from branch to branch and tree to tree, peering beneath the twigs and amongst the new leaves to pick at tiny insects. Two nights of light frost and a powdering of snow do not seem to dull their enthusiasm, and by the 18th even the most isolated tree-island on the moor is colonized.

On the 18th a single swallow turns up in the Red Lion farmyard by the river, and word spreads round the village. In 1935 my father saw one near Bolton Priory on the 8th April, but in most years the first sighting is within 3 days of the 18th. Swallows arrive in trickles rather than floods, and keep to the valley bottom for the first few days. It will be another week before they reach the upland farms to check their old nest-sites on mistal roof beams.

Whilst swallows are still confined to the main water-course in search of early mayflies, the sandpipers arrive, already paired. Each pair lays claim to a stretch of river which includes a bank running down almost to the water's edge. It is on this bank that they will hide their nest in May, but before then they have to strengthen the newly-formed pair bond, chase off rivals, and feed themselves up to peak condition on the water larvae that abound in the river's shallow margins. They also need to check that their proposed nest-site is really as suitable as it first appears, and is not, for instance, subject to regular invasions by tourists and their dogs. As with all waders, these processes are associated with a good deal of noise, and our walks near the river from now on will be accompanied by the urgently piped "kitty-needie" calls. The birds may be seen either flying low over the water on trembling down-curved wings, or walking by the river's edge with heads and tails a-bobbing.

The arrival of the sandpiper brings our population of breeding waders and their allies up to the full complement of eight – lapwing, golden plover, oyster catcher, curlew, woodcock, snipe, sandpiper and redshank. Greenshank used to nest here, and perhaps still do in some parts of the Dales, for they are regularly seen around the larger tarns and reservoirs for a few days about now, together with the odd stray dotterel, dunlin, or whimbrel. Whilst these fly-by-nights move on towards their breeding grounds in the northern mountains, the waders here are already irrevocably committed. Sandpipers may be still just settling in, but curlew, redshank and oyster catcher are all about to start laying and the rest are not far off hatching.

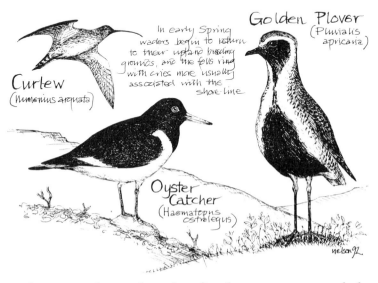

Curlew (*Numenius arquata*)

In early Spring waders begin to return to their upland breeding grounds, and the fells ring with cries more usually associated with the shore-line

Golden Plover (*Pluvialis apricaria*)

Oyster Catcher (*Haematopus ostralegus*)

nelson 92

Oyster catchers, when they first began to nest regularly in the Dales in the 1960s, chose the most foolish of nest sites. Commonest was a bed of shingle beside the river, where the eggs would be washed away with the first fresh, but nests were also made in fields in mid-cultivation, and I even heard of one on top of a fence post. Natural selection operates very rapidly in such circumstances, and oyster catchers began to move up to the higher pastures favoured by curlew and lapwing. However, they remained nostalgic for the sea shore, and persisted in nesting amongst pebbles, even if these were quarry-bottoms that had been used to fill in a boggy track or gate-hole. Most recently they seem to have made a fair compromise by nesting amongst dead twigs on the bare patches where heather has been burnt off. If a peregrine does not get the parents or a moor owl the chicks, the oyster catcher will be back again next year to bring a breath of sea air to our moorland tops. The fool has many friends, and I for one wish him well.

Whilst our moor owl, or short-eared owl, prepares to nest, the first eggs of long-eared and tawny owls are already hatching. Long-eared owls are not common, have a quiet moaning hoot, hunt almost always by night, and spend the day hiding in the tops of coniferous trees. They may therefore exist in an area without ever being seen, though if you are going to see them in the Dales it is likely to be in the few weeks from now onwards, when they are feeding their young. Look where water runs by or through hillside larch plantations, particularly near the old crow or squirrel nests which they renovate for their own use. And whilst you are looking for a long-eared owl, keep your ears open for the soft churring twitter of redpolls. Although these little finches are traditionally associated with stands of birch and alder, they seem to have a fascination at this time of year for the newly-opening flowers of larch and ash. The tufty sprays of ash flowers precede the leaves, making it difficult to identify the dull-coloured redpolls against the sky, but against the new larch foliage it should be possible to pick out their dark red foreheads amongst the little pink flowers.

I am not sure of the status of these wandering bands of redpolls, for the species rarely nests in this area and yet most finches have already paired and settled down. Perhaps these are the first year adults or other non-breeding individuals, since all populations contain a percentage of birds which do not breed in any given year. Certainly the chaffinches and goldfinches are already paired, and indeed there is a pair of goldfinches back in my garden for the third year running. These prettiest of finches well deserve the collective name of 'charm' for their bright markings alone, never mind their tinkling fairy-bell song.

Other birds already nesting in the garden include blackbird, wren and pied wagtail. Poor John Clare wrote 150 years ago of the blackbird's propensity for nesting in odd situations, and there is never a Spring passes without a newspaper article about a blackbird's nest beneath a car bonnet, on bicycle handlebars, or somewhere similarly incongruous and inconvenient. The 17 I have found so far this year have been in fairly conventional situations, though one was on the ground within six feet of a badger highway and another at eye level in a wall beside a busy footpath. The one in my yew bush contains newly-hatched nestlings now, and both parents are busy stuffing the hungry orange gapes. Jenny wren has finally accepted a nest amongst the old hay in a disused hay-rack, and after lining it with feathers she has begun to lay her clutch. Within a week she will have laid 7 eggs, and together they will weigh more than she does. And the neat and trim pied wagtail picks her way daintily across my lawn, and flies off with some scrap to add to her nest in the garden wall.

The pied wagtail is so much a bird of the farmyard that we still call it 'muck-bird' even when most yards no longer have muck-middens. The grey wagtail, by contrast, thrives only by running water. A third wagtail, which should occupy the fields in between, is now sadly declining. This is the gentle yellow wagtail, which used to arrive this week to flitter about amongst the new flush of dandelions, catching little black March flies and newly emerged spiders. We still see a few, but most will pass on up the dale to the high tops around Malham, where the pace of farming practice is slower and the yellow wagtail can still feel at home.

Our own tops give way to heather before they reach any great height, and there are relatively few insects amongst the heather. The plant is, however, the be-all and end-all of the grouse's aspirations, providing it with food and shelter, home and nursery, cradle and grave. The nest hollows which last fortnight were empty now have clutches of 8–10 closely-speckled eggs, and with the hen grouse incubating you may literally step on one before it flies away. I once did just that, and as she struggled free to fly off, the hen broke one egg. Knowing that she would return, and be none the wiser if one egg were missing, I removed the broken one and began to wipe the bits of yolk off a couple of others. To my surprise the blotches wiped off like water-colour, and although I managed to replace them speckled side up I have often wondered since how she manages to lay eggs with water-soluble colours without smudging the speckles.

You will not endear yourself to game-keepers if you go wandering through the heather disturbing grouse nests, and you should stick to paths even in the access areas. By the pathside the golf-ball sized lumps of 'sitting muck', dull green with a creamy-white coating, will signal to you that all is well and the grouse are sitting. You may find the odd grouse nest beneath a clump of heather even by pathsides on the wilder parts of the moor, though near the moor-edge you are just as likely to find a pheasant nest there instead. Over-stocking of the Estate woodlands with pheasants has led to the more pioneering cocks taking their hens beyond the protection of managed greenwoods, and their large clutches of pale brown eggs may now be found in any cover from riverside to ridge top. And if you have the chance to go probing amongst cover along the moorside, particularly in bobs of rushes, keep an eye open for young leverets, the fruits of mad March. If you find one, look in the neighbouring bobs for others, for there will be two or three cached separately away. Resist the temptation to handle these lovely creatures, for to do so may be to condemn them to starvation when the doe smells your hands and rejects them.

Also whilst you are out on the moor, keep an ear cocked for the ring ouzel. If you think there is an elusive bird calling "chrrt-chrrt-chrrt" from cover 30 yards away, look instead atop a stunted tree 300 yards away for the white crescent of a ring ouzel's chest, and marvel at the bird's vocal powers. It is no great tune, but it is a great voice.

And finally, no account of a week in April would be complete without some mention of its flowers. So many are blooming now that we can no longer cover them all. If you do not know them, you can make your own fun looking them up to discover their secret lives and their place in our folk-lore. Make a start by the wayside, differentiating the ground ivy from the red dead-nettle. These two get their English names from the resemblance of their leaves to those of ivy and stinging nettle respectively, but they are actually both relatives of the wild mint. The wild cabbage group, known as crucifers, are also flowering now. Thus on dry waste ground the shepherd's purse will soon be developing the tiny seed pods which give it its ironic name, whilst in damper sites the other wild cresses are flowering, first the hairy bittercress, then wood bittercress, then thale cress. Another crucifer, which resembles them in all but colour, is the pale pink milkmaid, sometimes known as the cuckoo flower because it will just be becoming noticeable when the cuckoo arrives next week. Growing alongside it in its favoured damp places may be an understated little rose called water avens, whose down-turned pink and yellow flowers are quietly opening now.

And on those same damp banks, so long as they are free from chemical fertilizers, will be found the first cowslips. These quaint old-fashioned flowers once almost disappeared locally, as the over-application of 'bag-muck' and the utilization of every field corner damaged their habitat. Milk quotas did them a favour, for it is no longer profitable to strain every field to its limit, and farmers can afford to leave some forgotten corners to be forever England.

April 24th – 30th

Another few showers, another few sunny periods, and
Nature hangs the pictures on the wall. Bright colours light
up the damp hedge-bottoms and sunny waysides which
suit so many of our native flowers, so that you can be a
naturalist now even if you cannot walk far. Coltsfoot may
be past their best and already seeding, but there are galaxies
of celandines still, and banks of primroses in the damper
places. Dandelions crowd the verges, but are held back
from the walls by ranks of stiffly upright Jack-by-the-hedge.
The large pale leaves of these latter taste of garlic, but
their heads of cross-shaped white flowers reveal them as
crucifers, so that they well deserve their alternative name
of garlic mustard.

Other white roadside flowers appearing now include the
common mouse-ear, with its eponymous leaves; its larger
relative the greater stitchwort, or 'stitch'; the white dead-
nettle, whose flowers children love to suck for their nectar;
and the first lacy heads of cow parsley, which next month
will froth up on every verge. If the road runs now and then
through woodland, as most roads do in the middle Dales,
we may see the stars of wood garlic beginning to shine
amongst the bluebells; the pink splashes of red campion,
a type of wild carnation; or the sickly-looking toothwort,
which sucks sap from the roots of hazel and elm.

But it is not only flowers which we find by the roadsides.
Hedgehogs have found plentiful supplies of worms during
the last few weeks, and are back in condition for breeding.
Unfortunately this involves a lot of running about in search
of prickly encounters, and there are now increasing numbers
of sad little corpses to show where the primitive insectivore
has encountered the twentieth century. Another insectivore may also be found dead beside paths and roads just
now, and that is the common shrew. Shrews are highly
territorial and combative, and if one is chased from his
home by a stronger rival he is at a disadvantage in the
territory of his neighbours, and becomes a refugee. Like
all refugees, he suffers badly from the combined effects of
stress and starvation, though in his case death supervenes
within hours because of his feverish metabolism. Thus his
tiny body, no bigger than the last joint of your thumb, is
often unmarked and is well worth examination, both to
study its structure and to check for parasites.

If you happen to find a grey beetle or two beneath the body, these are not parasites but burying beetles, attracted thereto by the smell of decay. They will entomb the corpse, attend to its preservation, and later feed it to their newly hatched young until they are big enough to help themselves.

Rabbits also form part of the roadside carnage, though they would seem to have enough enemies without the motor car. A feral tom-cat stalks up the blind spot below a hillside nest burrow, and then suddenly springs over the edge and runs straight towards the hole. The young rabbits are thrown into confusion, but one dashes towards its familiar refuge and into the jaws of the cat. Still alive, but dangling by the scruff with pathetic trust, it is carried away in stately grace and killed in the cover the some rushes. Across the valley a soaring buzzard, newly re-established in the area, spots a young rabbit that seems recklessly bold, and drops in on whistling wings to deliver the death sentence. And in a sandy new burrow by the river an inquisitive mink stumbles on a pregnant doe, and ends six lives in one.

Now that the mink population has declined, the birds that nest by riversides are back to normal numbers. Dippers have been frantically busy for the last three weeks catching river-bottom low-life to carry to their rapidly-growing young. To do this they may either wade by the pebbled edges, in competition with the grey wagtail and sandpiper, or dive into deeper, faster-flowing water. When diving they 'fly' down through the water on short stiff wings like minia-ture penguins, and then use their feet to scramble among the bottom probing for prey. The air trapped in their feathers gives them a silvery appearance, and as it escapes it leaves a trail of little bubbles on the surface. Their prey includes caddis-worms, stone-fly nymphs, water lice, fresh-water shrimps and small bullheads, and each parent may catch up to 500 of these items each day, calling at the nest every couple of minutes to deliver a beakful. The entrance to the nest is now streaked with white faeces, showing that the young are almost ready to fly. Within a few days the female will be laying again, leaving the male to care for any young that have survived the first dangerous week of life.

Surprisingly few do, though dipper chicks fare better than some bird species. The first flotillas of mallard ducklings are on the river now, paddling after their mothers with sur-prising vigour, and already able to dive and swim under-water. But within a few days these clutches of ten or twelve will be reduced to one or two by predation and mis-adventure, ensuring that only the fittest survive. The same is true of waterhens, which will start with about seven and be lucky if they rear two. Indeed, many waterhen eggs do not even hatch, for the bird insists on nesting just a few inches above running water, on a little island in mid-stream or on a branch overhanging a beck. One short rainstorm, one little flood, and all is lost. Can it just be luck that in most years there is only gentle rain during the four weeks from mid-April to mid-May when they are laying and incubating their eggs?

Waterside birds which nest rather later than this must take steps to protect themselves from the flooding of late May and early June. Thus great crested grebe nest on home-made islands exclusively on the larger reservoirs and tarns, where the water level remains constant. They may be viewed there now, engrossed in their strange courtship dances. These rituals take various forms, but the most spec tacular display is the one in which the pair rush towards each other with necks outstretched, and then raise them-selves vertically upwards on pattering feet, breast to breast, frill feathers raised, and heads nodding jerkily from side to side.

Black-headed gulls also nest by our reservoirs, though usually beside more acid upland waters than those used by grebe. They remove themselves from the risk of flooding by siting their colonies on raised ground set back from the edge, and indeed may nest around little black-pool peat hags well away from the main body of water. Where the ground is swampy they build low platforms of rushes for their simple nests, and from the beginning of this week we can find the eggs. Some nests have one, some four, but most usually there are two or three, with the colours quite variable even in the same clutch. We can spot the gulleries from a distance by the white squadrons wheeling above them. As we approach, the noise increases, except for the sudden hush as all the laying hens take off. Whilst we try to pick our way between the nests we are showered with watery droppings as the birds make repeated dive bombing attacks, supported by a constant screaming chatter. Such a colony of nests so easily accessible must attract foxes, but the wall of noise, the smell, and the confusion of fluttering white wings probably so disorientates them that we find few empty nests, and those only on the edge of the colony.

Another bird which nests in colonies near to water is

the sand martin, though it has little in common with gulls. It nests near the top of the little cliffs of sand along the river bank, well above the level of any spring flood. The nest is in a chamber at the end of a tunnel, and this week sees the birds renovating old tunnels and excavating new ones. The dull little martin has led the swallow all the way from Africa, and now reminds its more glamorous cousin that it is time to be breeding. The swallows seem to part almost reluctantly from the riverside, and make their way erratically up the becks until, sighting their native farmstead, they are suddenly seized with joy. They flit round my yard and roof-tops twittering "be quick, be quick" to their companions, causing the blackbird on the lawn to cock an eye skywards. This blackbird nested a few feet away from one of these swallows amongst the cowshed roof timbers last year. Whilst the one has remained within a mile of here through all that Winter sent, the other has made a round trip of 12,000 miles to skim over hippo pools and return to this same yard without benefit of maps or compass.

House Martin (*Delichon urbica*)

Swifts

The house martin is glossy blue-black above, with a white rump patch. The Sand martin is slightly smaller, is dull brown above, and has a brown band across its breast

Swifts indulge in noisy aerial chases, and often mate on the wing

Swallow (*Hirundo rustica*)

Even as a juvenile, the swallow can be distinguished from martins by its much longer and more pointed outer tail feathers. These are most developed in adult males.

Sand Martin (*Riparia riparia*)

nelson 92

The blackbird's young leave their nest towards the end of this week, as do those of a mistle thrush on the wooded bank below the house. The parents continue to feed them whilst their tail feathers grow and their wing muscles gain strength, but one drowns in a trough, another is killed by a cat, and a third flies into a window on its first strong flight.

Meanwhile the hen wagtail is lining her garden-wall nest with cattle hairs collected from hundreds of yards around, and the chaffinch is weaving the moss and cobweb foundations of its nest amongst the greenery of the hawthorn hedge. Last year linnets nested in this same hedge, so discreetly that I did not notice them until the young were hatched. This week small twittering flocks of linnets fall amongst us, and within a day or two of their coming a pair is back around the old nest site, the deep pink of the male once more surprising me with its brightness.

In the latter part of the week there is a spell of dull cold weather, and I begin to despair of hearing the cuckoo before May. He has almost certainly arrived, but he can be frustratingly elusive until he gives voice. Then on the last day of the month there is a warm foggy morning with the makings of a fine day, and I set off up the hillside behind the house. After a few minutes I emerge from the mist into a bright clear morning, and sit down on a bank of scattered oaks and hawthorn overlooking a beck. Around me little grassland flowers are making their modest *débuts;* ribwort plantain, with a garland of anthers around its knotty head; spring sedge, its tiny male spike tufted with stamens; and thyme-leaved speedwell, joining four other speedwells this month in the group we know as bird's eye.

As I study them with the hand lens, to get an insect's eye view of their charms, an insistent "psoot, psoot" call distracts my attention. We are apt to forget some of the calls of summer visitors whilst they are away, particularly since they often change voice within a week or two of their return. I recognize that this is something new, but cannot put a name to it until I spot the lovely cock redstart amongst the branches of a twisted oak. And even as I thrill to the perfection of the redstart's colours, my ears catch a familiar call drifting faintly across the valley. The mist clears from a patch of open woodland, the sun beams down upon it, and the carefree little lecher loudly sings cuccu.

5 May

Nature should not have a favourite month, but she does, and it is May. If you want to learn to love the Dales, and have only a fortnight to spare, choose the middle two weeks of May. It is the merry-merry month, the clout-casting month, the month when Nature fulfils all the promises she has been making since December.

Starting even before dawn, the chorus of songsters now reaches its peak. The last of our summer migrants returns around mid-month. Fox and badger cubs begin to play above the surface, sometimes together. Leaves appear even on the most refractory oak or ash. The flowers that peeped out last month now flood the fields with colour.

And in the woods, there is the inexpressible beauty of a carpet of bluebells in a cloister of beech leaves. To sit alone there at sunrise is to be in truly holy communion.

May 1st – 7th

The cuckoo vies with the nightingale and the lark as the bird most likely to drive poets to pen. But whereas the other two are almost universally praised, the cuckoo arouses mixed emotions. To Wordsworth, never one to understate a case, it is a blithe and blessèd bird, whilst to Bunyan it is a yawling bawling booby. Shakespeare has it mocking married men, though since the hen-bird is polyandrous the cuckolded cock may be simply mocking itself. Patrick Reginald Chalmers most accurately assesses the bird as 'little else beyond a captivating vagabond'. It is certainly a most effective self-publicist, for almost the entire population of the European community can both recognize its song and give some details of its life-style.

Booby the bird may be, but it is no fool. It times its arrival in this area to coincide with the start of the titlark nesting season, for it is with this pipit that it prefers to place its eggs. Once arrived, it flies around inviting small birds to mob it for its hawk-like shape and its constant calling. It is then a simple matter for it to choose an area with a high density of host birds, to watch where they are making their nests, and to await the promiscuous female. She passes freely from male to male, but lingers longest where there is most work to do.

The cuckoo's arrival is also timed to coincide with a sudden increase in the numbers of the larger invertebrates on which it feeds, and with a peak of feeding activity amongst over-wintered caterpillars. It is one of the few birds that can cope with the irritant hairs of so many of these latter, having in its gizzard a disposable lining which can be periodically regurgitated and replaced. Even the cuckoo does not seem able to consume white butterflies, which take glycosides from their food plants and distil them into irritant poisons within their bodies. The first emergence of these white butterflies coincides with the cuckoo's arrival and with the flowering of the cresses on which they feed. Damp places are suddenly alive with the fluttering of small whites, green-veined whites, and the increasingly common orange tips. We never saw orange tips as children, but now they are everywhere.

Up on the moors another butterfly is on the wing, though it is harder to find than the whites. If you walk through bilberries with the sun behind you, you may spot amongst the pale new leaves the richer colours of the green hair-streak. This little butterfly favours different plants in different parts of Britain, but in the Dales it is most easily found sunning itself amongst bilberries in May. And whilst you are up the moor, watch out, like the cuckoo, for small birds gathering nest material. If you find a titlark's nest, remember to check it a few days later to see if a cuckoo has found it too. If you are on stony ground, watch out for the wheatear, flitting away into his hole amongst the rocks. Incredibly, cuckoo eggs have even been found in wheatear nests, well below ground level.

Cuckoos are far less common than their calls suggest, for what appears to be the calls of several may just be the work of one, moving rapidly around his range. They are far more often heard than seen, and when seen in flight may be mistaken for hawks. The size, the long tail, and the blue-grey back are suggestive of a cock sparrowhawk, but the pointed wings and shallow fluttering wing-beats tend more towards the merlin. Merlins are already nesting when cuckoos arrive, and whilst you walk the moor-edge looking for cuckoos you may be lucky enough to see a cock merlin carrying some luckless pipit to his sitting mate. The nest is on the ground amongst heather, but it is an offence against both Nature and the law to disturb it.

Grouse are also incubating amongst the heather, hidden from view. At most times of the year grouse produce two types of droppings, one of which is a sticky brown excretion from the twin appendices, or caeca, which gives the bird its strong gamey smell. During incubation healthy hen grouse cease to produce this, but heavily parasitized birds cannot control the caecal excretion. They therefore smell more strongly, and are more easily located by ground predators. Thus on over-keepered moors, with predators strictly controlled, there are higher numbers of birds with significant worm burdens, whereas on more natural moors the birds are fewer but healthier. In recent years keepers have even taken to leaving little piles of anthelmintic-treated grit on their moors so that grouse can doctor themselves to be healthy when shot.

Breeding also continues apace on the lower ground. Blue tits, reassured by the appearance of white butterflies, have begun carrying feathers to our nest-boxes; a treecreeper has made her simple nest in a dry crevice within an open hollow tree, and is laying; the pied wagtail reposes within her cup beneath the top-stones, also laying; the fitful little wren covers her seven eggs in their snug sphere, and feels like a giant; hedge sparrows in the garden and grey wagtails by the stream are both proud parents, their eggs newly hatched; and starlings carry empty egg-shells away from their nests to shower us with their bounty, so that from now onwards we find the pale blue casings discarded about the countryside like gay wrappings after a children's party.

By moorland bog and on upland pasture the fluffy chicks of snipe, lapwing and golden plover tritter about on over-sized legs, learning to probe for food in wet places. At a signal from a parent they flatten into invisibility amongst the vegetation whilst the adults mob the passing crow or gull, or you. Plovers and snipe have only one brood each year, and will continue to care for them until they are fully grown and flying, towards mid-June. They nest early because the young have to be capable of moving away to lowland marshes before the hot weather dries up the hilltop bogs.

The blackbird, by contrast, looks after her surviving young for only a few days before turning her attention to nesting again. One at my house has decided to try a site alongside the swallows on the cowshed beam where it, or one of its relatives, nested last year. Whilst the swallows renovate their old nests with new pellets of wet mud, the blackbird gathers great beakfuls of moss to lay the foun-

Lapwing (Vanellus vanellus)

Both sexes have crest feathers, but those of the male are longer. Male also has more black on throat and breast

Males make steep twisting display flights accompanied by characteristic calls from late February onwards.

The first chicks hatch towards the end of April.

The bright white hind-neck of the chick is "switched off" when it squats down to hide

nelson 91

dations of hers. The last remaining young from the previous brood follows her in, and is later found dead and forgotten in the mistal window. The blackbird, it seems, nests early not because its food supply might dry up, but because two or three broods are needed each year just to keep pace with the effects of infant mortality.

As the swallows are mending the gaps in their nest walls, their relatives the house martins are just arriving, together with the unrelated swifts. The smart little house martins arrive in dribs and drabs, and consort with swallows and sand martins, so that we may not notice the first arrival. The first swifts are much more noticeable, for they loiter downriver until rainfall is imminent, and then come screaming in like miniature jet fighters, high and fast, ahead of the downpour.

When the rain has cleared the sun breaks through, and we notice that there are new voices in the woods as well. Male pied flycatchers started to appear a couple of weeks ago, and have spent the time since then carving up the oak woods into territories, each containing at least one suitable nest-hole. This week the females arrive, and spread through the trees eyeing up the talent, selecting males with the same taste in nest-holes. The males advertise their presence with variations on a theme of "chi-pizza-pizza-pizza-pi-pi", delivered with squeaky gusto from an exposed branch. In the same trees another new arrival, the wood warbler, stutters his clickety wing-shaking song with almost irritating frequency. And then a little further along there is a stirring amongst the new leaves, a glimpse of a dull warbler, and a sudden burst of clear liquid song that seems too big for the bird. A slight movement to one side brings its head into view, confirming that it is indeed a blackcap, one of our finest songsters.

As I move towards the blackcap for a clearer view, there is a rustling away to one side and I catch sight of a roe deer slipping away into cover. It stops on the edge of a belt of young conifers about a hundred yards away. It is a male, its shiny antlers now clear of velvet and its coat glowing with the reddish pelage of Summer. Roe deer give birth in late Spring and mate in Summer, so that this male will be already defending his breeding territory. Even as I watch, he gives an angry snorting bark and trots away with his head up, barking once more at my intrusion.

There is the nursery drey of a squirrel here too, though I am unable to climb to it. In this week in 1971 I took two well-grown young squirrels from separate dreys to keep as pets. One killed the other, but later developed into an entertaining little charmer. It had a passion for cream crackers, and after I released it into the garden it could always be called to hand by the sight of one. It would perch on my shoulder or on the top of my head nibbling anything that was passed its way, or chewing my hair when there was nothing better. Unfortunately it became so destructive in the garden that we eventually sent it to be released several miles away. I often wondered afterwards if it surprised some passing stranger by landing on her head and chewing her hair.

Young squirrels will be leaving their nests during the next few days, and will face many hazards as they learn to climb and jump, and to follow tree-top pathways. Not the least of these hazards is the tawny owl, which hunts day and night when feeding young. I know of an owl nest by the old fish-ponds, and decide to check it now, before the young start to leave the nest. It is more a scramble than a climb, with constant pauses to watch for the parents, but finally I attain a perch beside the nest.

Inside are two ugly owlets, their feathers beginning to show through the white down. They blow themselves up and click their beaks, but move away to the back of the nest. In with them are one dead wood mouse, untouched, and the remains of one adult and three young rats. I have most often found rabbit and rat remains in tawny owl nests, making them truly the farmer's friend, but also squirrels, water voles, starlings, blackbirds and numerous young duck-lings. Many other prey items are too small to be worth storing, and it is surprising to think that earthworms form an important part of the diet. Worms certainly provide easy pickings at this time of year, as the largest adults haul out of their holes for their frothy couplings in the dew.

In the pond beneath the owl nest, a single duckling paddling after its mother shows the source of some of the owlets' sustenance. Frogs and toads have both left the pond now, the toadspawn has hatched, and the frog tadpoles are almost full-grown. Palmate newts are beginning to lay, though their eggs, wrapped singly inside folded leaves, are not easily discovered. Some of the adult newts can be found under stones on the banks of the pond, the females fat-bellied with spawn, the males with their thumb pads and tail strings. Forget-me-nots are flowering here, where the knight flung them as he drowned, and amongst them the first crane-flies dally, tail-to-tail in their long-legged love. Primitive horse-tails thrust up between the patches of flower, the hollow stems of their fertile shoots topped by cone-like spore capsules. The broad width of meadow from the pond to the wooded hillside is yellow with dandelions, at their peak now with not a seed-head in sight.

On the wooded bank itself the sycamores are all at least partly in leaf, as is the hawthorn underbrush, but the oak and the ash are still bare. The elm appears to be bursting into leaf, but what seem to be yellowish young leaves are in fact clusters of winged seeds, called samaras, from the flowers of March. And beneath the elm on this bank, looking as if they have just landed from outer space, are a dozen or so newly emerged morels. I fill my pockets with the fungi and take them home, to steam in their own juices with a little salt-butter and milk. Even now that cultivated mushrooms are available all year round, the chewy old-fashioned taste of the morels makes a pleasant change from the bland familiarity of supermarket food.

May 8th –15th

Nearly all our migrant birds are now back with us, and the next fortnight sees the peak of bird nesting activity. Some species, such as the blackbird and mistle thrush, are already weaning their young. Others, such as the chaffinch and greenfinch, are still gathering nest material. And a very few, the most notable of which is the spotted flycatcher, have yet to arrive.

It must not be imagined that birds automatically nest in the same order in which they return, starting with the permanent residents. Skylarks may be seen in any month of the year, and have been back on their breeding grounds since late February, but they only begin to lay this week. The nest is a simple cup of dried grass hidden beneath a tussock on rough ground, and the four eggs are mottled brown. You are more likely to find the nest by chance than by observation, for the parents land on the ground some distance away and approach it through cover.

Our common grey partridges are, of course, with us throughout the hardest weather, and have been paired since mid-Winter, but even they only begin nesting now. The nest is well concealed beneath brambles and nettles on a rough hedge-side between green fields, and a large number of olive-brown eggs are laid. I have known a pair to hatch 16, and clutches of up to 20 are recorded, though about a dozen would be more normal. Red-legged partridges are said to sometimes make two nests, both containing eggs, with one clutch being incubated by the cock and one by the hen. Despite repeated introductions the red-leg has never really established in this area, and I have no personal experience of this odd breeding behaviour.

Summer visitors which begin laying this week include sand martins, sandpipers and ring ouzels. The sand martins have completed their new nest-holes, and are now laying their four white eggs into a simple bed of dried grass and feathers in an end-chamber smelling of damp sand. Sandpipers are nesting on the bank above, their nest a simple scrape beneath a tuft, lined with dead grass and an odd leaf or two. We may see them mating now, sometimes on a riverside sandbank, sometimes on scraps of flotsam caught in a pool on the river's bend, and by the end of the week they will be laying. The four blotched eggs have a pinkish tinge, and like those of the snipe and lapwing, and for the same reasons, they are large and pointed. The ring ouzel's nest and eggs are similar to those of the blackbird, but the nest is rather more rough and bulky, with stems of bracken, heather and crowberry woven into the outside layer. It is usually concealed amongst the clumps of grass and heather on the rock-face of a moorland outcrop.

The willow warbler, which so loves to sing from tall trees, actually makes its nest on or near the ground, albeit in the undergrowth beneath or near to trees. The nest is domed, but without the intricacy that dome-builders like the wren, dipper and long-tailed tit have led us to expect. Rather the willow warbler's feather-lined nest seems functional but disposable, with a grassy shell more for camouflage than protection. When the red-speckled eggs are laid towards the end of next week they will be plainly visible to us through the wide entrance, almost as if the bird is so full of the joys of spring that it cannot bear to be cut off from a clear view of the sunlight whilst incubating. It is certainly full of song, and will respond aggressively to the most amateur quality recording of its voice, even settling on the cassette player in search of the source.

Birds whose eggs hatch this week include kestrel, wood-pigeon and jackdaw. In its natural state the kestrel nests in the hollow top of a blasted oak, on some rocky moorland ledge, or in the abandoned nest of a carrion crow. For centuries now, however, it has been equally content in ancient ruins, disused barns, old quarries, and even urban rooftops. The nest is the simplest of works, as if the bird disdains to sully its beak and talons with domesticity, and the rounded eggs are closely mottled red. There may be five or more, but then after hatching you find only three chicks, for there is deadly competition within the nest and only the fittest survive. When there are few kestrels the parents find plenty of food, and all the chicks survive. When there is over-population, and food is more difficult to find, the chicks which hatched first are fed and the smaller late-comers die. The controller of small mammal populations exercises a ruthless self-control on its own.

Gentle woodpigeons have little trouble in finding food for their chicks, since pigeon food is all around. Buds, leaves, roots, seeds and berries, particularly ivy berries just now, are all grist to the gizzard mill. The problem is that such items are not easily digested by nestling birds. Most seed-eaters solve this by feeding their young on flies and caterpillars until their digestive systems can cope with adult food. The pigeon, however, has a unique solution in 'pigeon's milk', a special secretion produced in the crop of both parents to be fed as an infant formula to the chicks.

Jackdaws have a very catholic appetite, and would be equally at home with the food of the hawk or the dove. But again the chicks require simpler fare, and from now onwards we may see the frantic parents chasing heavy black Saint Mark's flies through the grass, seeming from a distance to be dancing. The jackdaw's problem is how to carry such small items back to the nest in quantities sufficient to sustain four large and rapidly growing young. The solution is a beak pouch, visible as a lump in the throat immediately below and behind the beak, in which squirming bundles are taken back to delight the chicks.

carrion crow   jackdaw   rook

nelson 79

A closely related species, with the same solution to the same problem, is the rook. Rooks use their pouches at all times of the year, often travelling considerable distances in search of food, but for the last month they have been specifically filling them with pickings suitable for their waiting chicks. The nestlings are now almost fully grown, and have begun to perch on the edge of the nest or to scramble through the branches to greet their parents. In the days when it was considered essential to control rook numbers, the 10th May was the usual time for the rook shoot. Attention was concentrated on the emerging fledglings, which could often be shot two or three at once with a 12-bore. Alternatively they were knocked out of the trees using catapults, or shaken from the branches by climbing boys, or simply caught amongst the grass where they had fallen whilst learning to fly. The dead birds were not wasted, for the breast muscles were trimmed off and cooked in a pie with potatoes and onions. Up to a couple of dozen were needed to make a family-sized meal, hence the four and twenty black birds baked in a pie. I ate crow pie several times as a youth, and it was pleasant enough when meat was scarce.

Young tawny owls are also just beginning to emerge from their nests, though with less synchronized timing than the rooks. During the next month or so odd ones will be found hunched on the ground beneath their nests where they have fallen whilst exercising their wings. For their first few days out they are more fluff than feathers, and well-meaning people tend to 'rescue' them. You should never do this. Their beak and claws are much stronger and sharper than you might imagine, and they are hardly ever truly abandoned. The parent will be watching somewhere, even if you cannot see her, and if you touch the owlet you may be attacked. I was once hit from behind by an owl whilst inspecting the chicks in its nest. The blow was a hard as a good left jab, and lacerated my ear. Other people, including the celebrated photographer Eric Hosking, have been hit in the face by owls and lost an eye as a result.

There is a young owl out this morning on the wooded bank near the fish-pond nest. I greet it urbanely and pass it by, but stop to watch it through binoculars from cover a safe distance away. The golden feathers are plainly showing now through the closely barred down, but the small birds around seem to sense that it is no great hunter as yet, and poses no threat. A song thrush with a nest nearby mobs it intermittently, but other birds do not join in and the parent owls are nowhere to be seen. After a while I am distracted by a high-pitched trill amongst the waterside sedges, followed by the emergence of a dabchick with her newly-hatched young. The glossy chestnut feathers of her neck and the yellow button below her beak catch the morning sun, but the chicks look uniformly dark brown at this distance. In the hand they can be seen to have longitudinal stripes of black and brown, and a pink beak tipped with yellow. They can swim and dive expertly almost from the moment they hatch, and are not easily caught for examination.

There are coot chicks also on this pond, scampering around their fussy flat-foot parents through the blue and white beds of bugle and scurvy grass. Their chick-down is pure black, but their yellow-tipped scarlet beaks reveal that they have evolved from a waterhen-like ancestor some millions of years ago. Actual waterhen chicks are even brighter, having all the colours of coot chicks but bright blue heads as well. To add to their exoticism they even have a functional claw on the front bend of each wing, which they use to help them scramble up steep banks until they are strong enough to manage without.

It is very pleasant sitting amongst trees overlooking water on this bright morning. The early sun on the water's surface glistens through the sail-wings of dying mayflies, mayflies which crawled through the mud for the first 24 months of their life just to spend their last 24 hours in ecstatic ephemeral flight. A wasp passes by me, looking for dead wood to pulp into nest paper. Then a hover-fly zooms in to hang motionless before my eyes, as if demonstrating that he is altogether a more up-market model than the wasp. Most naturalists can tell the difference between a wasp and a hover-fly, and some of us can recognize three or four species of each, so it puts our knowledge into perspective when we read that the two groups total over 500 species in Britain.

Small tortoiseshells flutter over the large bed of nettles below. A single peacock butterfly poses on a willow branch above them, wafting her eye-spotted wings. Across the field a crab-apple tree is bursting into pinky-white blossom, and beside me on the bank dangle the fragrant-flowered spikes of bird cherry. Ermel moths have visited this latter bush already, and the tips of its branches are even now being consumed by hundreds of tiny caterpillars inside their cob-webbed tents. In the boggy patch near the pond, white butterflies dilly-dally amongst the pink milkmaid and violet-anthered large bittercress, laying their eggs.

We have already mentioned that milkmaids are known as cuckoo flowers, because they bloom when the cuckoo calls, but the cuckoo name is tagged onto similarly coincident items, particularly those of a ribald nature. Thus the blebs of frothy liquid that developing frog-hopper nymphs blow out through their anus to protect themselves are called cuckoo spit, and the rude little arum lily is called cuckoo pint. Pint, pronounced to rhyme with tint, is an abbreviated form of pintle, an old English name for the male organ. The flowers are actually contained within a hollow at the base of the phallic spadix, and tiny flies attracted by the smell are trapped in this globe to perform the pollination.

Cuckoo pints, sometimes sardonically called lords-and-ladies, expose themselves beneath the hedges every few yards as I walk home, but there are many other new flowers to distract me from their importunity. Two little wild pea species, bush vetch and bitter vetch, are attracting bees and bumbles bees; the neat white flowers of wild strawberry give us promise of their delicious little fruits in July; crosswort and common sorrel delight us with their sleepy-smelling flowers and their tangy-tasting leaves respectively; meadow buttercups give children the chance to learn if their friends like butter; on the rougher waysides the equally yellow tormentil and the dew-pearled lady's mantle provide medicines alleged to cure everything from toothache to drooping breasts; and in stony places the tiny white flowers of whitlow grass and rue-leaved saxifrage reward those who will take the trouble to look carefully at simple things. At a time when we are being almost overwhelmed by Nature's munificence, it is still a trouble well worth taking.

May 16th – 23rd

The blackbird's overture signals the start of the matutinal performance. Within minutes there are a dozen other players competing for attention. The dawn chorus is not really a chorus, more a symphony, a collection of *virtuosi,* not grouped in the orchestra pit but scattered around the auditorium. It is delicious to awake to it pouring in through the open window at four in the morning. It is lovely to luxuriate in bed, now listening, now dozing, knowing that there is no rush to rise. But every naturalist owes it to Nature to be in the woods at dawn on at least one morning each May, even if it does mean rising at 3.30 to attend.

The woodland around the Strid near Bolton Abbey has been rather obtrusively tarted up in recent years, but it remains one of the best places in the Dales to hear bird song. A steaming hot mug of tea, a five minute drive, and I am there. The willow warbler's delectable cadence greets me as I step from the vehicle, and pours down on all sides as I walk through the ancient riverine woodland between massed ranks of bluebells. Egremond walked this path nearly a thousand years ago, and heard the same sweet song.

Cock chaffinches vie with the willow warblers as to whose voice shall dominate. For the moment the warbler leads, though the finch on his exposed perch is more visible. The two have songs which are actually rather similar, though the last three notes of the chaffinch's distinguish it. "It's-too-too-too-too-nice-to-be-here," he sings, and I have to agree. Against a lightening sky the beech leaves are still delicate and unblemished. The silver birch trees beside them are hung with long trailing catkins, just stirring in the faint breeze. Holly trees still bearing berries from last year have new white flowers dotted along their branches. The flower clusters of oak and sycamore are bursting out from amongst the newly-opened leaves, and even the bare-branched ash is showing tufts of green.

Uplifting though it is to wander wide-eyed through this greenery at day-break, it is also frustrating. Of course we know the songs of familiar residents like the song thrush, robin and wren, and our ears have become re-accustomed to the tappety call of the wood warbler, but is that a blackcap or a garden warbler we hear now? Our heads tilt backwards, mouth gaping, until our necks ache, and then we spot a movement amongst the leaves. In the second or two it takes to focus the binoculars it is gone. Then another movement here, another there, and a tantalizing glimpse of a dull little warbler with its head hidden. And finally a clear view of the head, with its rather thick stubby beak confirming it as a garden warbler. The garden warbler sings longer phrases with shorter pauses than the blackcap, and is not so loud or clear, but each Spring I confuse the two until I have heard them both.

And what is that now, high in an oak tree, with its scratchy "p-p-p-prrt-pzoo-pzoo-tsee-see-see"? An easier one this, for it keeps reasonably still and is brightly coloured. A cock redstart, which even as I watch flies onto the topmost twig of the tree to spotlight his fiery feathers in the first rays of the rising sun. My breath catches at the glory of it. Nearby a pied flycatcher perches atop a nest-box, singing to entice his female inside to breed. She is doubtless unaware that he already has a wife occupying a nest-hole some distance away across the river. He will only provide for the family that hatches first, but there is no shortage of food and the hen can cope alone if she has to.

Then there is a song which I do not recognize, in a clearing overgrown with nettles. In the centre stands a hawthorn bush, its flowers just opening. The flowers of hawthorn are commonly known as may blossom, and will only open when the risk of frost has become minimal. This has given rise to the proverb 'Ne'er cast a clout till may be out', with the clever pun on the name. The first may blossom is always seen in May round here, at any time from the 3rd to the 28th according to the weather. Once it is out you can safely cast a clout, or even put away the thermal underwear and turn down the central heating.

Just now I am more interested in the bird song from the centre of the bush, though the vernal fragrance of its flowers does not go unnoticed. "Heigh-ho, PIP's-in-it-too," sings the bird repeatedly, and after listening to a few phrases I am able to whistle a poor imitation back at it. When it momentarily stops singing and moves position I know that the bird is puzzled. In the interchange that follows it finally comes out onto an exposed perch to challenge me, and I note straight away the contrasting grey and brown of its plumage, the high forehead, and the white throat. It is in fact a whitethroat, a common enough visitor to the lowlands but one rarely seen here.

Onwards through the wood I go, eyes and ears agog. A robin by the pathside has a mouthful of small grubs for its young, but swallows them all itself when it sees me. To further convince me that it is really nowhere near a nest, it flies to the top of a sapling and sings a few phrases. Despite the subterfuge I find the newly-hatched young in a nest on the bank above the path.

It is not only the great songsters which are giving voice. The canopy is alive with chirps and peeps, and there are little movements everywhere. Here a great tit emerges from the nest-hole in which she is laying, and there a pair of blue tits pick aphids from the leaves. A treecreeper runs up a trunk carrying a beakful of spiders to its day-old chicks.

Young treecreepers look much like the nestlings of any other small bird at this stage, but within a week they will have begun to develop the long pointed beak. By the time they leave the nest at two weeks old they will already have the specialised physique of the adult.

The first pheasants are also beginning to hatch, but many cocks are still strutting round the woods shouting "KORK-kuk", accompanied by a quasi-orgasmic flapping of their wings. On the river there is a surfeit of ducklings now, and in some cases the clutches of two or more females have mixed together. If we chance upon a family by surprise, the duck will splash out over the water pretending to have damaged a wing. Where two clutches have mixed two females may cooperate, one distracting our attention whilst the other quickly leads the young away. There is also a clutch of goosander ducklings on the river today, sticking close to their fierce-looking mother and ignoring the mallard *hoi-polloi*. These chestnut-headed baby goosanders started their adventure in a hole up a tree, and almost their first act in life was to take that leap of faith into the void.

The behaviour of mallard ducks guarding ducklings is typical of many ground-nesting birds. It is such a deeply rooted instinct that I have even seen ostriches, flightless for millions of years, pretend to have broken wings when surprised in open spaces with their young. In the Dales the behaviour is most perfectly seen in grouse. The main hatching of grouse eggs up on the moor begins this week. If you stumble upon a clutch of young chicks, both parents will run round you within a few feet, crouching low, clucking constantly, trailing one wing as if injured, and seeming to be making pathetic attempts to fly with one wing. I doubt if an old fox would be taken in, but most foxes are not old. The large, noisy, flapping parents floundering in the heather will trigger a reflex hunting response, and a pursuit will follow. By the time the parent grouse miraculously recover, the fox will have been drawn several dozen yards away and the young will have had chance to scatter and hide.

You can find grouse families even by pathsides for the next few days. and I recommend a walk over the moor to see them. Keep an eye out for adders on sunny banks, for this is their mating season. They are there to be found if you go looking for them, particularly where there are patches of moor grass mixed in the heathsward, but they are timid and wary unless provoked. You may also be lucky enough to spot a common lizard basking in the sun. Although they are not at all common on this upland heath, they can occasionally be glimpsed where rocks and grass and heather meet.

The same environment is home to the wheatear, the cocks smartly turned out in grey and buff with an inverted black T on their white tails. The duller females are not often seen now, for they are in their nest-holes in rocky ground incubating their pale blue eggs. On the ground surface nearby, particularly where there is bilberry growing, the first meadow pipit eggs are hatching in their grass-lined cup. These are the lucky clutches that were laid before the cuckoos mated, though when the same pipits lay a second clutch towards the middle of June they may not fare so well.

Amongst the bilberry around the titlark's nest there are the darker and shinier leaves of the evergreen cowberry, with its clusters of tiny white bells just opening. A few yards below, in a boggy patch, lousewort is also flowering. The hooded pink flowers have something of the orchid about them, whilst the sprig of leaves could be a spray of fairy ferns: Nature imitating Art, in miniature in a moorland bog.

These little upland flowers are always rather special, because they relieve the monoculture of heather which makes the moor what it is. When all below has turned bright green the moor sticks stubbornly to its winter colours, though on closer inspection there are new shoots of heather growing and curl-tipped fronds of bracken surging up through last year's fallen dead. No close inspection is needed to see the flowers in the fields below. You cannot miss the explosion of colourful growth, even driving past in your car. Buttercups are replacing dandelions as the dominant yellow, and in old-fashioned meadows the grass and ribwort plantain compete for height. Where pastures are well grazed by sheep and fat lambs, the ungrazed beds of nettles are becoming obvious, and nettles on the road-sides are up to the height of car windows. The profusion of growth is nowhere more apparent than along the sides of walled lanes. There an effervescence of cow parsley flowers tops a tangled jungle of leaves and stalks, grass and goosegrass, nettles and thistles, dock and bramble. Where grassy banks run down to the roadside without hedge or wall, there are the first flowers of two plants named sweet, the sweet woodruff and the sweet vernal grass. Both these smell of newly-mown hay, a smell which triggers the same atavistic responses as do leather and freshly-baked bread in even the most urbanised of minds.

Pignut is also flowering here. If you have never dug for its rounded, parsnip-tasting roots in Autumn you can find them now, a couple of inches below the ground surface. It is probably illegal to do it these days, so confine yourself to one for curiosity's sake. Two members of the pea family are also beginning to bloom on these sunny banks, the red clover, so beloved of bees, and the bird's-foot trefoil, known to us as lady's slipper. If cuckoo pint is an abbreviation of cuckoo pintle, then an examination of the yellow flowers of this latter pea might convince you that lady's slipper is short for lady's slippery. If that is so, then the rare lady's slipper orchid, about to come into flower near Grassington, must be etymologically hermaphrodite.

Cuckoo
(Cuculus canorus)

Though it only spends three months each year in the Dales, the cuckoo is one of our best-known birds. It is most readily seen in rowan and hawthorn bushes along moor-edges, in late May, when it is typically vociferous

The meadow pipit is the preferred host of the cuckoo in this area.

nelson 92

Now that there is useful light for nearly eighteen hours a day, we can go for walks in both morning and evening, and still do a full day's work in between. This morning saw me up before four to listen to the bird song, and this evening sees me setting out to watch fox cubs at play. Unlike badgers, foxes are normally only seen playing near their holes for a very short season. Up to early May they come above ground rarely and unpredictably, and by the end of the month they leave the earth separately and slink away through the undergrowth. Just for a few evenings about now they can be seen playing together like puppies, outside the earth at sunset.

I set off while the sun is still high, so as to be settled in position well before time. Swallows are laying now, and they flick out of the out-houses with a nervous twitter as I step into the yard. House martins do not like my house because of the bevel on the window transoms, but they nest at my nearest neighbours on both sides, and I see their nests, still drying in parts, as I walk past. The birds themselves are lazily hawking amongst the abundance of insects, which seem to float like plankton in the evening light. Even as I wonder why the spotted flycatcher is not yet back enjoying them, one makes a foray up into the air from a hawthorn tree and catches a fly with an audible snap. In another day or two the hedges will be full of them.

I settle down on a rough bank of gorse across the little ravine from the fox earth, and make myself comfortable. Woodpigeons coo in the trees nearby, and a little party of swifts scream and chase overhead. A pair of linnets and a goldfinch watch me warily from the gorse, for they are nesting there and would like to go to roost. Gradually the bird song fades, with the noble blackbird singing the sweetly sorrowful finale. The swifts give way to noctule bats, roughly the same size and shape and almost as fast and high. The first midges of the year find me, and I shrink into my clothes like a tortoise. The cubs should be out by now, and I begin to look more carefully at the holes across the little valley. Then there is a sinking feeling as I notice that one hole is blocked, and by moving higher up the bank I can get a view that confirms by suspicions. All the holes are blocked, and the keepers have been. Deep within the earth the litter lies dead, poisoned by cyanide gas.

It is a bitter disappointment, but we must be philosophical about it. Gamekeepers are paid to control foxes, and if I can find occupied earths, so can they. It is quite legal to gas foxes, and yet they survive despite this. We can no more criticize the gamekeeper for killing foxes than we can the carrion crow for stealing grouse eggs. Both have their job to do.

The evening is not wasted, however, for I go to visit a badger sett instead, knowing that badgers tend to emerge slightly later. I have no sooner sat down than the sow emerges, followed almost immediately by what seems to be a yearling female. Whilst these two are scratching and sniffing around, the boar emerges from a separate hole several yards away and trots off into the trees. Then right on the edge of dark, but still clearly visible through my

8×50 binoculars, three cubs come tumbling out and throw themselves into play. It is a merry rough and tumble, chasing each other's tails, push-fighting shoulder to shoulder like pigs, and even rolling down the bank. After a few minutes I lose sight of them in the undergrowth, and tiptoe away. I walk home in the dark listening in vain for nightjars, but hear only a restless cuckoo calling to the moon.

May 24th – 31st

Dalesmen tend towards pessimism, to minimize disappointment. They do not anticipate a long spell of dry weather, and rather resent it when it comes. Farmers complain that it is hindering grass growth. Park wardens put up fire hazard warnings. Old folk affirm that a dry May means a wet Summer.

Nature holds back until most waterhen clutches have hatched, and then gives us four or five days of driving wind and rain. By the end of the third day the hazard notices are weathered to pulp, and old folk all have rheumatism, and the farmers are lamenting that it is going to be too wet to make silage. When a wild wet night gives way to a calm sunny morning, we are caught napping without a ready complaint.

The birds certainly relish it. Starlings poke at the lawn with half-open beaks, and fly off with easy pickings to their noisy brood. The wall below their nest-hole is now streaked white with bird lime, and by the end of this week the first young will be on the wing. Hedge sparrow chicks are already fledged, and are hiding beneath the bushes on the rockery waiting to be fed. There are pied wagtails also in the garden, picking crawlies from amongst the grass as they pitter about on the lawn, and jumping up to catch the flies they disturb. Their young have only just hatched, and each one will require something like 100 insects every day for the next fortnight.

I watch this throng of activity for a while from an upstairs window, and then take my mug of tea out onto the old stone garden seat. It really is a lovely morning, the air sparkling fresh, the sunlight flooding down, and the garden full of bird song. Along the hedge a spotted flycatcher picks insects from the air with casual accuracy. By the end of the month she will have started nest-building, and by the end of next month she may be laying again, for there are few birds that reproduce faster.

High-spirited house sparrows chirp from the hen house roof. One flies up there from the garden carrying two fat green caterpillars for his rapidly growing young. His stubby beak is made for seed-eating, but his nestlings need an infant *purée* to get them started. There will be plenty of caterpillars right through to the end of his nesting season in August. An agitated little wren flies down from the hen house and lands a few feet away on the garden wall, giving me the sharp edge of her tongue. Her young have now flit from the hay-rack nest, and she has brought them into the garden. As I walk along the flower border they scatter around, and even between, my legs. Their flight is still weak and their tails too short, but within a week the only noticeable difference from the adult will be the yellow of the baby gape still visible at their mouth corners.

Yesterday news reached me that a vixen with a litter of cubs is leading the keepers a merry old dance up the moor. She bore the cubs in an old stone land drain which could not be successfully gassed, and now keeps them in short-term shelters on the surface, moving constantly. I would like to meet this pimpernel, and plan a walk out through fields and woods and back over that part of the moor where she was last spotted.

The dairy cows have been out at grass for several days now, and muck-flies are very much in evidence down the fields. There are house-fly types about too, and a host of mayflies, March-flies, crane-flies and nameless dainty gnats. Some species must be floating high in the heavens, for swifts can be seen up there making the comparatively slow glides they use when feeding. They feed with their mouths agape, catching small flying insects on a coating of sticky saliva inside. Swifts are said to even sleep on the wing at times, though I am yet to be convinced that this is the nightly norm. They will certainly mate on the wing, for I once saw this happen. The female was gliding with wings slightly above horizontal when the male landed on her back with his wings more steeply raised, and the two glided together for several seconds.

Swifts begin nesting about now, using their sticky saliva as a glue to bind their nest materials into a shallow cup. Where they actually obtain their nest materials is open to debate. They never willingly alight on the ground, though they are able to take off again if by some mishap they land. It has been claimed that scraps lifted into the air by the wind provide the grass and feathers they use for their nests. In late May 1990 I saw a swift carrying a piece of sheep's wool almost as long as itself, which I am sure it did not find floating in the air. I believe they probably strip the old nests of species like starlings and house sparrows for their own nest materials, and this may partly explain why swifts are so often plagued by external parasites. Incidentally, the wool was more likely being used as a plaything than a nest lining – I have often seen a swallow repeatedly drop a feather and swoop down to catch it, perhaps for fun or perhaps as part of a mating ritual.

From the heavens above, back to the ground below: specifically, to young lapwings, which have been running around now for weeks and still cannot fly. The recent rain has been a real boon to them, for they need plenty of muddy ground when learning to feed. The parents are fiercely protective, dive-bombing rabbits and pheasants which stray too near to their chicks, and even squaring up to grazing sheep. Now that there are cattle in the fields, the hen lapwing sees no reason to be any less determined. I am amused to see one running at the head of a grazing cow, flaring her wings and crying "Tsia!Tsia!Tsia!". The great oafish bovine looks on in puzzlement as the chicks run off to safety with little wings outspread.

Young curlews are also afoot now, their hatching timed to occur after the first flush of plant growth. The large and long-legged chicks will remain safely hidden amongst the meadow grass and flowers, at least until silage-making commences. Away from the fast growing meadows, many flowers have been grazed off by cattle, though there is still a good show on the rough bank above the beck. Lady's slipper and pignut are the dominant species, with beds of germander speedwell making patches of deep blue. Near the top of the bank the much paler blue flowers of heath milkwort are earning their name, putting in an appearance just to coincide with the spring flush of dairy production. The little wild geranium called herb-Robert adds touches of pink to stony places, nicely setting off its flowers against bright stems and pale ferny leaves. Miniature forests of sheep sorrel give a red flush to bare peaty mounds. And on the wetter ground the bright blue spikes of brooklime and the pale pink heads of lesser valerian dab splashes of colour in dark dank places.

I follow the beck downwards to where the little valley flattens out into open farmland. The countryside is bursting with life, and my notebook, binoculars and pocket lens are hardly ever still. Here three recently fledged grey wagtails skip from stone to stone along the beck edge, the shortness of their juvenile tails making them look oddly bare and unbalanced. There an old heron rises heavily from a pool, legs trailing as he circles for height. His gawky young will now be perched on the edge of the nest platform exercising their wings, waiting for the horrid regurgitated mess to be brought to them from up to 20 miles away.

In the main river valley I begin to encounter majestic horse chestnuts. Although these trees are amongst the first to come into leaf, long before the risk of frost is past, they do not grow beyond the sapling stage on our exposed higher ground. There is something quite exotic, almost tropical, about their appearance, and this is reinforced when, as now, they are illuminated by thousands of white flower spikes. Our woodland trees, our stately oaks and beech and sycamore, are also in full flower now, though they do not flaunt it like the chestnut. Their little flower tresses are an understated green, and thanks to the recent wind and rain there is plenty of opportunity to examine some closely, where they have been knocked to the woodland floor.

In the wood the leaves are still dripping, and it is cooler and more restrained. The few days of cold and wet have given the forest creatures a longing for sunlight, and all the life seems to be in the clearings and around the wood edges. A noisy family of long-tailed tits plays follow-my-leader from bush to bush as I enter the wood, the parents pausing briefly to scold me as I pass. Deeper into the trees I go, working uphill as quietly as possible in the hope of surprising a roe deer. The does give birth about now, but the kids are hidden away in thick vegetation where they are very difficult to find. From two or three weeks of age the captivating little twins may sometimes be seen walking out with their mother, but I have never yet managed to stumble upon one in its most helpless first week of life. My chances today are ruined by a buck, which spots me first and runs off barking, alerting every deer in the wood. The angry hollow bark of the roe buck has something of the near-human quality of baboon or howler monkey calls, and is vaguely disquieting in these dark woods.

It is with some relief that I reach the more open wood-land below the edge of the moor, at the place where I came to look for woodcock nests in early April. As I round a bend in the track I surprise a family of five of these very birds, apparently two adults and three well-grown young. It is only as they spring into flight that I see the third young, for one of the adults is carrying it between its legs. The hindquarters of the fledgling are clearly visible in the undercarriage as the plucky parent rises away from me. I have seen this twice before in my life, both other times around the end of July, but both in similar circumstances. Doubtless the woodcock can carry its chicks at any age, but this behaviour is most likely to occur and is most easily seen when one of the young cannot fly as well as the others, and there is no chance of relying on camouflage and immobility. Think of the power in those wings, that can carry almost double the bird's normal weight in steeply rising rapid flight!

I pass obliquely up the moorside to get to where I need to be, climbing through a belt of scattered rowan trees. They are just beginning to blossom up here, and the creamy flower heads are plainy visible even from a distance. In the tops of the higher rowans sit tree pipits, singing both from the tree and in their display flights. The bird resembles the meadow pipit, but is more clearly marked above with less streaking below, and has more noticeably pink legs. The display is also similar to that of the titlark, but in the downward glide the wings are more openly spread, and the flight always begins and ends on a tree branch or post, never the ground.

I might hope to find nightjars here, for I saw a pair nearby in this week in 1972, and they nested here the following year. In the 1920s my father heard them along this hillside every Spring, but there were corncrakes and glow-worms around the village then. Times have changed, but there are new species colonizing the area as fast as others leave it. One of these stands before me now, perched atop a clump of over-grown heather singing his scratchy tune. This is the whinchat, streaky brown and buff, which is profiting from the decline of its close relative, the wheatear.

Meadow pipits were common in the time of my fore-elders and are still common now, fretting around me as I pass through their territories. They manage to maintain their numbers despite the depredations of all the small raptors and the parasitic attentions of the cuckoo. There are ring ouzels here also, and as I approach a rocky crag one flies over carrying a beakful of food to its young. I find a vantage point amongst the rocks and sit there for an hour or more, scanning the moor for any sign of a daylight-hunting fox. Then I work methodically across the heath from rock to rock and hole to hole searching in vain for the vixen's hiding places. The time is not wasted, however, for from the rocks I saw lesser black-backs amongst the heather, and made a mental note of the place. Now I am able to walk straight up to one nest, and find two more nearby. The nests are in grassy patches amongst the heather, and are lined with bracken, moss, and dead grass. Each contains three eggs, the size of a curlew's but paler and rounder. All around the nest sites loose pellets of fur, fish bones and most especially scraps of plastic show that a good part of the gulls' diet is obtained from waste tips several miles down river.

The nest colony of black-headed gulls is not far away, though it is much more discrete and concentrated than that of the lesser black-backs. I call in on the way home, and find several nests empty, with hatched eggshells nearby. There must be several dozen gull chicks hidden in the rushy bog within a few feet of me, but it is only after considerable effort that I manage to find one. It is buff in colour, with small dark flecks, but the shower of faeces from the screaming adults is so sustained that I do not linger long to examine it. Quite near the gullery an oyster catcher nested on a burnt patch, but when I check the nest there is no sign of eggshells or young. Possibly they hatched success-fully, for one parent flies round me at a distance, or possibly they went to feed young carrions or neighbouring gulls.

A tiny trickle from this bog joins with other tiny trickles to make the beck below my house. I follow it down, lost in thought, but suddenly stop to listen to a chat-like noise amongst the bracken on the opposite bank. By moving slightly from side to side I can pinpoint the direction from which the sound is coming. There is no bird there. The sound begins again at another point a few yards further up. The bracken stems have begun to branch but the fronds are not yet open, and I can see clearly between the stalks. No chat, no ring ouzel, positively no bird at all. As I stare hard at the place I catch a movement off to one side, and the mystery is solved. The noise is coming not from a bird but from a stoat, running about in a maze of tunnels beneath the dead bracken, and spitting fire and venom at me in defence of its hidden young. It pops up now here, now there, moving so fast that it is tempting to believe that there are two. I crouch low, cross the beck, and then advance on hands and knees. I squeak a little through pursed lips, and it briefly pops up a few feet away from me. Moving very slowly on all fours, I approach the hole where it has most often appeared. When my face is just over a yard from it, the stoat suddenly runs out and charges towards me, looking quite startlingly large and savage at such close quarters. We stare at one another from two feet apart, neither moving. Then it scuttles back to the hole and is gone, leaving a faint whiff on the wind. Later I hear that a stoat has been seen here carrying her young to a new nest site, no longer feeling secure after her encounter with me.

So many of the things we have considered today have been linked by the common thread of selfless maternal devotion. Wren, lapwing, woodcock, vixen and stoat have all in their own ways put their life on the line to protect their young. In these sad days of battered babies and latch-key kids, we still have much to learn from our lesser kin.

Stoat
(Mustela erminea)

6 June

Midsummer sees the day at its longest, and the best of the summer weather still to come. Farmers are run off their feet, cutting some fields for silage in the first days of the month, and some for hay towards the end. Those with sheep are also busy clipping, and hard-worked farm lads glow with pride at a job well done.

For the naturalist, this is a time of calm after the hectic days of May. There is still much to be seen, but it tends to be a repetition or continuation of what has gone before. What in May we only snatched to taste, we now have time to savour.

Thus nests with eggs become nests with young, chicks become fledglings, and second clutches begin. Flowers that peeped out in May glow brazenly in June, and yet more flowers appear. Insects and other invertebrates begin to demand more attention, some by their beauty, others by their nuisance. Midges, flies, wasps and bluebottles all must have their season, and it starts here.

By mid-month the bluebells are seeded, the beech leaves feed aphids and grubs, and the bird song is waning. The New Year's dream comes true at Midsummer, in the flowering of the wild honeysuckle, but a few days later the emergence of stinkhorns signals the onset of a slow but inexorable decline.

June 1st – 7th

June may flame, but not just yet. This first week of the month tends to be wet and dull, or worse. On 2nd June 1975 there was a covering of snow over much of the Dales, and on the night of the 4–5th June 1991 there was a hard frost, the only time I have ever seen hoar frost on cut silage. Very few Dales farmers made silage up until a generation ago, and then only as a subsidiary to hay. Nowadays some farmers make no hay at all, not even a few bales of calf-hay. There is no need for them to carefully gauge the weather, or to maintain good relations with likely-looking hay-makers. The whole silaging process can be completed in hours, and by outside contractors if necessary.

I always try to have a look round the edges of newly-cut

fields, though there may be some gruesome sights. The curlew called her gangling chicks out into pasture-land as soon as the tractor made its first round, but other birds have survived thus far by immobility, and cannot change. The pheasant near the field edge instinctively remains on her nest, for has she not escaped detection a dozen times already? The great noisy machine approaches, the wheels pass by, and at the last moment she sees the cutting edges. I find her nest laid bare, half the eggs smashed, and a roughly severed leg lying nearby.

Nature ensures that there is no waste, for there are carrion crows to be fed. To hold a carrion in your hand is to look into an eye as ancient and wily as the crocodile's. Archaeopteryx must have had an eye like this, and from a crow-like ancestor evolved all the birds of the world. I must confess to an admiration, even a liking, for the great old crow, though that might dissipate if I ever saw one truly picking the eyes from a live lamb. Come to think of it, I used to quite like crocodiles too, until I saw one with a woman inside it in Barotseland.

Young carrion crows leave the nest this week, provided the nest has not been blasted by shot. At first they cannot fly far, and practise from a steep slope nearby. Until now the parents have scattered the left-over food remains far and wide, to help keep the nest site a secret, but now the litter accumulates on the bank. The eggs of grouse, pheasant and lapwing predominate, though those of mallard, both partridges, curlew and other waders may be found. There may be 20 or 30 strewn over an area a few yards wide, and if you remove them you will find a dozen more next day. There will also be the remains of young rabbits, for the carrion will kill live ones as well as collecting fresh corpses. This litter will give you a fascinating insight into the life of the crow, as well as letting you see which of the larger birds are still incubating. The first knowledge I had of a red-legged partridge nesting here was when I found its egg-shells amongst this discarded booty.

It is astonishing that the beady-eyed crow can so effort-lessly find so many nests. Most of the eggs it finds now will be in the later stages of incubation, and each makes a perfectly neat bundle of easily-digested meat pulp for the waiting young. The crow's technique in searching for nests is to float a yard or two above the heath where the breeze catches the shoulder of a hill, sidling this way and that, in the hope of either spotting the nest or driving the incubating bird off it to attack. Late-nesting grouse are particularly susceptible, though the main bulk of the population now has chicks which are well able to fly.

Grouse chicks can fly quite strongly at two to three weeks of age, long before they are fully grown, but other birds are not so lucky. Where the cotton-woolly seed heads of hare's tail grass fleck the moor edge, in the very places that carrions favour, there are young redshank afoot, and teal ducklings too. The teal performs her wing-down trick just as well as the mallard or grouse, but the old carrion gives the corvine equivalent of a cynical snort, and pecks up a baby or two anyway. Nor is it only the crow up there, for kestrels and sparrowhawks are both feeding nestlings. Kestrels may specialize in small mammals, but if you find an accessible nest you will be surprised at the number of pipits' and larks' feet piling up around the downy wide-mouthed young.

Sparrowhawks hunt small birds for a living, and although they usually leave the open moor to the kestrel and merlin, they love the moor-edges. Here the scattered trees and bushes provide nicely exposed perches for cock whinchats and tree pipits to sing to their incubating hens. They all watch the skies as they sing, but the sparrowhawk comes low and fast from the woodland below, and for one or another, sooner or later, the struggle for survival is over.

Further down the hill the spotted flycatcher is equally at risk, for he also has a taste for exposed perches. Whilst his hen sits laying in her nest amongst the ivy, the cock catches flies to present to her. But the sparrowhawk catches the flycatcher, and another piece of protein shifts higher up the food chain. This is Nature in the raw, the movement of protein from species to species and from generation to generation.

Thus a tree sucks up minerals and water from the soil, mixes them with fresh air and sunshine, and makes leaves; the eggs of winter moths hatch there, and the grubs eat the leaves; a blue tit harvests the grubs, and takes them to its newly-hatched young in their nest-hole. In the river a crayfish ate insect larvae last year to make protein for its eggs; it carried the eggs all Winter beneath its tail; they hatched during the last fortnight; and now one of the larval young is caught by a sandpiper and fed to a day-old chick. Along the wood-edge a violet ground beetle crawls out from under its stone at dusk; it catches a bristletail in the leaf litter; in turn it is eaten by a little owl, which has owlets on the point of flying; the beetle's remains are regurgitated in a pellet, which drops to the ground; it is broken down by bacteria, and soaks back into the soil; and the minerals from it go back up into another tree to help make more leaves.

Those larval insects which are missed by the crayfish and sandpiper, not to mention the many other hazards of aquatic life, are emerging now as flying adults. The air is full with them, particularly near rivers in the evening. The trout love this lazy time of year, when the water is still fresh and cool, and the anglers love it too. For the swifts and swallows and martins it justifies their calling this place home, for there is nowhere south of the Equator that has such long days and so many flies. This is the reason they nest here, the swifts and swallows now incubating, the sand martins already beginning to hatch.

It is not only birds which feast on winged insects, for bats are busy now, some at dusk and dawn, others throughout the night. Bats are not truly blind, but eyesight is much less important to them than their sophisticated echo location system. A specialized larynx emits short bursts of ultra-sonic energy, which bounce back from flying prey and are received by sensory apparatus in the ear flap, or tragus. The pea-sized brain acts as radar, ultra-scan and homing device all in one, and acted thus for millions of years before we invented poor imitations.

The noctule's high, powerful wheeling flight, long narrow wings and large size make it rather resemble a swift in flight. It roosts in colonies, usually in hollow ash trees near to water. The large scent glands on the face help roost members to recognise each other in the pitch black inside the tree, and help mothers to identify their own young.

Noctule Bat
(nyctalus noctula)

nelson 92

Bats are truly marvellous little animals, and over the years I have looked after several different species that have been handed in to me. In my teens I had a pipistrelle in a bat box in my bedroom, and let it out to fly round my room each night until it was strong enough to be released. Most injured bats do not survive long in captivity, and I no longer accept them for treatment, but I still like to watch them, and find myself drawn to the riverside on calm summer evenings.

There is always a sense of excitement about walking out at dusk, for it means that we anticipate seeing something out of the ordinary. As always I set off too early, and find myself approaching the bat roost before time. Midges delight in a sitting target, so I linger on the path, listening to the last of the bird song and talking to the weeds. By the damp shady pathside there are two new flowers, the lanky greater celandine, with its wart-curing yellow juices, and the star-like flowers of the yellow pimpernel. The yellow theme is continued on the drier bank where I eventually settle, for there is hop trefoil blooming here, and the closely related white clover. White clover will soon dominate our pastures, like so many summer hailstones, but the dominant white just now is the fragrant hawthorn blossom, so tightly packed on the branches that the bushes in this half-light seem to have been snowed upon.

Then quite suddenly, at about a quarter to ten, noctule bats begin to pour out of their hole in a branch of the hollow ash by the river. I count 74 in a minute, and two or three later, large swift-like bats which rise up over the tree-tops and spread out in all directions. Who could believe that these creatures are nearer kin to elephants than birds? Who can really understand that this high rapid flight, with its gliding turns and headlong dives, is all powered by flaps of skin stretched between modified finger bones? There is nothing supernatural about bats in the commonly accepted sense, but of all mammals they do most closely approach the literal meaning of the word.

About fifteen minutes after the noctules, tiny pipistrelles begin to appear between the trees, flying at about 15 feet high, with sudden downward swoops. And then right on the edge of dark the almost equally tiny Daubenton's begins to flutter low over the river surface, earning its alternative name of water bat. There are other species also out tonight, whiskered, Natterer's, and Brandt's, but these are less easily identifiable on the wing, and we will have many more chances to observe and discuss them between now and September.

June 8th – 15th

There is a flower that is familiar to every Dales farmer, though few could put a name to it. It grows in every farmyard, though our fore-elders would not have known it. It is regularly trampled underfoot without a thought, but thrives in the very places where it is most likely to be trampled. When I see my son pluck a head off the flower and rub it in his palms to sniff, I smile at the thought that at least three generations of his family before him have done the same within a mile of here. It is called the rayless mayweed, it has a flower the shape of a pigmy acorn, and it is a foreign relative of the daisy. It was introduced to Britain in Victorian times, and because of its smell it is sometimes known as pineapple weed, though to me it is redolent of fresh apples.

There are up to a couple of dozen new flower species appearing every week at this time of year, and we cannot even mention them all, let alone devote a paragraph to each. We are fortunate in Britain that well over half of our wild flowers are wayside species, so that we need only walk along quiet lanes with open eyes to find plenty to exercise our minds. Meadow cranesbill, a sort of blue wild geranium, is immediately obvious amongst the whites and yellows, as are the thin red spikes of common sorrel and the bright blue flowers of alkanet. The tiny white flowers of the goosegrass could hardly be less significant, but its climbing vines have been used by generations of country children to stick onto the backs of unsuspecting victims in play.

Two plants which superficially resemble the dandelion are usurping that plant's place in the wayside mosaic, though neither will ever be as common. The one is the mouse-ear hawkweed, with its soft downy leaves, and the other the rough hawkbit, which is slightly larger and more vigorous. Growing below them, right on the edge of the road, is another yellow flower, the silverweed, so named for the silvery leaflets of its creeping foliage. Heath bedstraw is also a wayside plant where grassy slopes run down to the road, though it can be found on sunny banks almost everywhere, even along the moor-edge. Its flowers are tiny white crosses which make themselves apparent only *en masse.* Its soporific scent and bactericidal properties made it ideal, when dried, for stuffing pillows and mattresses in olden times, hence the name.

Two plants not normally found by the wayside are yellow rattle and common spotted orchid. The yellow rattle is a declining species, found particularly in old-fashioned meadows. Its roots tap into the pipeline of certain ·grass roots, from which it obtains nourishment, but it abhors chemical fertilisers. The orchid, by contrast, is on the increase, thanks especially to the closure of many rural rail services. Damp shady railway cuttings with a bedding of limestone aggregate provide ideal conditions for several wild orchids, and this one has spread out into our woodlands and even into the edges of pastures. Beeching was not totally bad, after all.

In the woods there are fewer flowers now, though herb-Bennet is opening around the wood-edges. As the tree canopy thickens and cuts out the light, bluebells go to seed and the woodland floor darkens. Bracken is rather unusual in that it grows equally well amongst the heather on exposed sunny hillsides, and alongside shade-loving ferns and brambles in the deep of the woods. It is amongst it in this latter habitat that the wood warbler is now incubating her eggs, for she lays late in the season and has only one clutch. The domed grass-lined nest is built in some cup-sized hollow on the ground amongst bracken and brambles, and is beautifully camouflaged by an outer layer of woven fern fronds.

Most other birds are further ahead with their breeding programme. The woods are teeming with fledgling black-birds, song thrushes, robins and great tits, many of which are unfortunately providing food for young jackdaws, magpies, and the occasional jay. Nearly all of our young starlings have also flown. Indeed they are now to be seen in small flocks in the fields, having been joined by earlier-nesting families from the flat-lands, and some non-breeding individuals. If you hear what sounds like the raucous calling of starling nestlings now, particularly near the edges of woods, it is likely to be the noise made by the larger and louder young of a great spotted woodpecker. With a little patience you can find the source, and the arrival of the parents to shout "pik, pik," at you will confirm that you have the right nest-hole. Find yourself a convenient bank overlooking the site, and settle down to watch for a while. It is astonishing to see how little time it takes each parent to collect a beakful of plump white grubs of a type you never even knew existed.

And whilst you are sitting out of sight in the undergrowth, keeping quiet and still, you are opening the door to other bits of magic. It may be nothing more than a hover-fly in a ray of sunshine, or the gilt-winged longhorn moths trailing their antennae along the edge of the clearing, but there are many young mammals about now, rather more carefree and foolhardy than their parents. Thus a few feet away a young shrew runs across a bare patch, then another and another, until half-a-dozen or more have passed; and then two or three run back, and back again, confusing your attempt to count them. One runs past holding another's tail in its teeth, and then two stop to roll and tumble and squeak, actually bouncing off the ground in their tiny fury, until you laugh out loud and they are gone.

There are young squirrels about too, though they have sharp eyes and will have seen you. Still, they are inquisitive and you are novel to them, and they cannot resist investigating. At this stage they are all head and legs, with a tail so sparse you can see through it. They also cannot grip or balance as well as the adults, and there are touching scenes of parental concern when one seems of have stranded itself, and an anxiously chattering parent exposes herself to you to guide it to safety. And if you are very diligent and persistent at keeping quiet in the woods, especially near sunrise, you may be privileged enough to see the roe deer lead her twins out to browse. The beautifully dappled wide-eyed fawns are no bigger than lambs, but can bound powerfully away alongside their dam at the merest sniff of danger. The sight of them is more thrilling to me than that of any badger or fox cub, for it can never be planned or anticipated, only yearned for and awaited.

Although we can see many rare and interesting things by hiding in the woods, we can see a wider variety by getting away from the undergrowth and canopy, and out into the open countryside. By the reservoir edges the eggs of great crested grebe are hatching now, and the chicks are being coaxed by their parents off the nest island into the lapping wavelets. By smaller meres and ponds the lovely yellow flag iris is in flower, as is the tasty watercress. Beneath the water there is a living soup of arthropod life, with the occasional helminth oddity, a specklety-brown leech, perhaps, or the long thin filament of a horse-hair worm. A few inches above the surface, electric-blue damselflies are starting new life, clinging daintily together in nuptial embrace. They are sometimes mistaken for dragonflies, which we rarely see before July, but they are much smaller, and their wings are folded back over the body when at rest.

Over the water there are swallows, now swooping to pick hatching larvae from the surface, now flicking over the tree-tops in pursuit of soaring imagines. Within a minute or two their beaks are full, and another little ball of chitinous protein is carried back to their newly-hatched offspring in the mistal nest. On the barn roof nearby a family of four recently-fledged pied wagtails await similar fare from their parents, making practice forays from the roof to strengthen their wings as they wait. A barn roof is a convenient place for small birds to practise flight, but around these upland farms it leaves them horribly exposed. Today it is not a sparrowhawk which takes one, but a merlin ranging out from the moor. Before the little puff of feathers reaches the ground, the hawk is gone from sight with its booty. Within ten minutes it is delivering it, ready plucked, to its little white chicks beneath a tuft of heather, having first thoroughly checked the moor for watchers.

Pipits are, of course, the merlin's main prey, and there is no particular shortage of young pipits for it to harass. Parent titlarks are now preparing for their second clutch, and it is during this week that the hen cuckoo lays most of her eggs. For the last month she has been dallying with this male and that, but now her bubbling voice is increasingly heard as she scours the moor-edge for nests to parasitize. Her young will never know their mother, for she will be long gone before they take wing, but her genetic message is so strong within them that her pitiful parenting does not blight their lives.

Mammals have perhaps the strongest maternal bonds of any class of animal life, as we have already noted with species like the stoat. We have followed the progress of some of the larger species, rabbits and hares, foxes and badgers, stoats and squirrels, and our elegant little roe deer. But we do not need to hide or stalk or lie in wait to be near to young mammals, for they are all around us as we walk, hedgehogs and shrews, moles and voles, rats and mice. Unfortunately we cannot look into their nests and walk away, as we can with birds. Many of our smaller mammals take their protective instincts to ridiculous extremes, pre-ferring to kill their young rather than have them exposed to unfathomable danger. Thus if we go searching for shrew or vole nests in the centre of grass tussocks or beneath old logs and stones, we are condemning the young to death by either the scent of our fingers, or simply the disturbance of the nest wall.

We should therefore avoid the temptation to go poking about where we are not wanted, though there will be times when we might accidentally expose a nest. I once cut through a shrew's nursery when scything thistles, and kept the surviving young alive on condensed milk for several days until a hen-house door banged onto my pocket and killed them.

I also once uncovered a hedgehog nest when clearing brambles from a corner of the garden, but my best efforts to repair the damage were to no avail. The returning dam dimly perceived that her poor blind young, naked but for their soft white spikes, were about to be subject to a fate worse than death. She bit swiftly through their necks and blundered away, red in tooth and claw, to start another family in a safer place. Nature can be cruel, but such apparent cruelty has allowed the primitive old hedgehog to survive almost unchanged for a million years or more. For really mindless cruelty we must consider the motor car, for every other hedgehog run over during the next few weeks will be a lactating mother, leaving behind a family to die of starvation in their thorny fortress nest.

June 16th – 23rd

And then suddenly it's Summer. You step outside one morning before seven, to find the air warm, the insects humming, and the last wisps of overnight mist yielding to a radiant sun.

By ten the dew is off the meadows, and the fields are buzzing with machinery. Most of the grass is being cut for silage, and will be cleared by this time tomorrow, leaving a patchwork of bare yellow stubble. That which is to be dried for hay will take a little longer, though with enough diesel and machinery, and favourable weather, it is still possible to cut it one morning and have it baled and cleared the following evening. When I first started hay-making, the cut swathes used to be turned and shaken and rowed up by hand, then piled into hubs and pikes for carting away. Today's methods produce, on average, a better quality feed for less toil. But they have nothing of the romantic innocence of a half-dozen lads and lasses sitting with their backs to a pike, sharing from a basket of home-baked bread and cool bitter shandy.

Once a few fields have been cleared the rooks flood in, to goose-step across the stubble. They search for exposed mouse-nests, confused insects, and other luckless small fry whose world has suddenly and drastically changed. The young rooks can still be differentiated from the adults by their dark beaks, cleaner-lined underparts, and occasional reversion to juvenile begging behaviour.

Young curlews also become visible now, since the clearing of the long grass has left them with fewer hiding places. The sentinel parents increase their vigilance, for their young cannot fly yet, and must protect themselves by flattening into what little cover is left. When you are still a quarter of a mile from their chicks, the adult curlews circle noisily around you crying "killilly-loo, killilly-loo" or "ploo-lilly" or similar, generally alerting everything within earshot of your approach. If you do mark a chick from a distance, or stumble upon one by chance, it will run off on long legs at a good speed, little wings outstretched. The lengthening beak is still straight at this stage, though when it has reached an appropriate length it will grow downwards at the tip to resemble that of the adult.

Curlews are classed as nidifugous birds because, like most waders, and indeed like the majority of large ground-nesting birds, the young leave the nest within hours of hatching. Those species which remain in the nest until fully fledged are called nidiculous. Some nidifugous birds, notably partridges, are still incubating their first clutch of eggs. Most, except of course the woodcock, do not yet have young on the wing. By contrast, many nidiculous birds, such as wagtails, pipits, and the thrush family, have already weaned one clutch and are busy with another. True, there are odd ones, like spotted flycatcher and whinchat, which are still incubating the first clutch. Others, like pied flycatcher and wood warbler, have only recently hatched. But a couple of dozen nidiculous species now have young on the wing, and another half-dozen will join them this week.

Thus on a grassy wooded bank we find a family of willow warblers in the branches of a rowan tree. The anxious parents call "tsoo-it, tsoo-it" at our intrusion. The fledglings try to imitate their parents' admonitions, but all that comes out is a comical croaky squeak. A little family of tinkling linnets moves through a full-flowered patch of gorse nearby, whilst around our gardens there are newly-flown green-finches. If we fill the nut hopper in anticipation of young blue tits, we find instead two squabbling families of glutton

Previous page: Garden robin amongst February snowdrops
Above (top): Meadow pipit with fostered cuckoo chick

Above: Long-eared owl at nest in conifer
Opposite (bottom): Pair of wheatears on limestone outcrop

Above (top): Winter fieldfare in search of berries
(bottom): Yellowhammer at nest amongst tufted vetch

Black-headed gull at moorland nest

Above: Badger amongst the bluebells in May
Opposite (top): Small tortoiseshell butterfly on spear thistle
(bottom): Hill primroses by the water's edge

Common toadflax and rosebay willow-herb

greenfinches, emptying it with vigour.

Up the moor young wheatears are emerging from their sunless holes to find, like Larkin's lambs, a world utterly unlike that to which they have been accustomed. On the heath beside them there are young ring ouzels, and the odd woodpigeon or two, scouring bilberry patches for the first ripe berries. They will find a few, but we do not need to start looking ourselves until we see the mistle thrushes begin to congregate there in early July.

There are other young birds up on the moor top, nestlings that will not leave the nest until July, and which break the rule about large ground-nesting birds being nidifugous. These are the raptors, most especially the merlin and the short-eared owl. You will need a lot of patience, and some skill, to find their nests, and if you get anywhere near you are likely to be moved along by a Park Warden or RSPB volunteer, who has been watching you all the while.

Moor Owl or Short-eared Owl
(Asio Flammeus)

nelson 91

It is illegal to photograph or disturb the nests of most raptors, though you can often find an obliging kestrel that you can watch without disturbance. I know a kestrel nest within two hundred yards of one of the busiest footpaths in the Dales, which gives close-up views into the nest for no more effort than sitting on a grassy bank. It is in a large hole on the uphill side of an old ash trunk. From twenty yards away I can nosey into the family life of the kestrel with all the ease of watching a nature film from an armchair.

An unhatched egg lies abandoned on the doorstep, half-covered by two dead bank voles. The satiated fledglings still appear downy, though the feathers are showing through. From time to time one raises itself on its toes to flap its wings. By the end of this week they are out on a branch. For days afterwards they hang around the area pleading "ki-ki-ki-ki" to their parents, and being mobbed by swallows and martins each time they fly.

House martins are quite localized in their distribution, according to the availability of suitable nesting sites. But for a few days about now they can be seen around any sycamore tree, even along the moor-edges, as they feast on an aerial plankton of greenfly. The life cycle of aphids is very complex and variable, but always around this time of year a winged generation takes flight. Aphids are prolific little plant bugs, and if you doubt their numbers you need only park your car beneath a tree, and watch their exuded honeydew falling on your windscreen. Fortunately they provide soft juicy prey for dozens of larger insects, which protect us from a greenfly plague. One of the most notable of these predators if the green lacewing. It rather resembles a huge greenfly, if an inch can be called huge, but is distinguished by the most remarkable shiny golden eyes.

Whilst sap-sucking aphids are damaging the leaves, other invertebrates are busy with the rootlets. One of the most serious of these subterranean pests is the shiny orange wireworm, which may spend up to four years below ground before emerging as a click beetle. Click beetles are at their most visible now. If turned on their backs they flick up into the air with an audible click, landing right way up to squeals of delight from budding naturalists. Like so many insects, they will easily pass unnoticed unless you have learnt to look for them. The same is true of the small copper, which may be found in a variety of habitats, but is especially attracted to sheep sorrel. It is a much brighter little butterfly than most books show it to be, and is well worth seeking.

For really insignificant insects we need look no further than the hogweed, which begins to flower this week. Many types of tiny insect are attracted by its boar-like smell, and slightly larger invertebrates congregate there to eat them. There may be several species on a flower head at any one time. It is a simple matter to catch them in a plastic bag for identification, though attempts at identification can prove frustrating.

Many other wayside flowers are opening alongside the hogweed. Tall plants like the foxglove, which gave us the base for life-saving digoxin; stinging nettle and marsh thistle, unwelcome to us but essential to some of our best-loved butterflies; hedge woundwort, its leaves foul-smelling but all-healing; few-leaved hawkweed and goat's beard, two more relatives of the dandelion; and little white raspberry roses, soon to yield delicious berries.

In the fields many flowers approaching maturity have been cut off in their prime. All the wonderful grasses that typify our upland meadows, timothy and cocksfoot, fescue and rye, annual meadow grass and good old Yorkshire fog, have laid down their lives for our winter pint of milk. The bare cleared meadows have the air of the graveyard about them. But this is illusory, for they will soon be rippling with lush new growth. Even now there is a strip around their edges which is teeming with survivors.

Few plants survive more tenaciously than the ground elder. It is now finally flowering, after seeming for weeks to be about to open. Above it in the hedge is its unrelated namesake, the elder bush, showing its first creamy-white flower heads. Soon we will collect a bucketful to mix with lemons and sugar for elderflower champagne, a startlingly refreshing drink with a marvellous bouquet. Next to the elder there is a guelder rose, a type of wild viburnum which will later produce bright red berries beside the purple-black ones of elder. And in the strip around the field edge, where the machinery did not reach, there are some of the archetypal plants of damp fields; meadow vetchling and salad burnet, snakeweed and ragged robin, and the ox-eye daisy that we call dog.

I flit from one flower to another like an evening moth, but a heavenly scent catches me and draws me away upwind. There, pure and prim amongst an exuberant tangle of vines, blushing modestly, the creamy flowers of wild honeysuckle pose upon a wall. In the depths of Winter when all seemed dead, her twin leaves gave us hope. Now, as she pours her glorious perfume on the breeze, she gives us the sad sweet message that the year is at its best, and will never be as good again.

June 24th – 30th

The hot weather continues, though it becomes overcast and sultry. There are brief localized thundershowers, but the hay swathes dry quickly without spoiling. Silage-making is hardly even interrupted.

On the meadowland over 750 feet ASL the growing season starts late, and hay-making is seldom contemplated until well into July. Even then the greensward is of a poorer quality than that a mile or two away down the hill. Agronomists say that the leaf to stem ratio is too low. We say you can see the mouse-runs.

You can also see young lapwings, for they are now as big as their parents. At a glance they closely resemble the adults, but on closer scutiny they can be seen to have shorter crests and duller colours, with grey on the neck. This week they begin to fly, and pewits from several fields join together in small flocks. In flight the young can be seen to have a whitish patch near the middle of the upper surface of each wing. This enables you to compare numbers, and you may be surprised to note that there is already less than one surviving young per adult.

Snipe nest at roughly the same time as lapwing, and their young grow at a comparable rate. Unlike young lapwing, however, young snipe can fly when still very small, from about two weeks of age. The adults tend them until they reach full size, and in these upland areas they usually stay together in family parties even after weaning. On permanent marshland, the parents may drive away the first brood and go on to produce a second. This is a risky business on our hills, for the boggy patches can be baked dry in a hot Summer, making food unavailable to the second-clutch chicks. Nevertheless a few dominant pairs do make the effort. For a couple of weeks about now we can hear them drumming and chukking again on fine sunny mornings, as they re-draw their territories.

A few skylarks also go on to produce second broods in the same high-ground habitats, and the song of the lark mingles with the call of the snipe to give a brief rememoration of Spring – all too brief, for both songs fade away again in early July. Further down the hill the woods are already falling silent, though there are snatches of willow warbler and wren song, and the blackcap is still in good voice. Blue tits have flown now, and their noisy family parties help cover the silence with squeaks and churrs.

Other youngsters which fly this week include goldfinches, from their nests in bilberry or gorse or garden, and swallows, from our outbuildings. Whether the weather be dry and cold or hot and humid, the interval from the swallow's first egg to the young flying is remarkably constant at about 38 days. If it looks like going beyond this, you need only stretch out your hand towards the fully feathered young, and they will be off. Having never flown before, they flit out through the door and high over the roof in strongly sustained flight at the first attempt. Their parents and other adults swoop in to join them, chittering excitedly. If you have ever taught a kid to ride a bike, you will know something of how they must feel.

Herons also fly in late June, and the youngsters may be seen in the company of their parents along our becks. They have a blue tinge to their grey plumage, with less vivid black and white markings, shorter necks, and duller beaks and legs. Once they separate from their parents these features are not so obvious, though if you see a lone heron now which seems too bold or too sleepy, it is likely to be a juvenile. And whilst you are looking for herons you are bound to disturb sandpipers, for they have chicks at foot. They make a terrific fuss up and down the riverside as you walk past, though you will only find their chicks by the sheerest chance. Not only so they have an abundance of waterside cover in which to hide, but they can swim surprisingly well, and even dive if the need arises.

Another bird which hatches its chicks this week is the partridge. We may be walking along some country lane when suddenly a cock partridge runs out into the middle of the road, looks both ways, and calls out his family to cross. A dozen or more little brown balls of fluff go running past him, shepherded by the hen. He stands his guard till they are past and then follows, always the perfect little gent. Or again we may surprise a pair round a bend in a track, and walk up to within a yard of them. Both parents sit there, frantically afraid but determined to hold their ground, whilst the chicks hide beneath them and stir amongst their feathers.

Such courage deserves recognition. Why should the hawk or eagle be thought bold and brave when there are birds like the partridge around? But life is not fair, and so the hen is injured by a tourist's dog or the cock is hit by a passing car.

There are certainly plenty of road casualties now, and not only amongst birds. Of course there are rabbits; there are always rabbits, whether quick or dead; but as more fields are cleared, other mammals begin to move. Moles live mostly on the surface in Summer, scurrying through the tangled undergrowth around the base of grasses and flowers. When a field is felled, they escape harm by going below ground. When it is cleared they move to the hedgerows and wall-bottoms. But this sudden depletion of habitat occurs at exactly the time that young moles are leaving the nursery to become independent. In seeking suitable territories they cross roads, and are sometimes run over.

Just as young moles find themselves in reduced circumstances at the time of greatest need, so do young rats. And whereas the mole will eventually find refuge in uncultivated woodland, the rat reverts to the farmyard. Suddenly I see a rat or two around the buildings at dawn or dusk, and know that for every one I see there are another ten in hiding. Between trap and gun and poison they are soon gone. The rat is an admirable little beast in many ways, but so long as he carries leptospirosis he must not live where we do.

The cutting of grass for hay or silage does the naturalist a great favour. Within a few days, everything worth seeing in the fields is concentrated round their edges. If you know of an old bridle path or green lane that passes between two meadows, particularly on a south-facing slope, then go there now. Go prepared to sit and watch, and take a little bait. Cheese is the classical lure for small mammals, but I prefer a kipper head, or a cream cracker pasted with butter and cocoa powder.

If you go at dawn after a wet night, there will be great black slugs, often in pairs. Their slithy coupling is positively obscene, but they have the decency to do it in the dark. Beneath some hedges there will be large yellow-and-brown striped garden snails, though these have a very localized distribution. As the day warms up, the sun-loving insects come out. If there is a bed of lady's slipper and bit of limestone there will be common blue butterflies, almost invisible when resting but bright as the sky when in flight. And where there is pignut there will be chimney sweeper moths, fluttering low over the grass on sooty black wings.

But even if you see not a speck of animal life, even if it rains all day, there are masses of flowers to enchant you. Two or three types of dock make a wash of rusty red, obligingly close to a bed of nettles. Creeping and spear thistle follow the lead set by the marsh thistle. Nipplewort and figwort, two very different small flowers on large plants, are open in shady places. In the drier pastures there are yarrow, self-heal and betony, all famed for their healing properties in the days before antibiotics. Along the old railway embankment the first rare bee orchids are coming into flower beside their common spotted cousins. And almost everywhere the pure White Roses are lighting up, followed two days later by the blushing Reds, Yorkshire and Lancashire nodding to each other in the breeze. We have a lot more in common than either of us likes to admit.

7 July

J uly is the pivotal month of the year, when life and death hang in the balance. On one side of the scale there is an abundance of insects and young birds; a glorious kaleidoscope of flowers; an explosion of small mammals; and a hot sun providing the energy for them all to thrive. On the other side there is the fading away of all bird song; dark thickened tree leaves riddled with holes; face flies and berry bugs; maggots and putrefying flesh; and the gradual appearance of saprophytic fungi, sucking their life from another's decay.

In the Dales it is also the month when tourism is at its height. We are naturally flattered that so many people, from all over the World, want to come and look at what we hold dear. But is is undeniably pleasant to pack a few sandwiches, get away from the honeypots, and flee to some hidden valley. The sun on my front as I doze there; the springy moor grass beneath my back; the sound of grasshoppers calling to their mates; the luxuriant smell of jungley bracken: this is July in a nutshell. And if, at some little distance, there is the reassuring laughter of my wife and children splashing in the beck water, then life is very nearly perfect.

July 1st – 7th

The sky becomes heavy and overcast, and the hills seem to close in around us. Every exertion brings out beads of sweat. Finally the storm breaks. Warm rain pours down, with the full Wagnerian accompaniment.

After an hour or two the thunder fades away into distant rumblings, leaving the sound of rushing water all around. Becks that had barely a trickle this morning are now raging torrents, smashing out through their banks and flooding fields. Ponds form in slack spots, and mallard come gliding in to splash and quack. The drakes have lost their gloss now, and could be mistaken for females or juveniles. Only their dull olive beaks and greyish necks distinguish them.

The sun beams through again, and four fledgling redstarts pop up onto a wall-top to dry out. They fluff out their feathers, looking almost like young robins, and make excited chuttering noises as their parents approach. But the calls of the young redstarts, and the solicitous "pwit, pwit," of their parents, only draw attention to the silence. Where is the stormcock that thrilled us from these scattered oaks after winter showers? Where is the blackbird that fluted here each evening around Midsummer? And above all, where is the cuckoo? Last week we heard him, and realised that it had been some days since we heard him last. Now we listen for him in vain. Both cock and hen cuckoo have ceased to call, and are already leaving the hills. We see odd ones resting in strange places, or see twos and threes together flying swiftly away towards flatland fens.

The silence in the woods is even more profound. The only noise is the sporadic squeaking of a family of coal tits, high in the branches of a stand of conifers. A rabbit thumps the ground with its back feet, and we hear it two hundred yards away. It is not our presence which has alarmed him, but the whiff of a fox as the breeze stirs the air. The fox cub emerges thoughtfully from amongst wild rhododendrons, searching the ground for beetles and slugs brought out by the rain. He has a lean and hungry look, accentuated by his short thin tail-brush. He freezes like a pointer dog and then dashes forward, but the young pheasants have seen him. They clatter noisily into the low branches of a tree, and then work their way up higher, their parents nowhere to be seen. The cock pheasant, like the drake mallard, is in eclipse plumage, and wants nothing to do with his offspring. Even with his tail feathers missing he still tries to strut, but merely succeeds in looking ridiculous: all pomp and no circumstance.

Fox cubs spread out across the countryside during July, spurned now by tetchy vixens and forced to fend for themselves. They may be seen by daylight, even in city parks, and are often killed on the roads at night. Young tawny owls have the same problem. They have been fed by their parents since leaving the nest in May, and have slowly learned to hunt for themselves. Just as one thinks it knows all the angles it glides down for an easy kill in this bare open space, and is clipped by a car. Next day children draw its body at the local primary school, and write poems about it.

There are many little bodies by the roadside now, but not all have been hit by cars. The population of common and pigmy shrews, even water shrews, has built up to a peak, and there is a shortage of territories. The shrews born

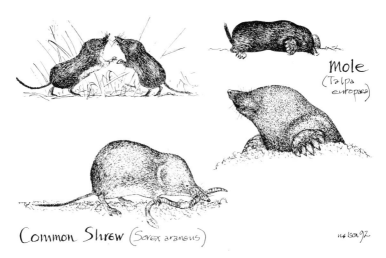

Mole
(Talpa
europaea)

Common Shrew (Sorex araneus)   nelson 92

last year are now quite elderly, and are unable to compete against this Spring's robust and aggressive youngsters. We hear their squeaking matches in the hedgerows as we walk, and sometimes see a half-dazed shrew tottering along a roadside, allowing us to approach it quite closely or even pick it up. More often we find an unmarked body huddled on the verge. The shrew needs to eat nearly its own weight of fresh food daily, in regular courses three hours apart. Weakened by age and reproduction, driven from its home, it runs and runs through the undergrowth, attacked by all it meets. Only in an open space does it find respite, and there it dies. The appearance of these little pathside bodies in thundery July led the ancients to believe that they had been frightened to death by thunder. In reality they die of old age and poverty, like farmers.

Shrews have skin glands which produce a sour-smelling musk, making them unpalatable to many predators. This does not bother owls, and you will see the red-tipped teeth of shrews in most owl pellets. Cats, in their uniquely wanton way, will stalk and kill shrews, and then leave the bodies to rot. Stoats and weasels, however, do not kill many shrews, though they have plenty of other prey available. This is a good time of year to see these two mustelids, crossing roads or working along wall-bottoms. You may even be lucky enough to come upon a family of stoats, half-a-dozen or more running in a pack, one of the most thrilling sights I know.

Up on the moor there is a silence of a different kind, the sort of open silence that is typical of deserts. Our two

ground-nesting raptors have fledglings on the wing now.
If you see two moor owls or two merlins together, they are
likely to be a parent with the largest offspring. Look around
in the area from which they took off, for the more backward
younger siblings may be still hiding there, unable to fly far.

Smaller birds will mob these inept youngsters, their alarm
calls punctuating the stillness. "Peu, cht-cht," cry the whinchats, perching atop bracken fronds near their nest. The
two phrases of the call are so dissimilar they they seem to
come from different birds. "Tit, tit, pipit," calls the titlark,
flying round and round a few feet above the heather. Is it
a second brood of young or a great coarse cuckoo chick
which it is trying to protect?

Mistle thrushes and ring ouzels fly off from a patch of
bilberries with harsh churrs and chacks of their own. Many
bilberries are ripening now, and in distant suburbs purple
pigeon droppings suddenly begin to fall on polished cars.
I like bilberries cooked or made into jam, I like them raw,
but most of all I like to sit and pick them, in some primaeval
reversion to hunter-gatherer. In the same way that oysters
have the taste of the sea, bilberries have the taste of the
wild moorland that is my ancestral home.

Other fruits are ripening down in the valleys; little wild
strawberries dotted on stony banks, red but not quite full-
flavoured; or wild goosegogs, hidden in a prickly hedge,
green amongst greenery. But flowers still predominate, and
have not even reached their peak yet. Upwards of three score
more species will flower during the month of July, though by
the end of it there will be more in seed than in flower. This
week a dozen or so new plants come into bloom, including
such delightfully named species as enchanter's nightshade,
woody nightshade, wild sage, tufted vetch, Good King Henry
and knot-head. On wall-tops and old barn roofs there are
galaxies of yellow stonecrop in flower, protected from
desiccation in the drought weeks ahead by the water stored
in their leaves.

Many of the flowers now, particularly the showier ones,
are those which grow in permanently wet places. Thus we
see the red-spotted yellow of monkey musk and the sweetly-
perfumed heads of dame's violet, both flowering by the
beckside; whilst a little further back are the blebs of bladder
campion and the pink heads of sedative valerian, the one
on the gravel bed, the other in the bog. In moorland bogs
there is the cross-leaved heath, with its greyish-green stem
topped by little pink bells; and beside it the lovely violaceous

flowers of butterwort, surrounded by basal rosettes of pale insect-eating leaves.

Whilst plant leaves are busy eating insects in peaty hags, insects are getting their own back in wooded valleys. Nearly every leaf on every tree is perforated by caterpillars or warty with galls. The galls are growths produced by the plant around invading gall-wasp larvae, in a process not entirely unlike the production of pearls in an oyster. Indeed spangle galls rather resemble pearls, shining red on the underside of oak leaves. Perhaps the strangest of galls is the robin's pincushion, often seen now as a tangled mass of crimson fibres amongst the leaves of a wild rose, more like a flower than an insect's nursery.

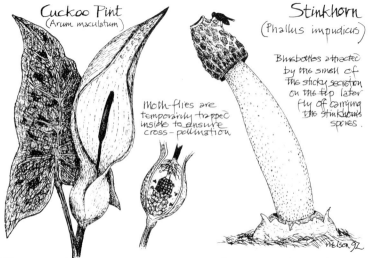

Cuckoo Pint
(Arum maculatum)

Moth-flies are temporarily trapped inside to ensure cross-pollination

Stinkhorn
(Phallus impudicus)

Bluebottles attracted by the smell of the sticky secretion on the top later fly off carrying the stinkhorn's spores.

Two completely unrelated species linked only by a lore of rustic phallic symbolism, preserved in names like Lords-and-Ladies for the cuckoo pint, and in the stinkhorn's Latin name

Another interesting relationship between plant and insect is that of the stinkhorn and bluebottle. The stinkhorn's Latin name means 'immodest phallus', and the phallic symbolism is unmistakable. Even my five year old daughter calls them white willies. The warty glans is covered by a foul-smelling greeny-brown slime which is ambrosia to bluebottles. They flock there and crawl about in it, becoming so stupefied that they sometimes fall off. Later, probably with something like a hangover, they fly away carrying the shameless one's spores inside them.

Many of our most interesting insects fly by night, and it is surprising how many common species we do not know.

As a youth I had hardly seen cockchafers until my brother put up a little greenhouse near his cottage at Bolton Bridge. Then, over a period of two or three weeks in late June and early July, there were fresh chafers in the greenhouse each night. They had entered the soil as larvae a couple of summers before, when there was no greenhouse there, and emerged to find themselves temporarily trapped. But you do not need to build a greenhouse, or even a moth trap, to see night-flying insects. Leave the light on in an open outhouse, splash around a boiled-up mixture of beer and black treacle, and you will have a dozen or more new friends by morning. Putting a name to them all is another matter.

July 8th – 15th

There are days in July when I go for a walk and come back with nothing but a list of flowers in my notebook. Animal life has not ceased to exist, but for the next few weeks it seems to be doing little that is new or noteworthy. If you have not previously had an interest in flowers and insects, now is a good time to start. If you are obsessively ornithological, I can only suggest that you go away on holiday, or send in your binoculars for that overdue service and cleaning.

In an age where any unusual bird is reported down a hotline, and surrounded within hours by a gang of twitchers carrying half a hundredweight of equipment apiece, there is a lot to be said for flower watching. It has a sort of cool scientific certainty about it. Each flower can be checked and re-checked, identified, recorded, talked to, smelt and photographed. And there are a lot more flowers than birds in the Dales, including some of extreme rarity.

So this week I record over eighty species actually in flower, not including grasses and sedges, which can be difficult to identify, or non-flowering species like mosses and ferns. Of these four score flowers, 44 are on the verges of a 300 yard stretch of lane along which car loads of tourists pass almost nose to tail. At least a dozen of them have opened during the past week: rosebay willow herb, meadowsweet and ragwort, which grow together in such perfect harmony of colour and form; hairy and slender St John's wort, which are not supposed to grow together but often do; the busy-Lizzie Himalayan balsam, its lower sepal formed into the shape of a bobby's helmet, perfectly sized to fit the pollinating bumble bee; creeping cinque-foil, which looks like silverweed, but for the five-fingered foliage that gives it its name; prickly sow-thistle with its thistle leaves and dandelion flowers; lady's bedstraw, which clots milk and unclots blood; and the unpretentious greater plantain, with its tough little spike and tongue-like leaves.

Away from the hedgerows there are other new flowers, wherever they can escape from being grazed or mown. Thus on dry sunny banks we see twinkling eyebrights and nodding blue harebells, both childhood favourites of mine; and on moor top peat bogs the common cotton grass, insignificant when in bloom, is showing its full shock of white hair as it runs to seed.

These wet patches amongst the heather become increasingly interesting as the rest of the upland dries out. The permanent ponds, often no more than a few feet across, draw in dragonflies from miles around. The golden-ringed dragonfly, over three inches long, is the largest and commonest, particularly if there is woodland not too far away. Further out onto the moor you may see the smaller blue aeshnas, though on these little pools the two species do not easily mix. Dragonflies are superbly predatory, one moment hovering or sliding slowly through the air with iridescent eyes aglow, the next streaking away to hit a passing bee.

There are other invertebrates here in the pond; skaters and whirligigs on the surface skin, boatmen and backswimmers jerking about below. On the heather nearby there are the hairy brown caterpillars of the oak eggar moth, woolly bears with a row of white tufts down each side. The heavy tawny-coloured moths themselves may also be seen, flying swiftly but erratically upwind. And there is vertebrate life too, little tadpoles with four legs now, and with rapidly shrinking tails, ready to leave the water over the next couple of weeks.

The snakes up here will love them. There are both grass snakes and adders on this upland heath, though the adder is the more common. I have never been lucky enough to see a grass snake yet, but many of my friends have, particularly in rush beds near reservoirs. The adder generally prefers drier ground. A warm afternoon, a bank facing the sun, a mixture of grass and heather, and a stream nearby; these are the adder's delight. You are not likely to see him unless you go looking, and you are extremely unlikely to get bitten so long as you keep your distance. He does not move as fast as you can walk, and he will run away from you if he can.

If you are bitten you may get cold sweats and nausea and develop a nasty local reaction, but the bite is very seldom fatal. Keep calm, make your way to the nearest hospital, and be sure that you are not allergic to the anti-venin if they decide that you need it.

Many of the birds up on the moor are already thinking of leaving. Male oystercatchers have been down in the valley for a week or two, but can still be seen commuting back to the moor, high and lonely in the sky, their plaintive piping alerting us of their approach. Within the next week or so their families will join them, and they will move west to the Lune valley to congregate on the tidal flats. Many young curlews are still downy, and most are not able to fly far. They run away through the rushes and into the bracken if they see you approach, though by the end of the month they too will have gone. Golden plovers already have young on the wing, but they will stay longer than most, long enough to be shot as grouse by myopic old peers. Black-headed gull chicks also take to the wing this week, and begin to join their parents foraging in the newly-mown fields. They are easily distinguished by their pale heads and the brownish patches in their plumage, and once again you may be surprised to see how few have survived the first two months of life.

But black-headed gulls are tremendously versatile birds, and will always prosper. Over the last month I have noticed that they are even becoming crepuscular, hawking insects over meadowland with an almost nightjar-like agility at dusk, and continuing to work there until it is too dark to see them. Today they show another facet of their character, harrying young kestrels all over the fields, with a great hue and cry. There are many kestrels about now, the young being similar to the hen birds but paler, especially on the tail.

At about the same time that young black-headed gulls begin to appear in moorside fields, lapwings begin to leave. A few late nesters stay on, but most will be gone by the end of the month. They do not always go far, and can be seen in flocks further down the dale, huddled disconsolately on arable land or playing fields. This dejected appearance will be seen in many birds over the next few weeks, as their levels of sex hormone fall and they go into the summer moult. It is particularly obvious in rooks; they will even take to roosting overnight in flocks on the ground, as if they cannot be bothered to fly into the tree-tops during their seasonal menopause. I suspect also that they leave the tree-tops to get away from the hordes of insects amongst the leaves – their bare faces must make them particularly susceptible to midge attack.

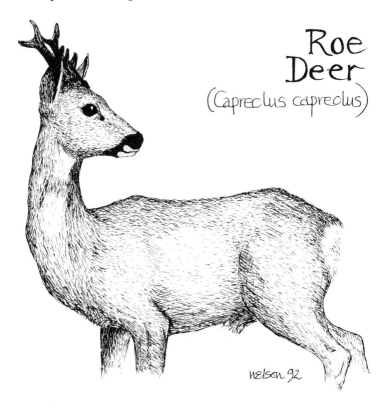

Roe Deer
(Capreolus capreolus)

nelson 92

The breeding season of many mammals is also drawing to an end, though the roe deer is a notable exception. This is the height of the roe rutting season, and pairs may be seen out in the open at any time of day, well away from their usual haunts. They have a foxy red summer pelage now, very noticeable against the grass in our July sunshine. They almost seem to enjoy being conspicuous, for where a road runs through the woods they may lie on it. If they are forced to move by an approaching car, these normally shy wild creatures will move only a few paces, and then bark angrily at the passing intruder. But all this is show and bravado, for their real business takes place in the twilight in some small clearing in the wood. Here the male has browsed away the vegetation around a little sapling, bitten off some scraps of its bark, and rubbed it with scent from his head glands. As the female nears oestrus he brings her to this trysting place and begins to chase her around the sapling, gently shepherding her back into the circle if she playfully tries to break away. After much running and walking round the ring, the doe becomes excited by the strong scent of the buck's heel glands and urine on the well trodden run. Mating then takes place, and is repeated many times over the next few days and nights, accompanied by more merry-go-round and a good deal of grunting and squealing. Development of the embryo does not start now, however, for the doe still has young at foot and does not want to be burdened with another pregnancy. Instead the fertilized egg is stored in her womb until it is needed, in a process known as delayed implantation. Only in the dead of Winter, just after the shortest day, will the biological alarm clock go off and the development begin.

July 16th – 23rd

There is a taste of the Tropics in the Dales in July. Garden weeds seem to break through the soil one day, and be a foot high the next. The lawn needs mowing twice a week. A lush green growth of fog covers each meadow as soon as it is cleared. A day with temperatures in the eighties is followed by a night with an inch of rain.

And above all, there are insects. If you live long enough in the Tropics you become immune to flies crawling all over your face, but here their season is too short. You walk with your head shaking and one arm waving, and you share your picnic with guests of uncertain provenance.

But to birds which spend half their lives in the Tropics, this is very heaven. Spotted flycatchers arrived late to be sure of finding such a boon, and now their first youngsters are sallying forth. Inexpert as they are, they still manage to take their fill with a leisurely ease. The hen bird helps sustain her offspring for a day or two, and then begins to lay another clutch. The new nest is already waiting, having been started by the cock in his spare time. He will keep an eye on the first brood as the hen incubates the second, though they are pretty much left to their own devices.

Swallows, martins and swifts are also having an easy time of it. They all have young on the wing now, and may be seen well away from their nesting sites, across the front of rocky crags or beneath moorside sycamores. Often you will see a loose association of 30 or 40 swallows and house

martins, where several families have converged to exploit
a superabundance of insects. Swifts also form little parties
as the adults put the young through their paces, screaming
low over rooftops in frantic chases, or soaring high over
hills in lazy splendour.

Many of the smaller insects seem totally defenceless,
relying only on numbers for their survival. Others, however, carry arms and are prepared to use them. Best known
amongst these latter are the wasps, with their re-chargeable
stings. Social wasps are increasingly noticeable now, and
their nests are becoming larger and more obvious. Some
species, such as the common wasp, nest in the ground,
taking over old mouse-holes and clearing a little runway by
the entrance. I once gassed a wasp nest in a sandbank, and
later dug it out intact. It was eighteen inches from top to
bottom, and almost as wide. Nests of other species are found
in hollow trees or suspended delicately from the branches
of a bush. They are masterworks of insect architecture, well
worth a closer inspection. The wasp was collecting wood-
pulp and making it into paper long before we began to
experiment with tree bark and stretched goat skin. And the
interior of her nest shows us most of what we need to know
about insulation and air conditioning.

The colours of the wasp give due warning that she is
dangerous, and she only attacks if provoked. The horse-fly,
by contrast, comes in quietly from behind and stabs you in
the back. There is nothing menacing about her appearance,
apart perhaps from her fiery eyes, but she has a wicked
proboscis that feels like a hot needle, and she lives by
sucking blood. She is most at home around livestock, but
if you get your shirt off in a damp meadow on a hot day,
she will find you.

But for every insect that bites or stings, there are a
hundred that do not, and many that give pleasure. Butterflies
are particularly pleasing, being associated in our minds with
flowers and sunlight, colour and heat. High on the intakes
and rough peaty pastures the small heath butterfly is on the
wing now, whilst further down the valley side a new generation of small tortoiseshells is much in evidence on honey-
smelling thistle flowers. Not all these pretty creatures are
quite as defenceless as they seem, for most are distasteful
to birds, and some are positively poisonous. The six-spot
burnet moth, now on the wing, contains cyanide, or at least
precursors thereof. Its forewings are glossy dark green with
red spots, giving reasonable warning to any predator. If any

bird is tempted to have a taste, a flash of the scarlet hind-wings will reinforce the threat. The bird's caution is innate, like our fear of snakes.

The burnet moth flies in damp limestone dells, where red and white clover are dotted amongst lady's slipper and hop trefoil. In these very places two lovely new flowers are blooming this week, the fragrant orchid and the showy yellow toadflax. The flower spike of the fragrant orchid is of a much deeper purple than that of its common spotted relative growing nearby, and unlike most orchids it has a strong and pleasant perfume. Other new flowers this week include salad burnet and sheep's bit scabious, joining the harebells on ungrazed grassy banks; and two large plants of moist waysides, the lanky burdock and the giant bellflower.

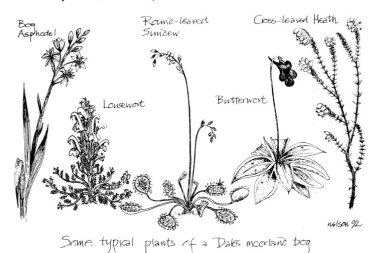

Some typical plants of a Dales moorland bog

But perhaps the most interesting of this week's flowers are two species growing beside the butterwort in moorland peat bogs. One is the bog asphodel or mountain lily, with its spike of yellow stars. It disdains the sheltered woodland habitat of other lilies, and blossoms proudly on the fell tops like a proper dalesman. The other is the round-leaved sundew, with its curly-topped stalk of little white flowers. The sundew looks innocuous enough until you lie down beside it with a hand lens. Then its pretty red leaves are seen to have glue-tipped tentacles, trapping tiny midges which settle there, and folding over them with stealthy grace. Magnified and speeded up on film, and dubbed with a belch as each leaf re-opens, the sundew would pass as a monster from outer space.

The young cuckoo has something of the monster about it too. Squat and ugly as a toad, with a great orange gape and a wheezy rattling voice, not even its own mother can bear the sight of it. But its foster parents are still besotted with their prodigy. They continue to feed it long after it has outgrown their home, sometimes perching on its back to better reach into its mouth. From this week onwards the young cuckoo may be seen hunched on some rocky prominence or moorside wall. With its barred brown plumage and the white patch on its nape, it looks rather like a young sparrowhawk. Its shorter tail and more sedentary behaviour distinguish it, at least until it is fully weaned.

Young merlins and young moor owls are also on the wing now, and are beginning to move away from the moor. We notice young merlins around upland farms in pursuit of sparrows and young swallows, and see moor owls at sunset flying low over marginal land. In good vole years, when every bob of rushes seems to have a field vole nest, there may be three or four owls at once quartering some rough boggy field. Let us hope that our conservationist farmers will continue to neglect these fields, so that our wild and noble moor owl can escape the fate of his lowland cousin. The hunting grounds of the barn owl have been drained and ploughed and planted with corn, not to feed the hungry but to fill the pockets of businessmen and the warehouses of Europe. Between insecticides, fungicides and weed-killers, they have been converted into that most paradoxical of wastelands, a fertile desert.

Even in the Dales we are not immune, for it is both easier and more effective to spray thistles and nettles than to cut them. This is the right time of the year for spraying thistles, when the flower heads are up, but before they go to seed. Can it just be coincidence that for a week or two about now I find several dead hares in lowland woods, with swollen livers and damaged kidneys?

Dales farmers get little enough leisure time. Anyone who has worked amongst them would want them to enjoy the full benefit of modern technology. But, please God, let them not enjoy it too much.

July 24th –31st

Most meadows have been mown now. On the ridge tops farmers are still busy with their first and only hay crop of the year, whilst two miles away in the valley bottom the second crop of silage is being felled. Five hundred feet of altitude can make a world of difference.

Mixed flocks of jackdaws and rooks are shuffling gravely about in the recently cleared fields. If disturbed they will fly off with less noise and more effort than usual, leaving the odd wing or tail feather spiralling down. Many show gaps in their wing primaries, and a few have no tail feathers at all. This must considerably affect their aerodynamics for a week or two, but Nature gives us all more than we usually need, and so they get by.

Clans of black-headed gulls huddle around the edges of crow flocks, or mix in with them. The heads of the adults are already fading, and the brown patches on the young are being covered by grey, so that the difference in age is becoming less obvious. Larger flocks will form soon, and the gulls will move away to arable land, waste tips and estuaries for a while. Starlings also drift away to similar sites in high Summer, for they feed by probing the ground, and cannot work here when it is dry. We barely notice their absence until we see a passing flock, and realise that it is a week or two since last we saw any.

With all the grass now short, we can get an idea of just how many rabbits there are. If it has been a good year for rabbits there will be few hares, for these latter will be up on the moors. If rabbits are well controlled the hares will be more widespread, though their numbers are generally lower. Both species ceased breeding around Midsummer, and from now onwards the percentage of fully grown individuals will gradually increase.

Partridges are also visible in the bare fields and fresh leafy fog. Chicks are now about half-grown, and are able to fly. Those hens which were barren or had their nests raided or lost their chicks in infancy, and those whose cock bird has died or been killed, will tag on to nuclear family parties. After a day or two they will be accepted in as aunts, which they may well be. Similarly, small families may latch onto larger ones, for the parents probably spent last Winter together, and have kept on nodding terms across their borders. Thus we will often see three or four adults with a group of between six and twenty young, all living peaceably together in one big happy family.

But it is not only birds and animals that we can see in the meadow aftermath, for the time of fungi is upon us. Large, often colourful, fungi will become progressively more common as flowers fade. Many are edible, including dozens that we think of as toadstools, but many are not, and some are deadly poisonous. If you can reliably identify the edible species you can have great fun gathering and sampling them. I have tried several, but have yet to find a species that can match the good old field mushroom. Mushrooms will reach their peak in September, but country folk usually get their first picking in the last week of July, provided there has been a bit of rain. They grow best in what we call fog, which is the new green grass that appears after a field has been mown. They are not actually killed by chemical fertilizers, as many people believe. But they grow on decaying straw in the soil, and so will only thrive where a field has been spread during Spring with a good layer of old-fashioned muck.

Other fungi that begin to appear this week include such quaintly named species as the shaggy ink cap, puffball, parasol, and blusher. All of these are said to be edible, though I can only vouch for the puffball. The blusher in particular closely resembles a poisonous relative, and is best avoided.

And of course there are still new flowers to be seen, and old flowers doing new things, like forming berries. Bilberries are at their peak now, and the moor-edges are throng with feasting pigeons and thrushes. If you decide to join them, pause awhile to think how lucky you are, for bilberry picking is one of the most therapeutic of diversions. It can take an hour or more to get enough for a pie, particularly if you eat two for every one you keep, and all that time you are up on sunny hillside in the clean fresh air on a summer's day. As you pick you move, and as you move you find new things. Where the bilberries run into patches of moor grass at the bottom of the bank, there are the ventriloquial susurrations of grasshoppers calling to their mates. Further up you may find the large warty green caterpillar of an emperor moth munching its way through the heather. And the heather itself is coming into flower, not yet the full glorious carpet of August, but the first few pricks of colour in sheltered places. We have three species of heather up here: ling, which covers the moor; bog heather, which flowers around peat hags beside sundew and asphodel; and bell heather, which makes patches of a darker purple where ling cannot reach, particularly on rocky ledges.

If your taste does not run to bilberries, or you can no longer make it up the hill to pick them, there are raspberries on shady waysides, and perhaps even the first blackberries too. Be prepared to suffer from berry bugs, which are in fact tiny burrowing mites. These make the long march up your arms and legs and dig in where the digging is good, causing itchy lumps on your delicate parts. Across the road from the berry bushes, the trumpet flowers of bindweed are blaring white. Also by roadsides, but more particularly in ploughed fields, the two weeds that we call redshank and fat hen are in flower. If you tire of fungi and berries you can pick and boil the leaves of fat hen, which taste rather like spinach. They are best when chopped up half-and-half with scrambled egg, and served on toast.

But, as might be expected in this hot dry time of the year, it is by the waterside that you find most new flowers. Growing out in the open water, with their leaves intermingled on the surface and their flowers poking through it, are amphibious bistort and broad-leaved pondweed. In the shallow water and on the mud banks are two tall species with extensive root systems, the great hairy willowherb and the reed-mace or bulrush. The bulrush has one of the most striking flowers of any British species, though most people are familiar only with the seeded remains of the female part. In full bloom the anthers will shed literally spoonsful of pollen, and will cover your hand with yellow dust at the slightest shake.

It is always worth looking for flowers around the borders of a pond in late July. In addition to those already mentioned there may be a variety of sedges, and several species or hybrids of wild mint that we group together as cat-mint. But if you go on a warm evening after a wet day, you may find yourself at the centre of a 'rain' of half-inch toads or frogs, for these tiny amphibians have decided to live up to their name and leave the water. Apart perhaps for the stump of a tail, they are perfectly formed bright-eyed little creatures, small enough to fit onto your fingernail as you view them through a lens. One day there may be thousands, so that you can hardly put down your foot without treading on one. The next they are gone, mostly dispersed throughout the surrounding woods and fields. A small proportion will have fallen prey to birds and animals through whose territory they passed, but by moving *en masse,* almost as a plague, they ensure that their enemies are soon satiated so that most can survive.

For a night or two the hedgehogs feast on this manna, before reverting to their usual catholic diet. Hedgehogs are true omnivores, in that they will eat just about anything they can catch, dig out or climb to. Young hedgehogs are at weaning age now, and may be found after dark scavenging about with their mother or breaking out on their own. In southern England hedgehogs have two litters every year, but up here the season is too short. As we leave July, the first frosts of Autumn are but a few weeks away.

8 August

By August the trees appear dusty and drab, and some of the leaves have gone brown round the edges. In the morning there are cobwebs draped over the grass, and in the evening there is thistledown on the breeze. Some birds have already left the hills, and others are forming flocks in preparation for departure. By the end of the month even the swallows and martins will be collecting on overhead wires.

But there will still be some in their nests through into September, and the year is not over yet. She has a tired smile and her wrinkles are showing, but the old girl can still take our breath away when she sets out to dazzle. So one morning we wake up to see the hills turning pink, and a few days later the heather is at its peak, mixed with splashes of emerald bracken and set against a blue and white sky. It is a display of serene confidence, of a landscape with nothing to prove. I could sit and watch it all day, just to imprint it on my mind's eye. Indeed I often have, and it is truly glorious. What a pity that without the Glorious Twelfth it would never be as perfectly conserved.

August 1st – 7th

The lack of bird song is now almost absolute. You may walk through a wood where you heard a dozen species at once in late May, and hear nought but the hum of insects in the tree-tops. Perhaps the odd woodpigeon may start a coo, and then break off abruptly; or a willow warbler may make a vapid attempt at a song, and then another, and then give up. Certainly the wren will scold you with his clickety little rattle, since even when he cannot sing he cannot bear to be thought insignificant. He may even give quite a convincing short burst of song, for he is one of the first to come through the moult.

If you hear the wren scolding alone you need pay little heed, for it is in his nature to be vituperative. But if other birds join in they have probably found a predator to molest, and it will be well worth turning aside to check. At this time of year it will most likely be a tawny owl, or perhaps even two or three. Those which fledged first have been establishing territories for a month or more, but the less dominant pairs nested later, and their young are still not fully independent. They seem to have not yet learnt the art of lofty seclusion, perhaps because, having only partly mastered night-hunting, they are obliged to fly by day. Perching on exposed branches in search of food, their bulk padded out with an undercoat of down, they are easily spotted and mobbed by small birds. The slimmer adults, with their rich brown streaks and mottles, sit in dark evergreens next to the trunk, and merge into the bark. What material there is for the rustic philosopher in the contrasting styles of owl and wren.

The distribution of the owl population is very volatile now, as the juveniles attempt to establish themselves across the territories of their parents. At night we can hear the sharp kewicks as boundaries are re-defined, intermingled with the occasional moaning hoot. Most of the hoots sound quite comically hoarse and wheezy, for they are the first efforts of this year's young. The adults seem to indulge the adolescents' feeble braggadocio for the present, but by October there will be serious conflict as they stake out their winter claims.

Waterhens show no such indulgence, for as soon as their young reach a decent size they are mercilessly driven out. The parent will seem to quite suddenly turn on one of the largest of the chicks, pecking and chasing it, even treading it underwater. What instigates the attack is not clear, but the young bird evidently fails to give the right signal, and is treated as a rival. It is Nature's way that offspring should leave home, to avoid in-breeding, but what is odd about the waterhen is that whilst some are driven off with great gusto, a favoured few will be allowed to remain, and may even help to care for the second brood.

The fluffy black chicks of this second brood are on the water now, and are finding more food and better cover than did their siblings in May. Waterhens will feed on a wide variety of plant and animal matter, including grass, leaves and pondweed, insects and other invertebrates, and even small fish. The bird is no great fisherman, but with the low river levels of August there are easy pickings in riverside ponds. When I was a boy each of these riverside ponds had its shoal of darting minnows, with some individuals up to three inches long. They were lovely little fish, green and gold above with dark barred flanks and pale pink bellies.

Now I seldom see them, and if they are there at all they barely measure an inch. Their decline has been blamed on pollution, and there is certainly more nitrate in the rivers than there used to be, not to mention silage effluent. But there is more to it than that, for both the bullhead and the stone loach abhor pollution, but both still abound here.

Neither bullhead nor stone loach could be called lovely little fish, unless you are one of the young kingfishers that are trying their luck up our rivers now. The thick-lipped bullhead has broad flat forequarters bristling with protective fins, whilst the piggy-eyed loach has a mouth rimmed with olfactory barbels. Both are nocturnal bottom feeders, and hide beneath stones during the day, cheek-by-jowl with the crusty crayfish. Paddling kids have turned over these stones since men in skins lived here, doubtless for food at first, but now just for the relic thrill of catching things. So long as they release their catch at the end of the day there is little harm done. Better by far that they stare goggle-eyed at a crayfish in a sunlit jam-jar than at a televised cartoon in a darkened room.

Crayfish are especially easy to catch in riverside ponds, for they become trapped there after a late June flood, and find their little world gradually shrinking. When only a few gallons of tepid water remain, there may be a dozen or more under any one stone. One night when I was walking by the river after dark, I saw movements in the moonlit mud of a near-dry pond. Scores of crayfish were setting out to walk 30 yards over dry shingle to the river. Next morning there was no trace of them, though whether they made it across, or fell to some opportunist predator, I will never know.

There are some species which are obligatory and efficient predators, like the stoat, and others that will take a tasty treat if it hops past their nose, like waterhens and hedgehogs. One of the most opportunist of these latter is the squirrel. We think of him nibbling nuts, but he is just as happy eating nestling birds or stranded fish. Young squirrels, like so many other young birds and animals, are spreading out now, and may be seen following streams or crossing open fields. The squirrel's stronghold is leafy woodland, but he will range widely: the first grey squirrel to reach Bolton Abbey was shot by my grandfather on the open moor.

One of the most surprising pieces of opportunistic predation that I have seen was a squirrel eating a slow-worm. I managed to make it drop its prey by chasing it across open ground, and satisfied myself that it had killed the reptile rather than found it dead. Slow-worms are probably more common than we realise, for they move around in leaf litter and burrow under rocks and logs. They have a perfect neatness about them, these legless lizards, and are completely harmless, in fact beneficial. I have yet to see a live one in the Dales, despite repeated searches on sunny wooded slopes. But I have found three dead ones around the village over a period of almost 40 years, all about this time of year.

The time of new flowers is almost over now, though many that first appeared last month are still in full bloom. Rosebay willowherb in particular dominates the waysides; its tiny creeping relative the New Zealand willowherb is one of the few flowers that is only just opening. The harebell is also at its best, and we see showy clusters of its flowers in strange places, on the ledge of a bridge stanchion perhaps, or in the hollow side of a time-worn ash. Mints are livening up damp places with both the colour of their flowers and the fragrance of their leaves, whilst their close relatives, wild basil and wild marjoram, are opening in drier sites. None of them has the potency of flavour of their herb-garden namesakes, but they make welcome additions to the late summer flora.

Wren
(Troglodytes troglodytes)

The creeping thistles are just beginning to seed, but for every seeded head there are ten that are still in flower. They have a special attraction for butterflies: small tortoiseshells of course, but also a few peacocks and even the occasional painted lady. Other smaller insects flock there too, and soldier beetles gather to eat them, often copulating as they feast. But for all the colour that we still can find, there is no denying that most plant life is running to seed. This can be seen more easily in the larger plants, and is most apparent of all in bushes and trees. There are recognizable fruits on the crab-apple tree, and green hips and haws in the hedgerows. There are new little cones on the alder, and new big ones on the pine. There are clusters of double keys on the sycamore, and clusters of single ones, still green, on the ash. And on the yew trees there are yew berries, with their poisonous seeds. The yew is the most deadly of trees, to man and animals alike. I know of a cart-horse that snatched a mouthful of yew leaves when its master stopped to close a gate. The man pulled all he could back out of the horse's mouth, but the poor beast dropped dead before it reached the out-barn half a mile away. They don't come more toxic than that.

August 8th – 15th

The grouse-shooting season begins this week, on what is styled the Glorious Twelfth. It starts rather too soon for the well-being of the young birds, but those who shoot them have to consider the London season and the parliamentary recess. It is odd that our aristocracy, standard bearers of charm and urbanity, arbiters of good taste and fair play, can find nothing better to do on a moor in August than blast away at harmless birds. But we must not criticize too glibly, for grouse do taste very good. And if you had to spend months on end in the House of Lords, you would probably want to totter away to the hills and let off a few loud bangs.

There are certainly plenty of grouse to be seen about now, though because of the shooting you may need to go up on a Sunday to see them. The older birds seem to know which parts of the moor are least often driven by beaters, and will congregate there. The adult males are still not at ease in one another's company, and there is much posturing and cackling to ensure that none trespasses on a rival's temporary pitch. Their combs are not so large and bright now as they were in Spring, but their neck plumage is a rich ruddy brown, and the birds have a robust and well-fed competence about them. They have had a surfeit of food, fresh air and exercise all Summer, and are now gorging on crowberries, bilberries and bent seed to build up stores of vitamins and minerals for the leaner months ahead. No wonder they taste so good.

Unmistakable large bird of high moorland, usually seen in flocks. Remains on the bleakest of moorland throughout winter, and will feed beneath drifted snow if necessary.

In the breeding season the wattles of the cock bird swell up and glow bright vermilion

Red Grouse
(*Lagopus lagopus*)

nelson 91

Many birds which came to spend Summer with the grouse on our moors have already begun to leave. The gulls and oyster catchers have departed, as have most of the redshanks. Ring ouzels have moved down to the moor edges, and will soon be gone. Meadow pipits are still on the moor, but are beginning to gather together and move around in parties of a dozen or so. Those which reared young cuckoos have now parted from them, and the young cuckoos themselves are setting out southwards. Despite having been raised as meadow pipits, and having no mirror from which to take a pattern, these young cuckoos recognize each other on sight. In a story to rival the Ugly Duckling's, they unite joyously together in small groups. Towards the end of this week we see half-a-dozen fly swiftly over, heading unerringly towards some tropical feeding ground on the dictates of instinct alone. We shall not see them again until the last week of April next year.

In the valley other birds have noted the dwindling day-length. Freed now from the responsibilities of parenthood, they are reverting to winter haunts and habits. Pied wagtails are leaving the upland farmyards and can be seen in little flocks on valley-bottom lawns and cricket pitches, tripping through the morning dew. Blue tits, which have spent the last few weeks in the oakwoods, begin to visit our gardens again, checking for the presence of bird tables and nut hoppers. Young coots, driven out by their parents from the ponds where they were reared, are congregating in groups of up to a hundred on our reservoirs. They are full-sized now, and have begun to develop their bald white pates, though they are still recognizable as juveniles. On the reservoirs they encounter young tufted ducks and great crested grebe, or maybe a family of teal *en route* from moorland bog to flatland ings.

Perhaps the movement which is most noticeable is that of swifts, for they have screamed around even urban buildings for the last few weeks, and become familiar to most of us. Now that the last of their young have flown they are free to return to their wandering ways. They leave the towns and villages to fly with the clouds, running ahead of the rain. If the weather is sultry, swifts may still be seen regularly up to the end of August, though those birds that nested with us may be already hundreds of miles away: one swift ringed in northern Europe was recovered in southern Africa 11 days later.

The high flying insects on which the swift specializes need calm weather and a high temperature and humidity for their flight, which is why these birds like to run before a storm, and why they are amongst the first to leave us. But there is no shortage of other insect life yet, and many swallows and martins are still feeding unfledged nestlings. Some insects even seem to be more abundant now than they have been all Summer, a notable example being the crane-fly; or rather, crane-flies, for there are over 300 British species of what we commonly call daddy-long-legs. The recent emergence of a new generation of adults means that crane-flies are at their peak in mid-August. They particularly abound in low vegetation, either mating or looking for the right soil into which to lay their eggs. The eggs will go on to develop into the gardener's hated leather-jackets, which can do great damage to plant roots.

The presence of crane-flies in large quantities at ground level may partly explain why it is that we most commonly see green woodpeckers on the ground at this time of year. In the flatlands the green woodpecker spends much of its time at the soil surface in pursuit of ants and their pupae, which it can take from their tunnels and nest-heaps using its long sticky tongue. Here in the Dales there are fewer ants available, for ours, both black and red, take the precaution of nesting beneath stones. The woodpecker may still find foraging ants, and may be looking around for any early emergence of a flying generation, but here it lives mostly on arboreal grubs, like other woodpeckers. For it to be spending so much time on the ground at present there would have to be something more than ants to sustain it, and crane-flies seem the most likely contenders.

Another insect which becomes more common in August is the wasp, though it has not yet reached the nuisance proportions which make it notorious. Wasp nests have grown steadily larger throughout the Summer, and may now contain hundreds, even thousands, of larvae. It is at this stage that the badger strikes, for nothing is more to his liking than these fat juicy grubs. We see a little excavation, a football-sized hollow with scraps of wood pulp and a few dead wasps, and we know that Brock has done his job. He could not have timed it more perfectly, for the worker wasps have spent Summer collecting aphids and other plant pests, and have done us a great service. In turn they have satisfied their craving for sweetness by feeding on a secretion made by the larvae in their care. Some time about now a sexual generation develops which will quit the nest in September, leaving the workers with no larvae from which to obtain their syrup. It is because of this that they begin to plague our orchards and houses for sources of sugar, and by timing his raid now the badger has let us have our cake and eat it. There is little doubt that he does time the raid, for I have seen a wasp nest beside a badger track left alone all Summer, and broken open this week.

The wasp's mouthparts are not suitable for collecting nectar from most flowers, though even if they were it would find little other than heather on which to feed now. There are a few welcome late-comers this week, such as knotgrass, sneezewort and wild angelica, but there will be no new flowers after these until the ivy blossoms late next month. The flowering of the ivy will mark the onset of Autumn, but the year has Summer in it yet, and we will enjoy a few more hot days before then.

August 16th – 23rd

There are misty mornings now, with heavy dews and a chill in the air. But more often than not a misty morning heralds a sunny day, and when the sun shines in August it still has some force. We are as far after Midsummer as we were before it when the swallows came, but the ground is warm now, and loth to cool.

As the sun touches the rooftops, the starlings start to sing, a medley of whistles, gurgles and clicks reminiscent of early Spring. The flocks arrived back with last weekend's showers, newly noisy after their short trip away. They are not yet ready for the mass roosts of Winter, and disperse in the evenings to check their old lodgings.

As if not to be outdone by any uncouth *arriviste,* the robin also throws back his head to greet the morn, shrilling out a rolling tinkle of notes. His phrases last for just a couple of seconds each, but they are enough to evoke a vision of leafless branches and winter sun. He has not sung since early June, and will need a couple of weeks of rehearsals before he reaches full voice again in mid-September. The few young that are still in mottled baby coats this week will by then have attained their adult plumage, and will need territories of their own. We can look forward to a good old sing-sing.

The young of many species are developing adult plumage, and no bird shows this more clearly than the adolescent male pheasant. He has hardly anything that could be called a tail, and his neck, belly and rump retain the pale fawn feathers of youth. But over his shoulders, flank and chest the rich gold and purple mantle of maturity is showing through, giving him a distinctly patchy, almost sickly, look.

Young partridges have no such problems, for their first growth of feathers so closely resembles the adult plumage that the change thereto is barely noticeable. They are almost fully grown now, and without binoculars it is not easy to differentiate the ages. We see groups of up to two dozen birds together, and can perhaps pick out three or four adults, but we cannot say how many families constitute such a flock. We may also see groups of six or eight red-legged partridges re-appearing this week, though the two species do not mix. Red-legs are scarce enough in the Dales to have been inapparent when the vegetation was luxuriant, for they rarely fly. They are not well adapted to our rough hillsides, and these family parties will become smaller and smaller as Autumn progresses.

Another species which is becoming increasingly evident is the heron, for the young birds have completed their apprenticeship and are spreading to every pool and beck to practise what they have learnt. They seem to remain on good terms with their parents, for they will often roost together when not feeding. On the river they may be seen stepping loftily around throngs of gulls, which are strangely quiet now that their breeding is over. The gull flocks are passing along the valleys from coast to coast via well-known feeding grounds, always on the look-out for a ploughed field or a new rubbish tip to add to their staging points. Black-headed gulls make up most of the flock, through their dark heads have now almost completely faded, leaving only a trace of grey with a black spot behind each eye.

If you check carefully amongst these grey and white gulls you may find that they include one or two of the species known as the common gull, actually far from common here. There will also be a few lesser black-backs, standing out from the rest of the flock because of their larger size and diffferent colouration. Adult black-backs have the dark grey wings and back that give them their name, but juveniles are dull dark brown all over. A few greater black-backs are also seen at this time of year, but they tend to move singly or in pairs and keep away from other gulls, roving along the higher ground without reference to watercourses.

On the high ground both the heather and bracken are now at their peak. Seen from a distance the contrast between them is superb. At close quarters you can sit down in a bed of bracken and disappear from the world, like the child Hardy among the ferns. Or you can lie on your back in the open heather, feeling the sun on your closed eyelids and hearing the hum of bees across the heathsward. Every breath draws in the honeyed scent from a million tiny flowers, and every movement disturbs a pink cloud of pollen. Save perhaps for the bluebell in May, there is no flower that thrills me as much as heather in August. I so love the flower that I named my daughter Heather – I could hardly call her Bluebell – and can only hope that she will grow up to have the beauty and tenacity of this heavenly perennial.

Insects love the heather too, and bee-keepers will sometimes move their hives to the moor-edges in late Summer to be sure of getting something of the flower's essence in their honey. But one relative of the bee has no interest in flowers, for in its brief life above ground it never feeds.

This is the flying ant, which is simply the winged sexual generation of the ant we commonly find beneath moorside stones. Some time towards the end of this week, usually late in the afternoon when the humidity is high, a virgin queen ant will take to the wing, pursued by hundreds, even thousands of fertile males. The timing is quite precise, with nuptial flights from several separate colonies often taking place on the same evening. We rarely get the sort of swarms here that are seen in southern England – ants stopped play in a Home Counties cricket match in August 1990 – but they can be impressive enough. Within hours all the males have perished, including the lucky one that had the chance to mate, and the queen has shed her wings and gone below ground to form a new colony. She may live for several years without ever again seeing the light of day.

These late summer evenings are precious to us, for all too soon they will be gone. The yellow glow of the sinking sun casts long shadows as we walk, side-lighting the floating thistledown. Some thistle heads have simply burst open to cast their pappi on the wind, but most have been pulled apart by finches, which throw out four seeds for each one they eat. We see them now beside the path, flying ahead or rising into the trees with their twittering flock calls. In winter plumage, and accompanied by juveniles, they can be difficult to tell apart, but the yellow wing flashes of goldfinches and the double white wing bars of the chaffinch distinguish them from the chestnut-backed linnet.

When the sun drops from sight the dark encroaches quickly, bringing out the waiting bats. There are just over a dozen bat species in Britain, with the actual number varying as some species die out here and others are discovered. Much of southern England has most of these species present, but in the Dales we have relatively few – long-eared, noctule, Natterer's, Daubenton's, pipistrelle, whiskered and Brandt's. The latter two are so similar that young females can only be told apart by counting the cusps on one of their cheek teeth, which is why Brandt's has only recently been recorded in Britain. It is said that the adult male Brandt's can be distinguished from the whiskered by the more club-like shape of its penis. I have examined several whiskered bats over the years, but in my ignorance I never thought to look. I have also heard anecdotal evidence of lesser horseshoe bat colonies in the Dales, though I have not seen any here myself.

Undoubtedly the most widespread British bat is the pipistrelle, though over our slower moving stretches of river the Daubenton's water bat is locally more common. It is these latter that we see most easily as the darkness deepens, for so long as there is a hint of light in the sky it reflects off the river, showing their flutterings over its surface.

It is surprisingly dark as we turn away, and we are glad of the pocket torch we brought to look for moths. There are precious few moths about tonight, but as we walk home we find three separate toads on the lower hillside, each moving uphill across the road. These are not young toads setting out on life's journey, but wise old toads who know what Winter holds in store. They want to be near their hibernating holes in the woods before the first nip of frost, and the chill in the dew is hastening them onwards.

August 24th – 31st

Just when everything seems to be sliding inexorably towards Autumn, we get a hot spell. Suddenly it's high Summer again, with scorcher succeeding scorcher for days on end. The Dales fill up with great happy crowds from the old West Riding conurbations, intent on the Bank Holiday pilgrimage that is part of their Yorkshire season. As a youngster I used to open gates on these back roads for pennies from the few cars that were about then. August Bank Holidays still make me nostalgic for Jowett Javelins and threepenny bits.

The tourists of today are more numerous and better informed, but not necessarily more enterprising. Most still like to stay where the crowds are, and if they walk at all they move in platoons on well-beaten tracks. The seeker after solitude can find lonely places on the busiest of days, simply by following the lesser known footpaths that are not mentioned in popular guides.

One such footpath passes by my house up onto the moor, and I follow it alone today, heading for hidden places. There is no particular benefit in being out before dawn in late Summer, and so I set off when the sun is already high, to be sure of seeing what insects are about. Within a few minutes, whilst I am still between the hedgerows on the valley side, I have seen a couple of vapourers and several gamma moths. These are day-flying moths, common enough nationally but unusual up here. The vapourers are both males, chestnut-orange in colour with a single white spot towards the back of each forewing. The females are wingless, and simply pose on the branch where they hatch, releasing pheromones to attract mates.

The gamma moths, or silver-Ys, are recognizable by the distinctly gamma-shaped mark on each mottled forewing, and by the little furry tufts on their backs. These dull-looking little moths lead a far from dull life, for neither moths nor larvae can survive the British Winter. The individuals we see now, which will die with the first night of frost, may be offspring from moths which crossed the Channel in May, or they may themselves have started life on the plains of Picardy. Do they sense already, when they leave the French coast, that a great and welcoming island awaits them, or do they sally forth into the unknown with a bold blind faith, like ancient Polynesians exploring the Pacific?

On the hillside below the wood there is a patch of common ground over-run with ragwort, for this mildly noxious weed so thrives on neglect that the 1959 Weeds Act was drafted with it in mind. As I wander through it there is a wonderful buzzing all around, emanating from thousands of blow-flies, greenbottles, bluebottles, and other calypterate flies, as well as bees and a variety of hover-flies. We think of many of these species as predatory flies or carrion eaters, but in fact many are not, and even those that are often have nectar-feeding males. When most other flowers have disappeared or run to seed, these large yellow beds of ragwort exert a powerful attraction. I can count into the teens of different insect species without moving, and if I were a better entomologist I could double that number.

Further up the hill, where a trickling stream marks the boundary between wood and moor, several dragonflies flicker past me in the sunlight. They patrol the wood edge like border guards, alert for any victim breaking from cover. And when I lie down for lunch beside a little moorland pool, two appear from opposite directions and mate over the water in front of me, four pairs of wings beating as one.

There is a magic in these little upland pools, and it is never more apparent than on these hot cloudless days in late Summer. I spend an hour or more beside this one, now looking down into the clear cool water at the tiny dramas of invertebrate life, now gazing into the hazy heavens at the swirling flocks of swallows and martins. The birds are feeding where swifts lately fed, building up their reserves for the journey ahead, whilst the pond-dwellers are squiggling about in the mud. But late next Spring, when the swallows again venture over this high ground, their two worlds may meet. Little larvae that have spent Winter beneath the ice will emerge as adults and take to the skies, to be snapped up in their brief ecstasy by swallows back from the shimmering veld. Does some such fate await us all, that we can comprehend as little as these larvae now ken theirs?

Wheatear
(Oenanthe oenanthe)

These two small moorland chats occupy very similar ecological niches, though the wheatear likes rocky hillsides and the whinchat is fond of gorse bushes. As wheatears have declined, whinchats have prospered

Whinchat
(Saxicola rubetra)

nelson 92

Over the moor top there is not much to be seen, save scattered parties of titlarks and irrepressible sturdy grouse. Here and there I find grouse carcases, from those which have taken a few pellets over the butts but flown on to die later, alone and inglorious. On the further flank of the moor I encounter little flocks of whinchats, wheatears and ring ouzels, following the stream down into the main valley. Here, near to their summer quarters, they are easily recognizable, but as they follow the beck to the river and the river to the coast they will puzzle many a novice bird watcher. Even in the Dales it can be momentarily disconcerting to find a couple of whinchats in a flock of spotted flycatchers working along some lowland hedgerow, or a ring ouzel amongst the blackbirds in a garden cherry tree.

Willow warblers are also forming little flocks in preparation for departure, though they will remain in their breeding areas for a few days yet. As I descend into a belt of scattered trees along the moor-edge I see them flitting from tree to tree, and hear occasional snatches of their autumn song. They will carry this little tune with them throughout their migration, and still be whispering it when they reach the acacia savannahs of central Africa.

As I pass through the wood I can hear some of our resident birds as well, for they are re-gaining their voices after the despondency of their moults. The robin's song is maturing nicely, and the little wren is clicking and trilling. Wood-pigeons are cooing consistently again, and even the harsh call of the jay marks a welcome return. Most jays have been downriver for Summer, and even those which have not have kept very quiet about it. Now they are drifting back in search of fruit and acorns, with their bright smart plumage looking marvellously exotic amongst the green and scarlet of rowan leaves and berries.

The rowan berries are almost fully ripe now, and hang in evenly-spaced heavy clusters on every mountain ash. They are not poisonous, and in fact can be used to make a rather bittersweet jelly for eating with meat. Fieldfares and redwings will gorge on them in Autumn, but our resident thrushes are spoilt for choice just now. Not only is there an abundance of blackberries ripening, with many more to follow, but hawthorn and elder berries are starting to flush red and purple in every hedgerow. For birds that can handle them there are other fruits: blackthorn berries like tiny black plums; little red clusters lighting the tips of honey-suckle vines; and plump smooth hips that shine as if they have been waxed. In the 1950s we primary school children were paid through our schools to pick rosehips: threepence a pound, a badge after three pounds, and a free bottle of rosehip syrup after ten pounds. I often earned a badge but never a bottle.

The seeds in the centre of rosehips are coated with irritant hairs. These are supposed to protect them from being eaten, though I have known small birds peck open a hip to eat the seeds, and discard the fleshy skin. Some plant species, of course, have seeds which are fashioned to pass through digestive systems, like the berries mentioned above. But others go to extremes to protect their seeds from being eaten, such as hiding kernels in sealed wooden shells. For every natural defence, however, there is a natural attack. The hazel nuts that are ripening now will be pecked open by nuthatches and great tits when the shells are still green, and gnawed open by squirrels and wood mice when they harden.

One of the most ingenious seed defences, which also serves as a method of dispersal, is on display now on the sickly-scented balsam. The seed capsules of this plant explode at the slightest touch, scattering shot-sized grain in all directions. Any bird which might be tempted to have a peck at one of these jumping jacks would be in for a terrible shock, and would be unlikely to try it again. If you very carefully cut off a nearly-ripe seed head and place it in a child's palm, it will suddenly squirm open as it is lightly squeezed, causing a delicious thrill of alarm to the initiate. Even now I cannot resist trying one or two, and laughing at the memory of the small panic that the first one caused me all those years ago.

This seems to have been a day for metaphysical thoughts and childhood memories. There is a certain sweet sadness about this time of year that provokes such pathos. As the day draws to its end, the cold breeze on my arm reminds me that the season of melancholy is creeping in around us.

9 *September*

To those of us that know it well, the countryside has been looking tired since July. Throughout August there have been unmistakable signs of decline. Now that September is here the year can no longer pretend, and has to face up to growing old gracefully.

In the first days of the month the swallows begin to gather on the wires, though a few still have nestlings to feed. Little piles of grey leaves gather in wall corners below sycamore trees. The rivers and becks are scummy with brownish algae, and the ground is dry and cracked.

But by the end of September all the swallows will have gone, and full-feathered pheasants will be heard currocking through the misty stillness at dusk. And there will have been nips of night frost, leaving some branches already bare and others clothed in the flaking gold-leaf of Autumn.

The sun is moving lower across the sky now, and the evenings are drawing in. Autumn is upon us, and I am glad of the change.

September 1st – 7th

The fine weather continues through into September, starting talk of drought precautions and Indian Summers. Where the top-soil is thin the pastures turn brown, and anxious farmers watch the sky. The rivers are at their lowest, and cattle stray across.

With afternoon temperatures in the seventies, it is easy not to notice that the sun is lower and the days are briefer. But the illusion of Summer fades with the day, for at dusk there is no mistaking the chill in the air. These September evenings can be truly enchanting, with watery-red sunsets leaving a pink-rimmed horizon, and everything so calm and still that you can hear an old ewe call clear across the valley.

But one evening there are a few craggy clouds silhouetted against the orange glow, and next morning a heavy grey blanket covers the sky, under-run by a thin damp wind. It may not be official Autumn yet, but this is the end of Summer.

Winged insects feel it first, and populations of the smaller ones start to tail away. Birds which have relied on them for the major part of their sustenance must go now, following the warmer weather south. A few swallows are still feeding a third brood, but by the end of this week almost all will have flown. They will hone their flying skills in the early part of the migration, when there is no great rush, and then will have to make do or die. For a few days they remain near their birthplace, gathering in excited little flocks on the wires each morning, and then dispersing widely to feed. Over the next two weeks these little flocks will coalesce, following upland gills down to hillside hamlets, and streams down to rivers. For the moment they are still with us, and it behoves us to watch them a bit, and wish them well.

House martins often travel together with swallows, but sand martins tend to stay by themselves. It is a characteristic feature of migration that one day all the birds of a certain species seem to have gone, and the next they are plentiful again. This is because the resident birds that move away are replaced by others that are wandering through. These passing flocks know a good breeding site when they see one, and often drop in to check on the nests recently vacated by their colleagues. We may sometimes hear a great agitation amongst the swallows in our yard, as if there is late merlin amongst them, only to find that a flock of strangers is soaring overhead and has decided to establish contact.

The last of the wheatears and meadow pipits are coming down off the moor now, for they are not specially equipped for an insectivorous life-style, and must leave the tops as soon as invertebrates become less readily obtainable. By the end of the month all the wheatears will have left the Dales *en route* for warmer climes, but not all the meadow pipits will go. Many remain amongst us for several weeks, often forming mixed flocks with pied wagtails. Even when they leave the Dales some will remain in flatland Britain, and little bands of hardy pioneers may be seen crossing the Pennines during any mild spell throughout Winter.

Though there are fewer and fewer small insects to be seen now, many of our best butterflies are at their most abundant. Adults that were on the wing in May have multiplied through one or two generations since then, and are enjoying a final fling before the frost sets in. Some, like red admirals and painted ladies, came in from the Continent to breed in southern England in Spring, and are only now reaching the Dales. Others, like the wall brown, are lowland residents that only come into the hills when they have flooded all the more favourable habitats. And a loyal few, like the three smalls (heath, copper and tortoiseshell) are with us all year. Immigrant or native, downbred or dalesbred, they make welcome late additions to our records.

Night-flying moths also abound on still September nights, particularly after a shower, and now is a good time to treacle a few tree trunks. There is great variability in the results from treacling, with many moths being attracted one night, and hardly any the next. This helps to make it interesting, but not everyone can safely wander in wooded places by torchlight on the off-chance of finding a moth or two. You may prefer instead to try an ultra-violet lamp in your garden. What you lose in romance you will make up in efficiency, for insects are fascinated by radiation beyond the blue end of the visible spectrum. Their visual sensors are different from ours: many flowers photographed on ultra-violet sensitive film show patterns of insect guide lines which are otherwise indiscernible to our eyes. Other creatures may also be drawn to the lamp; a couple of bats, perhaps, or even a passing nightjar. Nightjars are working their way overland from traditional breeding grounds onto the main migration routes just now, and may be seen in unlikely habitats where there is a concentration of moths.

Whilst fly-catching birds are feeling the pinch, berry-eaters are replete to the point of surfeit. The glut of berries comes at just the right time for blackbirds, for they moult late and are still looking patchy. In any thick tangle of bramble vines there may be half-a-dozen blackbirds in various stages of moult, looking as baldy-headed and moth-eaten as any country parson. As we work towards them they do not fly away, seeming to accept us as fellow berry-pickers.

Finches will also pick at berries, though they prefer to put their beaks to proper use in eating seeds. Chaffinches, by far the commonest, have formed flocks again now, and can be seen roaming the countryside in search of beds of groundsel and chickweed. Redpolls are also about in flocks, but theirs are scarcer and keep to the tree-tops, picking seeds from dead catkins. With the adults in winter plumage, and with many juveniles amongst them, they can be difficult to identify amongst the thick dark foliage of a mature birch or alder. But their flight gives them away, for they have a distinctive churring twitter on the wing, and a convenient habit of flying out in a wide circle and returning to the same few trees.

Whereas the beaks of finches are adapted for crushing

small seeds, like tiny pointed pliers, the beak of a nuthatch is more of a chisel. And if we are vain enough to believe that only wise Man uses tools, we should study the nuthatch selecting his vice. From the top of the Scar opposite Bolton Priory you can look down onto his work-bench amongst the branches, and be part of his world. Watch him fly in with a hazel nut onto some gnarled and twisted branch. See how cleverly he sizes up the cracks and crevices, turning the nut this way and that, until he gets it firmly wedged in. And observe the coordination of muscle, beak and eye as he then hammers a neat hole through the shell and pecks out the nut. Other nuts and seeds will be cached away between or behind scraps of bark, hence his name, a corruption of nut-cache.

Nor is it only resident birds that are feasting on plenty, for the squirrel is doing more than his share, eating some and burying others for later. Even carnivorous mammals enjoy fruit and berries, picking them carefully off the bushes with bared incisors. They prefer blackberries, for their size and succulence, but will take almost any that are edible. At this time of year I have seen fox dung by moorside tracks that consisted mostly of compacted seeds and opaque orange skins, the digested remains of dozens of rowan berries. The berries of the rowan do not seem especially tasty to us, but the fox knows that they are rich in vitamins and minerals that it will need in the months ahead. When an animal

When the grey squirrel first began to establish itself in Britain, a bounty was paid for each squirrel tail. This failed to control the population explosion, and has now been stopped.

Grey Squirrel
(Sciurus carolinensis)

The introduced grey squirrel has now completely replaced the native red in all parts of the Dales. It is a bold, agile and aggressive species, active by day, and easily seen. Though it is an appealing animal, it can be a pest both to trees and bird nests.

nelson 92

breeds in mid-Winter it has to be well-prepared. Every extra mouthful now will increase the chances of its genes surviving to Spring, and the survival of genes is the essence of life.

September 8th – 15th

September is in many ways the mirror image of April, and the two months have very similar weather. So it is that the bright periods and squally showers that welcomed the swallows in Spring now come out to wish them farewell, and to ensure that they leave here well-fed.

The much-needed rain soaks into the parched ground, fostering a flush of late-season grass. The soil swells up and softens, closing the cracks and reactivating things squirmy and boneless. Adolescent dor beetles come up from their crypts, to drone around and feed for a few nights before digging in for Winter. Long-legged harvestman spiders clamber along walls, losing a leg or two here and there, but managing nevertheless. Birds such as song thrush and snipe, which thrive on worms and the like, seem suddenly common again. The song thrushes have been away on easier living for the last few weeks, and will leave us again in late Autumn, but for the moment they join omnivorous blackbirds on our lawns and fruit-bearing bushes.

There is an embarrassment of riches by our waysides these days, with blackberries leading the field. Village kids come home blue-lipped, suburban pensioners make fruitful roadside raids, birds and beasts guzzle and gorge, but still each new day sees just as many ripe. Some go to waste fermenting on the vine and others are gathered for rustic brews, though for the connoisseur of country vintage the best of all berries has not yet peaked. This is, of course, the elderberry, traditionally made into a richly flavoured tonic wine. In these days of year-round salads the medicinal properties of this poor man's port are not so relevant, but in times past its high concentrations of iron and vitamin C, coupled with heart-warming alcohol, perked up many an old widow or sicky child.

The nutritional value of elderberries is well known to birds, and as they ripen this week they attract much attention. Larger species such as woodpigeon and mistle thrush seem to find them particularly irresistible. They can reach many by perching on walls and fences, for the elder likes hedgerows and woodsides. But eventually they become so engrossed in their gluttony that they will flounder around in the outer branches, scrambling and flapping, even hanging upside down, behaving more like fruit bats than birds.

Hazel nuts are now hard and ripe enough for human consumption, though you are unlikely to find many left. They do not crop heavily in our North Country hills, and most are taken before they turn brown by an assortment of rodents and birds. As you seek out the odd survivor hidden amongst the leaves, you will notice that next year's male catkins are already developing. The same is true on alder trees, and it is comforting to know, as the first beech trees take on a blaze of Autumn gold, that the hazel and alder are already looking forward to Spring.

On oak trees there seem to be two types of fruit, the commoner being the familiar acorn, the other a similar-sized spherical structure, ripening from green to brown. This latter is often called an oak apple, but is in no sense the fruit of the tree. The nuthatch knows its secret, and breaks it open to get at the fat white grub that lies at its heart. It is in fact a marble gall, and the grub is a gall-wasp larva. It will spend the Winter in this insulated orb, and burrow out in Spring, leaving a single neat hole to mark its escape.

The acorns themselves are reaching full size, and becoming palatable to jays and squirrels. Squirrels are over the moon at this time of year, their bellies full with nuts, fruit and fungi, their bodies sleek with new layers of fat. They squabble and squawk in the tree-tops, chasing each other through the branches as they sort out their quarters for Winter. Some, especially this Summer's young, may have to roam widely in search of a place to call home, and many are killed on the roads. Their cousins, brown rats, are also on the move, following the hawthorn hedges back to our yards. The wise farmer freshens his traps and baits about now to prevent these malignant pests gaining a foothold in his buildings.

The berries on the hawthorn bushes are still not deeply red, though they are ripe enough for the little bands of bullfinches that return to us this week. These lovely birds go away to nest, but return with their families to the same favoured localities each Autumn. They seek out banks of hawthorn and ash, with a ragged undergrowth of tall weeds, and seem singularly at home on disused railway cuttings. They eat a variety of wild fruit and weed seeds, but concentrate on haws at this time of year, pulping the flesh with

Bullfinch
(Pyrrhula pyrrhula)

Goldfinch
(Carduelis carduelis)

nelson 92

their stubby black beaks, and discarding the stone-clad seeds. When the ash keys ripen in another week or two they will turn their attention to them, gradually separating into twos and threes as they search out each far-flung ash.

The return of birds like the bullfinch, song thrush and snipe is visible evidence that it is not only our summer migrants that are in a state of flux. We can see that the congregations of swallows on the wires have grown from a few dozen members to several score, but we barely notice that the family flocks of partridges are breaking down and mixing up, to give new little groups of six or eight. A solitary tardy swift reminds us that all his kin are long gone, but only the keener observer sees the two pochard that have arrived on the reservoir to mingle with coot and mallard and stripe-necked young great crested grebe. We take note of the last few spotted flycatchers amongst a newly-formed mixed flock of tits along the woodside, but miss the arrival of the first northern blackbirds amongst our resident stock.

And even our resident bird populations are not so stable as they might seem. We see, for instance, four different robins singing at each other in a small patch of shrubbery, or hear three great spotted woodpeckers calling at once, but we do not fully realise that when jaw comes to war only one of each will remain there. The rest must join in the chain reaction of displaced fauna jostling through the countryside staking their claims. Beneath the genteel façade of these tranquil September days, a thousand animal odysseys are enacted each instant. Great deeds are done in tree-top and hedge-bottom, countless tiny creatures are put to the test, duels are fought, and land is won.

These are times of death and disaster for our wildlife, but times of triumph too. This is not conflict between armies and regiments, but single-handed combat between evenly matched opponents, Robin Hoods and Little Johns meeting on disputed bridges. Their lives may be brief and often harsh, but they are very seldom dull.

September 16th – 23rd

As the ground cools, the weather becomes changeable. High winds, heavy rain, and bright sunny periods seem to follow one another in rapid random sequence, interspersed now and then with cold clear nights and misty mornings.

A few sickly sycamores, in exposed positions on poor soil, lose most of their leaves in the storms. Even the more robust begin to look a little sparse, with daylight showing through their middles. Several more beeches acquire touches of coppery distinction, but the woods are still predominantly dark green. On the hills there are reddish-brown patches where night frosts have nipped at the bracken. The heather flowers have mostly run to seed now, and the light has gone out of the moorland.

In the hedgerows there are still two or three dozen species in flower, though the high points of colour now come from the fruits. Bramble and elder berries, glistening black; shiny rosehips and plump little haws; sloes and crabs, bitter as gall; poisonous clusters of warning red, like wild arum and guelder rose; and the deadly deceptive little fairy lights on the yew.

Colour and poison also combine in various species of toadstool which are emerging now. Agarics, boletes and russulas vie for attention in exotic shades of blue, purple, red, yellow and green. Bracket fungi bourgeon out from the sides of rotting birch trees for country elves to sit on, and putrefying stinkhorns waft their musky perfume on the breeze. Unlike flowering plants, most toadstools do not have common English names, and those that do are not well-served by them. Slippery Jack, fly agaric and penny bun sound more like Dickensian low-life characters than fine upstanding young fungi.

Certainly toadstools have a less appealing physical presence than flowers, and because some are poisonous we are taught from childhood to avoid them, like snakes. In fact many fungi are simply inedible rather than poisonous, though most will make you sick if you eat enough of them. Some, of course, will kill with remarkable despatch if eaten in quite trivial quantities, and you can forget the idea that if a toadstool has been nibbled by animals it is safe for you to eat. Many animals can eat substances which are poisonous to us, and some of what seem to be bite marks have actually been made by slugs and beetles.

Even the common field mushroom, which is so edible and delicious, will cause headaches and stomach upsets if taken to excess. The larger, coarser horse mushroom can also cause nausea, though both are safe and highly palatable in reasonable quantities. You need to be eating a pound or two a day to experience any side effects, though in a good mushroom year, when we can fill a basket in a few minutes each morning and evening, this is all too easily done. To get a good mushroom crop you need a warm Spring followed by a hot Summer ending in a wet August. This year the August was too dry, and the rains did not fall until the soil was already cooling. The yield has not been good, but the recent wet weather has given us a welcome late flush, to add to the rest of Autumn's bounty.

The rains have also freshened up the tired rivers, washing clean the dipper's perching stones for the first time in weeks, and clearing the riverside scum. Dippers start singing again, and fish start rising. On every still stretch of water we hear the 'plop' that is music to the fisherman's ears, as trout come up to gulp insects from the surface. Some of these are insects which have lived for weeks on the wing, and have now fallen to the Autumn chill. Others, such as gnats and non-biting midges, have been provoked into life by sunshine and showers after the long dry weeks of late Summer. It is these latter, mainly confined to the watersides and lower slopes, that fuel the flight of departing swallows and martins following the rivers down.

Most swallows leave the Dales by the end of this week, though odd ones will still turn up around farmyards for a few more days. Both swallows and martins may also be seen in good-sized flocks along the valley bottoms until early next week. The flocks tend to be more-or-less mono-specific now that they are on the move, though as they collect in hosts of several thousand at places like Fairburn

Ings, prior to moving down the coast, the swallows and martins inevitably mix again, and form associations with many non-hirundine migrants.

One such migrant is the chiff-chaff, which tends not to nest in the Dales but does pass through. It is one of the first birds of passage to be heard in Spring, from the end of March onwards, and one of the last in Autumn. It is still calling as it wanders through now, and little snatches of "tsip-tsap-tsip-tsap" will draw our attention to its presence. Most chiff-chaffs will go on to southern Europe and north Africa, though a few remain all year in southern England if the Winter is mild.

It seems surprising to us now that early naturalists, up to the calibre of the Rev. Gilbert White of Selborne, sincerely believed that birds like swallows hibernated here in Winter. Witnesses were quoted who had seen flocks diving into water to burrow into the mud on the bottom, or who had found clumps of torpid birds when cracking open stone in quarries. It is a lesson to us all that we should trust only our personal observations, and take any other report with a pinch of salt, no matter how authoritative the source.

I have heard of a Dales swallow still having young in the nest on the 23rd September, though I do not know whether to believe it. But I know for sure of a woodpigeon that was still feeding nestlings on the 17th September, for I climbed up to look at them myself. Records such as these, at the fringe of normality, have little relevance to the natural history of the species concerned, though they are the very stuff of life to those ornithological addicts, aptly styled as twitchers, who need a weekly fix of rarities to keep them going.

I cannot easily understand what drives people to go bird-watching in groups, though Man is a social animal and it may be me that is odd. For me the relationship with Nature is a sensuous experience, a sort of meditative communion in which sight, sound, smell, taste and touch are all put to use, but in which the combination of senses adds up to more than the sum of the parts. Those who march in gang-handed with walkie-talkies, who watch through cumbersome tele-scopes from hundreds of yards away, or who sit in hides poring over a reference book, are often awesomely erudite. But if they are insensible to the poetry in the air about them, then they might as well be collecting stamps or spotting trains.

September 24th – 30th

It is now officially Autumn, and it feels like it. A few more empty branches stark against the sky, a fading of colours in the fields and hills, a sudden shiver in a brief gust of wind, a flurry of dry leaves eddying in a corner, all these are part of it. But the more subtle signs come from a quality of light and space, a sort of freshness and clarity that are hard to define. We see most things in life from the side, so that when the sun is lower the lighting is better, like a day-long dawn.

One thing which even the most torpid townie will have noticed is the decreasing daylength. With the passing of the equinox the nights are closing in, and working folk have little time left for rambles. We must make what we can of the dusk and dawn hours, for soon we will lose even these. No-one who sleeps soundly will relish rising in the dark, to get into cold clothes and set out into a grey dawn. But no-one who has done it will regret it, for these Autumn mornings have a special mood known only to a lucky few. Whether it is a calm new day with a touch of frost, or a wild one with blustery showers, the sense of nostalgia is there. Misty mornings are particularly atmospheric, for the mist absorbs distant noises, strengthening our feeling of being cut off from Man's world and enveloped in Nature.

The crowing of cock pheasants at the sunrise only adds to our awareness of the silence. Cock pheasants are forming bachelor groups now, of adolescent young led by adult males. They are working themselves up into a lot of empty-headed crowing, unaware as yet that their end is nigh. The adult cocks are back in full glossy plumage, and this year's young are almost so. Mallard are also becoming noisy and emerging from the eclipse, though some of the younger drakes are still rather patchy.

We cannot hope to see too much on these grey morning walks, for there is usually a slack patch between the departure of the summer migrants and the arrival of the winter ones. It is always worth carrying a plastic bag, for there are likely still to be mushrooms. If you spot some from afar, and find that they are only puffballs when you get there, take a few anyway. Sliced and salted and fried in batter, they are not below regard.

The few birds that you see are likely to be common or garden species, though they may behave in interesting ways. A roving band of magpies flies off as I approach, but one which has not yet seen me jumps onto the back of a sheep. Starlings and jackdaws in Spring will pick loose hairs from sheep for their nests, but at this time of year the magpie seems to be simply flying to the nearest vantage point for a better view over the bare field. I have even seen one perch on a pig's back in Autumn, though never on a cow's.

In a nearby oak tree there are rooks and woodpigeons feeding on acorns, clattering through the foliage as they twist the seeds from the twiglets and take them to more solid perches to eat. Some are swallowed whole and others split open, so that there is a litter of acorn cups, split acorns and empty skins on the grass beneath the tree. As I examine them a jay flies past, his throat bulging. I have never noticed jays pouching food before, but crows and jackdaws do, and he is a close relative. Doubtless he has several acorns in there, for no bird loves them better.

The big trees in the countryside, oak and ash, beech and sycamore, are still mainly green, albeit of a dull dark hue. But some of the smaller species are beginning to glow with colour, like live coals fanned by a breeze. Rowan and hawthorn are especially radiant, for the bright red berries are nicely set off against a flickering assortment of orange, russet, yellow and green given off by the dying leaves.

By lunchtime the sun is shining, so we throw open the doors and sit in the garden. The Michaelmas daisy is in flower, and so is the ivy. The ivy flower is small and green, and even in clusters it is far from ostentatious. But to insects it is very heaven, and it draws in winged friends from all around. The house front positively hums with life in the warmth of the sun, as bees, bumbles, bluebottles, wasps and hover-flies throng amongst its flowers. Even the aristocrat butterflies are there, peacocks and tortoiseshells taking what must be their last feed of the year, and a single red admiral taking the last feed of its life.

By late afternoon most have gone, though we find dying bumble bees clinging hopelessly to the blue spiraea, and an asylum-seeking tortoiseshell inside the front porch. And in closing the door we reveal a green lacewing, which has flown in during the afternoon and found a dark place to hide. Green lacewings often spend Winter hibernating in buildings, fading from green to dull pinkish-brown until they return to their aphids in Spring.

There is precious little time in the evenings for walks, but once the clocks change next month there will be no time at all. We must at least make the effort, for it will be six months before we have the chance again. Most birds have already gone to roost in this hour or two before dark, though little owls are notably active, sorting themselves out for Winter. They are out well before dusk, and are entertaining to watch, twisting and tilting and bobbing their heads with an expression that is at once startled and quizzical. Little owls are amongst the most endearing of birds, not especially uncommon but all too seldom seen.

There is still time to go watching badgers, though their emergence is less predictable these days, and the wait is less pleasant. Sitting still on cold wet ground is not to everyone's taste, and you may prefer to keep moving. If so you can go instead to have a last look for bats before they tuck themselves up for Winter.

Most bat species mate in Autumn, though they do not actually conceive then. The sperm is stored inside the female during hibernation, and embryonic development starts in late Spring. During pregnancy and lactation the sexes tend to roost separately, with the males paying little attention to their offspring. Following their birth in high Summer, the young cling to their mothers' undersides even in flight, but as they grow larger they are left behind. From mid-August onwards they begin to fly themselves, though they are not fully adept until mid-September. They then have to take full advantage of the longer nights to put on about one-third of their own weight in fat, and they thus become notably active and apparent. A calm mild evening in late September is therefore an excellent time for watching bats, for not only are the numbers in full flight at their highest, but the adults are coming up to the peak of their rut.

As they emerge at dusk we get our chance to pin-point their winter roosts, for in species such as the noctule and pipistrelle the sexes have mixed again now, and the roosts are large. But we may also be lucky enough to see some at close quarters, since this seems to be the best time of year for finding them in accessible crannies. If you get the chance to hold one in your hand and look it straight in its bulldog face, you cannot fail to be enchanted.

Thus I find two Daubenton's and a Natterer's together in a rock crevice at the entrance to an old lead mine, and three whiskereds behind an old wooden notice board nailed to a tree. These are species which are known to hibernate singly or in small groups, and the ones that we find at this time of year are mostly young males forced out into less than ideal accommodation by older stronger rivals. They may even be passing migrants, for bats at the edge of their range, as in the upper Dales, are quite mobile in Spring and Autumn. Localized migrations are more important to bats than is generally realised, and flocks of bats have even been known to land on ships and oil-rigs far out in the North Sea.

Bat-watching ensures that you make the best use of the failing light, but if you have access to a car you can carry on into the night. A quiet drive along the back roads will always turn up something, even if it is only a few rabbits. Most rabbits are fully-grown now, and despite the ravages of myxomatosis and the all-too-obvious road casualties, they seem plentiful everywhere. The rabbit Myxoma virus, spread both by fleas and by direct contact, reaches a peak in late Summer when the warrens are at their most crowded. It is always a pitiful sight to see a swollen-eyed rabbit stumbling along with myxy, but the population as a whole is now relatively resistant to the disease, and some affected individuals will actually recover if left. If you are too squeamish to put an end to one's suffering, console yourself that it might get better.

Badger
(Meles meles)

The badger is probably the most easily recognised of all our Dales' mammals. Although it is in fact a type of large weasel, it has character traits in common with the bear, the pig and the hedgehog

Badgers will often mark trees near their setts with scratches and scent marks by standing on their legs and reaching up as high as possible

On leaving the sett at dusk, badgers spend several minutes grooming before going off to forage for food.

nelson 91

As well as rabbits you may see hedgehogs by the roadside, far too concerned with stuffing themselves to pay much attention to you. You may even be lucky enough to catch a glimpse of some rarer animals, a fox slipping away over a wall, perhaps, or a wandering mink, quick, dark and strong, rippling across a riverside road. Many young mammals, including both fox and mink, are spreading out in search of their own territories just now, and a night-time drive is well worth while. Take a flask and a friend, or a couple of kids, and spend some time sitting in the dark, watching the harvest moon. Apart, perhaps, from the dancing flames of a nocturnal camp-fire, there can be few sights that so induce calm.

10 October

When I first started work in the Tropics, in Haiti in 1972, it was not the English Spring that I missed but the English Autumn. There was quite enough mellow fruitfulness in that warm and humid land, but no season of mists.

As soon as I returned home I made a short 8mm film of Autumn in the Dales, which I took with me on all future contracts. I could then at least conjure up a picture of falling leaves and Autumn tints on any white-washed wall, even when the Fahrenheit temperature and relative humidity were both in the upper nineties.

But you do not have to have lived six months without rain to appreciate a cold damp October. It is always uplifting to hear at last a full river roaring down the valley again, to see cobwebs draped over the grass bejewelled with dewy droplets, and to smell the rich moistness of leaves decaying to humus. After several weeks of rather dreary sameness, it is good to feel a bite in the air once more, to see the trees blaze into a brief flame of glory, and to hear the busy chatterings of a newly-arrived flock of fieldfarcs.

When the clocks go back there will be a lot less hopeful prospect than when they went forward in Spring, but at least the wheels of life will be out of the ditch and back on the high road again.

October 1st – 7th

The pheasant season opens this week, and the bang-bang of clay pigeon practice changes to the bang-bang of the pheasant shoot. Inasmuch as the noise tends to be concentrated on a Saturday morning instead of spread all over the weekend it is to be welcomed, though we cannot help feeling sorry for the oafish birds themselves. Pheasants do not deserve the same sympathy as, say, dalesbred grouse, for they are noisy, gaudy, witless creatures, lacking in nobility. It is tempting to apply a similar description to many of those who shoot them, but that would be unkind and not wholly true.

We tend to think of pheasant shooting as a flatland pursuit, with people from London standing around the Home Counties all day, dressed from catalogues. But there are some pheasant woods up here in the Dales, even on the grander estates. When I was younger and the pheasant were wilder I shot a few brace myself, and I have certainly eaten plenty.

The problem with pheasant shoots is that if you go for a walk in the woods, except on the most public of public footpaths, you are likely to find yourself in the middle of one. This applies any time between now and the year-end, and particularly on Saturday mornings. Since the shorter days mean that we rely increasingly on weekends for our wildlife rambles, we have to select our routes most carefully. But the shooting of game is not permitted on a Sunday, so we must not protest too much.

Pheasant (*Phasianus colchicus*)

In fact we need hardly protest at all, for as the beaters move through the coverts trying to convince pheasants to fly, they disturb many creatures which are wilier and more worthy. If we choose a good vantage point overlooking the sidelines, we may see much that we would not otherwise have seen. Perhaps a fox will slip over the wood wall as soon as the action starts, and trot off through the beck-side bracken to a higher and safer refuge. Perhaps a couple of roe deer will leap into view and bound gracefully past us, looking darker now in their winter pelage. Or perhaps there will be nothing more interesting than a few old crows and a heron or two, though as these commoner birds make their exit you should keep an eye amongst them for more notable species, such as woodcock, woodpeckers, or the odd disgruntled buzzard.

There is actually not that much in the woods that is seriously disturbed by the beaters' passing. Mixed flocks of tits move along the wood-edge canopy with a blithe indifference to the affairs of dogs and men. Badgers and rabbits are tucked away below ground, and there are few hares down from the hills yet. Squirrels bolt off to safety along tree-top highways, or merely press themselves flat atop a branch until the danger is past. And many normal residents of the wood, jays, woodpigeons, and three-parts of the squirrel population, are away day-tripping on banks of oak and rowan, feasting on acorns and berries.

But there is one life form that is mostly confined to woodland at present, and that is the toadstool. As children we were led to believe that all toadstools were poisonous, as were any mushrooms that grew beneath trees. In fact the separation between mushrooms and toadstools is a false one, for what we think of as mushrooms are simply species of agaric. Also there are several perfectly palatable types of wood mushroom, though to children the large white toadstool known as the destroying angel would look just like one. It is, of course, most deadly poisonous, so that the adhortations we received were based on good sense.

It may surprise you to learn that there are some ten thousand species of fungus in Britain, of which the majority are non-poisonous. But simply because there are so many, it can be very difficult to identify unfamiliar ones with any certainty. Avoid eating any which you cannot definitely recognize as edible. And remember that there is a difference between edible and palatable, for very few fungi are as tasty as the common or field mushroom.

Bearing that in mind, however, it has to be said that the quest for fungi will liven up many a dull ramble over the next few weeks. Even here in the Dales, which is not especially good fungus country, you may find two or three dozen species without much trouble. If you like to be with other people on your walks, you can join one of the fungus forays traditionally organised by local naturalists' societies about now. Or if you prefer solitude you can carry a little pocket book, and sit talking to your subject whilst you look it up.

So on Sunday this week I find 33 species, of which I am able to specifically identify 17, and narrow most of the rest down to family or genus. Of the 17, 14 have English names, including dryad's saddle and fairies' bonnets, two very different toadstools growing side by side on a rotting stump; blusher and stinkhorn, familiar to us from earlier in the year; the dignified parasol mushroom and the little amethyst deceiver, both in open woodland; the false chanterelle, false because it resembles the prized chanterelle but is virtually tasteless; the clumsily-named black-and-purple russula, smelling of green apples and tasting as hot as cress; the lemon earth-ball, always beneath oaks and always having larval wrigglies eating at its powdery heart; and King Alfred's cakes on an ancient ash, dry and hard as charcoal, with dull concentric rings. Few of these are edible, and none is highly esteemed, but to those of us who love words, their very names are delicious.

All of those named above are woodland species, for the toadstools of open pasture do not become prominent until the soil has supped its fill of October rain. As yet there has been no sustained heavy rainfall, and a few inches down the soil is still dry. But there have been enough heavy showers and hours of drizzle to bring the gorse into a second peak of bloom, and to revitalize several other wayside flowers which had been on the verge of capitulation.

The run-off from these rains has also freshened the becks and made a few short-lived floods in the rivers. The dippers have welcomed the change, and are suddenly conspicuous again. Two chase one another high above the river, cutting corners and flying over tree-tops, angrily calling "tzit, tzit". One stands beside rock-strewn rapids, his endless chirpy song clearly audible above the roar. And another dives repeatedly into the brown foaming water, returning to the same stone four times in four minutes to eat another little bullhead.

The crayfish under her stone sees his form swim past, compressed by the water and streaming bubbles of air. She too is feeling the effects of the new season's rain, and will soon be moulting and mating. Like the bat and the roe deer, though each in its own different way, she will carry the germ of life through all the winter months, until its time arrives in Spring. Even before Autumn grows old, the plans for Spring are being laid.

October 8th – 15th

I step out into a grey misty morning with a light fine drizzle.

It feels mild, almost warm, with not a whisper of a breeze. In the wood the drizzle seems more persistent, for water has accumulated on the leaves. Each little movement from a bird or squirrel releases a cascade of large wet drops. For a while the only sound is the pattering of these drops passing down through the branches, but then a robin sings, and another, and a pair of jackdaws goes chacking past. I have rarely felt closer to Nature.

There is little hint as yet of the great changes impending. Most large trees still have most of their leaves, and there is no great shortage of verdure. Fewer cattle are out in the fields, but the pastures are far from bare. Where land is ungrazed the grass is draped with millions of small cobwebs, slung from the higher stalks like miniature hammocks. Each is beaded with drops of moisture, and when the sun breaks through they glisten, making a ghostly silver sea. In the warmth of the day the image fades, the mist clears, and the hills re-appear to put bones on our land.

The bracken on these hills has died back over the last couple of weeks, and now appears dull reddish-brown. Where grazing land runs up to the moor-edge there is a nicely artistic contrast between russet and green, delineated by a dark stone wall. But on lower ground and in the woods the bracken is still putting on a show of reds, yellows, browns and greens, and is still upright enough to make walking a soggy-trousered job on a drippy day like this.

The colours of lowland bracken are particularly effective in birch woods, for birches develop a rich variety of Autumn tints earlier than most other trees, and are widely-spaced enough to let the sun shine through. If there are a few colourful fungi as well, large fresh specimens of fly agaric perhaps, we have a perfect picture of Autumn.

Arboreal toadstools still account for most of the fungi we find, though a few more species are appearing in the fields. There is quite a good show of common mushrooms even now, though they are diminishing in both size and flavour. Horse mushrooms, by contrast, are having a last fling, and there are some huge specimens about, weighing several ounces apiece. Another off-white toadstool, rather resembling a mushroom and growing in a similar habitat, is the miller. The skin on the miller's upper surface feels slightly less smooth than that of a mushroom, like the softest palest kid glove, and the gills below are creamy-buff instead of pinky-brown. But is perfectly edible, tasting like the smell of young bracken when raw, and vaguely like bread when cooked.

Other grassland toadstools about now are the shaggy ink-cap, the liberty cap, and a type of little grey Japanese umbrella. The shaggy ink-cap is by far the largest of the three, and is easily recognized. It tends to grow on recently disturbed grassland, and is said to be palatable. Unfortunately it softens to a wet black jelly when cooked, and has to be swallowed whole like an oyster. I have never felt the need to try one. Nor have I ever felt the need to try liberty cap, a poisonous hallucinogenic species known to ageing freaks as the magic mushroom. There is a lot more magic in our woods and hills than they will ever induce biochemically.

Mind-bending properties also used to be attributed to over-ripe blackberries, and any berries eaten after October 1st were said to have been touched by the devil. This may have simply been linked to alcohol produced by fermentation, but was more likely due to mycotoxins from microscopic moulds. In these well-fed times there are few country folk who would eat October blackberries, for they have a watery bitter taste. There are still plenty to be seen, but most are rotting on the vines, often whilst still red, and even those that look all right tend to fall apart when picked.

There are no nuts left on the hazel trees this week, acorns are unpalatable to humans, and the few sweet chestnuts that grow in the Dales rarely produce decent-sized roasters. But there is at least one nut that has a place in our hearts, and that is the noble conker. Which country boy has not marvelled at the shiny brown prize as he split open the three-seamed urchin, has not soaked his best men in salty vinegar and dried them on the hearth, has not taken aim one-eyed down a string, and felt the elation as his opponents gnarled champion shot to pieces on the playground floor? Conkers are ripe and hard now: water-bellies beware!

Though there are few fruits and nuts left in the wild that appeal to the human palate, our feathered friends are stuffed to the brim. Hawthorn and elder berries adorn every hedgerow, and the hillsides are dotted with rowans. What a welcome awaits winter thrushes from the treeless north when they blow down here later this month! A few, in fact, arrive later this week, little flocks of redwings down from Iceland, where they have spent summer around villages and in suburban gardens. They move past hardly stopping, appearing through the clearing mist to alight on a tall ash, chup-chupping quietly amongst the branches, and flying off again before we draw near. These are the first of the new winter species, but they are so obviously passing through that they hardly seem to count.

With snow already falling on high ground in Scotland, and barely a month away here, there is many a bird that is moving through southwards at present. Birds of passage that we saw heading for Scotland in early April can now be seen again on their return jurney. A golden eagle soars majestically over Gouthwaite reservoir, thrilling those who are scrutinizing the waterfowl there. An osprey is disturbed eating a trout on the wall-top just next to a fish farm, and flies off in a high circle, taking note of the place for Spring. A long-eared owl, down from the hills, spends several days roosting in a village thicket, poised ready to quit when the weather turns cold.

In some cases it is difficult to distinguish the migrating birds from normal residents. When pied wagtails return to our hillside farmyards, are these our own birds come back to clean up the insects now the swallows have gone, or Scottish birds working their way south, or even Scandinavian white wagtails crossing from coast to coast? When we see green woodpeckers making long high flights, instead of slipping quietly from tree to tree, are they residents showing off new territorial borders, or strangers passing quickly through? Certainly the scattered flocks of linnets must be mostly rovers, for they contain more birds than ever nested here, and the local ones left us at the first hint of frost.

Nor is it only birds that are quitting the Dales, for hotels are laying off staff, caravans are being towed away, and holiday cottages stand cold as tombs. There are many young dalesfolk living today in the strangeness of towns because they cannot afford to buy or rent these cottages. They have memories of the families that used to live there, often pooled memories going back generations, of tears and laughter, labour and love. When they see these old family homes standing empty for most of the Winter, can we blame them for feeling that market forces alone deliver a queer form of justice?

October 16th – 23rd

If we have a mild wet September, a sharp frosty start to October, and a windless calm thereafter, then we will see Autumn's glory full-flame. Too dry in September and the leaves will fall early, whilst they are still drab and grey;

no frost in the first half of October, and they will never develop full colour; too much wind, and they will be blown off before they are ready. The right combination of weather comes but once or twice in a decade, and the resultant production runs for barely a week. None who has seen it will rue the wait.

Up to the beginning of this week the omens are good. There have been a few showers and a few light frosts. Birches are changing from green to yellow, and beeches from yellow to gold. But then a breeze starts to fret and fidget, ruffling itself up into a squally wind. By dusk there is a raging storm, with a warning of gales to come. All night we hear the rain lashing against the windows, and feel the tempest's anger vent on our old stone walls. Throughout the following day the rain continues, fitful and sullen now, but towards nightfall it dies away, the skies clear, and the temperature drops.

Next morning there is a brush of white frost on the grass, and a lingering fog in the valley. All the sycamores round the house have been stripped of their leaves, and two or three of the smaller branches hang twisted and broken. But this is exposed hillside here, and down in the gill the trees are still well-covered. The loss of their best leaves has dulled their sparkle, but there is a thick enough foliage for a decent show yet.

As well as ripping the brightest leaves from oaks, the storm has littered the ground with acorns. This especially suits the ducks, which love acorns but are ill-equipped for perching and picking. As soon as the first grey light appears in the sky, they leave the river to gather beneath hillside oaks, waddling frantically about like old wives at a bargain sale. Later, full-cropped, they return to the water to splash and quack with noisy exuberance, the drakes resplendent in full dress plumage. And later still, near dusk, they fly back to the oaks for their supper, dropping down from on high with undeniable skill and grace.

During the night their place beneath the oaks is usurped by pop-eyed wood mice, ever watchful for owls. The wood mouse is quite capable of climbing most oaks to pick his own acorns, but at present he is filling his larder and has no time to waste. Back and forth twixt tree and store he travels, carrying acorns gripped in his teeth. There may be several mice at once below the spreading branches, for territorial disputes have no place in times of short-lived plenty. Neighbours must come in from considerable distances, for I have found acorns stored beneath stones hundreds of yards from the nearest oak. If one mouse were to try and defend his home patch around the tree, he could not carry away much in a night; there would simply be more for the birds next day.

And certainly birds love acorns. The pheasant, like the mallard, tends to pick fallen ones from the ground, stuffing thirty or more in his crop at once and ruining the cut of his jib. Pigeons, magpies, rooks and jays are up amongst the branches, grabbing and gulping. The jay, of course, is the doyen of acorn-eaters, and even plants his own oaks, for as soon as he has enough in his crop he carries his pickings away. Each acorn may be carried several hundred yards before the jay finds a site to his liking, and it is then hidden just below the soil surface in a hole dug and filled in by the bird's strong beak. Those which the jay forgets find themselves ready planted for Spring, and thus the oak extends its range.

Exactly how the jay retrieves the buried acorns is one of Nature's little riddles. Certainly memory must play some part, if one can use such an anthropomorphic term for the workings of a bird-brain. But most are probably re-discovered because they were hidden in likely-looking places. I have watched a jay carrying bird-table scraps for short-term storage onto a nearby bank. Each scrap was separately hidden, but always in the same sort of site, wherever there were a few square inches of bare soil at the base of a steep little face on the bank. When coming to retrieve his store, the bird would land near the bird-table, fly across onto the bank face, and peck around any disturbed soil on the small bare patches. They were simply the sort of place where any right-minded jay would be likely to have hidden a treasure. I suspect that if a jay were removed from his territory and replaced with a stranger, the latter would find a goodly part of the hidden acorns.

Much the same technique is used by the squirrel, though his task is made easier by a smaller territory and regular runs. He tends to bury his nuts near recognizable landmarks beside familiar pathways, and is equipped with a good sense of smell to help him find them again. Also, as a mammal, he has something more nearly approaching what we would understand as a memory.

Squirrels seem unusually bold about now, and if you move rather aimlessly looking at the ground, picking fungi or pretending to, you can walk up to the base of an old oak tree and sit yourself down amongst them. There may be up to half-a-dozen in any one tree. Provided you keep still, they will come down the far side of the trunk and carry on gathering and burying nuts within a few feet of you. They are strikingly handsome in their Autumn pelage, with red cheeks and feet set off against an almost blue shade of grey, and with a characteristically bright-eyed and bushy-tailed presence. They are not yet actually obese, but we can fairly say that they are pleasantly plump, and a little less light on their feet than of late.

Whilst oaks draw in the larger birds, many of the smaller ones are busy with berries. Elderberries are disappearing rapidly, for they can be swallowed and digested by all but the most insectivorous of species. Hawthorns seem particularly attractive to the finch and thrush families, with blackbirds the most obviously gluttonous. Since early July the black-birds have been in moult, and have kept a low profile near bramble-rich cover. Now they are posing once more on exposed branches to show off their new clean plumage, the adult males being especially noticeable. Song thrushes, by contrast, are becoming quite scarce, and those that we do see are just passing through.

As elderberries disappear there is more competition for haws, but for larger birds the hedgerows have their dangers, not least being the 12-bore shotgun. Thus when pigeon, jay

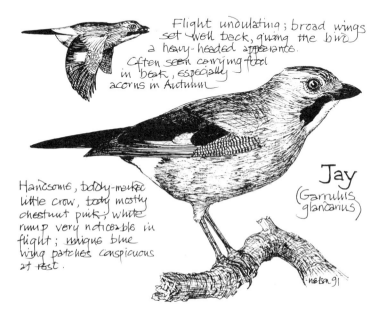

Flight undulating; broad wings set well back, giving the bird a heavy-headed appearance. Often seen carrying food in beak, especially acorns in Autumn

Handsome, boldly-marked little crow, body mostly chestnut pink; white rump very noticeable in flight; unique blue wing patches conspicuous at rest.

Jay
(Garrulus glandarius)

nelson 91

and pheasant need a change from dry hard acorns, they head not for hedges but for hillsides, to patronise little rowans. Like hawthorns the rowans lost most of their leaves in the storm, but that only makes their berries more temptingly visible.

Rowan fruit is actually not all that tasty. To birds which have been gorging on bilberries, blackberries, elders and haws it is pretty poor fare, barely better than holly berries. But there are birds on their way that will guzzle it by the cluster, that will flock to a bush and strip it bare in minutes. One clear night towards the end of this week, as I sit outside watching the stars, I hear a "chu-chu-chu-chuk" in the blackness above. The airborne invasion is underway. Next day there are fieldfares everywhere, wave after wave flying hither and thither, wild and restless and bent on pillage.

October 24th – 31st

The cold snap that followed last week's storm does not bite deep or linger long. It is soon replaced by the sort of dull drizzly weather that always seen to coincide with the potato harvest. My first paid job was tatie-picking, in the half-term holiday that was timed to release kids for that specific purpose. For 21 hours bent double I was given a one pound note, the first I had ever held. A bob an hour was big brass for a nine year old then.

Many things have changed over the intervening 35 years, but the natural cycle endures. Potatoes are still lifted this week on the few Dales farms that still grow them, and the peak of Autumn tints still coincides with their harvest. Some individual trees may not yet have reached full colour, but the woods as a whole are at the zenith of their glory.

Most regal of all are the beeches, robed in coppery-red. Stately horse chestnuts in riverside fields are dappled with orange and green. Graceful birches, ladies of the wood, trail lacy cascades of colour against silver-grey trunks. Oaks change with majestic gentility, through fiery gold to a warm nut-brown. Some sycamores and ashes in more exposed situations have already lost all their leaves, but those in the valley bottom glow with yellow light.

Amongst this riot of colour there are a few trees, such as beck-side alders, which have not yet lost their greenery, for their roots are standing in water. And a few others, protected by waxy coats, will remain green throughout, to spruce up our mid-Winter rites. Firs are classical members of this last group, though not all firs are evergreen and not all evergreens are firs. The larch is a common fir that sheds what pass for leaves, and the holly keeps its leaves but is not remotely related to the firs.

Holly berries have been quietly ripening over the last month, and some are now fully scarlet and ready for Christmas. Birds do not find them especially tasty, so that there will still be plenty around when we need them.

A good crop of holly berries is popularly thought to forecast a hard Winter, though in fact it is simply the result of a favourable growing season. But like most bits of folk-lore there is an element of truth: the berries grow best if the Summer is wet; a wet Summer tends to be followed by a dry Winter to allow rainfalls to average out; and a dry Winter tends to be a frosty one, because we need clouds to keep the ground warm. It is not a question of trees sensing the approach of an unusually hard Winter and producing more berries to compensate. Rather it is just another example of the way in which so many of Nature's plans dovetail so beautifully together.

Holly berries may still be bitter and unpalatable, but other fruits are being guzzled ounce, pound and ton. Elder bushes have been stripped almost bare, and their seeds are being scattered along the hedgerows with little splashes of fertilizer, exactly according to plan. Hips and haws now form the main food of species varying from vole to finch. Where hawthorns have reached out from upland valleys to mix with moorside rowans, the blackbird meets his wild Norse cousins and leads them down to pasture. Fieldfares and redwings, unapproachable last week, now move in small flocks along hedgerows and banksides, calmed by full bellies and new layers of fat.

Sitting on a steep bank in a thicket of thorns, I can watch them only a few yards away in the bushes below. Pick and gulp, and cock an eye skywards; pick again, and once more, then time for a change. A change of branch, a change of bush, then the whole mixed party takes to the wing, shuffles itself into a new order, and descends again onto the same few trees. What marvellous birds they are, these friends in need, these welcome winter guests. The boldly marked fieldfare, a mask on his face, every inch the handsome rascal; and the gentle little redwing, almost feminine, consorting freely with pirates. Seen as now, at close quarters through good binoculars, their subtle colours and lovely markings embody perfectly the spirit of Autumn.

Photographs of redwings and fieldfares all too often show them on berries in the snow, when their hunger allows a better chance of a portrait. But in fact they are most abundant in the Dales in late Autumn and early Spring, and tend to drift away to the flatlands in mid-Winter. We do not expect any really hard weather for weeks yet, and there will not even be any ice on the troughs until the second week of November. For the moment there are still insects on the wing, not only the dancing gnats and mottled grey moths of Winter, but warmth-loving species as well. Wherever there are fresh cow-claps there are the familar brown muck-flies, and wherever a stinkhorn protrudes it is surrounded by a swarm of blow-flies, either clustered on its sticky tip or lying drunk on the ground below.

The recent rains have generated a new flush of various toadstools, the stinkhorn being most noticeable because of its shameless posturing and evil smell. Species associated with trees still predominate, and although the stinkhorn prefers coniferous leaf litter most of the others should be sought in broad-leaved woodland. A bundle of sulphur tufts sprouts from a half-fallen tree, looking down on their ruddy relatives growing from the base of neighbouring oak. A charcoal burner stands boldly up from the soil beneath birches, whilst ashy little antlers of candle snuff grow almost unseen on the dead twigs beside it. A large brown roll-rim bursts through the rough grass on a wooded bank, over-shadowing the little group of moss pixy-caps huddled nearby. And three edible species appear, two being boletes – the bay and the downy – and the third the oyster mushroom. Although called a mushroom, the oyster is not closely related to our common field variety. Except for its gills it resembles a bracket fungus, dolphin-grey above, creamy-white below, and growing on old tree stumps. But fried in a little butter it tastes delicious, more like white meat than fungus, reminiscent of veal but with the chewy texture of shark meat.

Other species abound, but with so many of them coloured in shades of brown their identification is no easy matter. Slugs seem to have no such problem, for some fungal species will decay away without ever being touched by slugs, whilst others invariably have molluscan bite-marks from the dawn of their first day. It is a source of wonder that slugs continue to forage long after the first frosts, for lowly creatures as wet and unprotected as they are should surely freeze solid at the first touch of hoar. In fact they simply retreat into their slimy cellars beneath logs and stones, and re-emerge when the frost is past. The dry weather has not been kind to them, and they need to rasp up as much as they can now that the rains are here.

Much the same is true of earthworms, which aestivated deep in their burrows when the soil was dry, but are suddenly full of life again. Hundreds of worm casts appear on the surface of the lawn, and leaves which have fallen there are dragged below to be eaten. There is even a new peak of mating activity as the worms revel in the joys of Autumn. If we step outside on a mild drippy night we can catch them at it, stretched on the grass in moist embrace wherever the torchlight shines.

But there are other eyes watching that need no torch, and that gleam with a glint of hunger, for mating worms are carefree worms, exposed for most of their length. They may sense the badger's heavy steps and retract themselves in time, but the little owl has silent wings and loves their boneless flesh. We see him near dusk on a dry stone wall, now calling his "piu-piu-piu", now pouncing on luckless prey.

An owl eating worms may seem strange, but worms actually comprise a large part of the little owl's diet in Spring and Autumn. Even the tawny owl takes them as tasty snacks, and carries many to its young in their first month of life. Young tawny owls are now fully independent and have territories of their own, but some of these territories are not what they seem. A patch of wooded hillside which afforded plenty of cover to the inexperienced youngster in August is unexpectedly revealed as devoid of evergreens when the leaves start to fall. This causes a good deal of local mobility in the owl population as boundaries are re-defined. In the early mornings at present we often find tawny owls caught in exposed positions, and as we approach they fly up onto higher and barer perches, as if uncertain where to go next.

It is tempting to think that these are migrant birds passing through, but such evidence as there is suggests that the tawny owl does not move far. In another week or two these same owls will have settled into clumps of holly or yew or stands of spruce, and will roost there through Winter. A similar situation prevails with grouse, which also do not move far from their birthplace, and are also found in exposed situations this week. With grouse, though, the reasons are simpler and more obvious. They are hefted to the hillside, like sheep, and would fall ill if they moved far; they make limited local movements partly to escape the guns and partly because of territorial conflict; and they are seen in exposed positions because they love hawthorn berries, and do not mind looking ridiculous to get them. A grouse does indeed seem out of place perched atop a hawthorn or rowan, particularly when its crop is so full that even the fiercest-looking cock seems positively buxom.

A lot of good-natured posturing and squabbling is taking place amongst the grouse population at present. Most of the shooting is over, there are vacant possessions up for grabs, and the dominant males are carving up the spoils. One still morning, when it is misty in the valleys and clear on the tops, I go up there to listen to them. In addition to their normal cackles and gobbles they are making a babble of unusual contact calls, some sounding almost like distant human speech, some deep and croaky, and some almost falsetto.

It is lovely to sit up there and be part of their world, moor-side born and bred. But then the sun comes out, the mist clears, and the wooded valleys catch fire. There is really no other expression that does justice to the incandescence of colours, and I am drawn back down to them like the moth to its flame. Any one tree viewed at close quarters is utterly sublime, but to be surrounded by dozens in a sunlit glade is simply transcendental. I wander through the wonderland as if entranced, alone amongst giants in a palace of gold.

11 November

The glory of Autumn is all too brief, and fades within days of its peak. Wind and rain strip the trees bare, leaving the branches stark against a sullen sky. Frost follows the rain, and sleet follows the frost, forcing the farmer's hand. Dairy cows are taken inside for Winter, and the tups go out amongst the horned ewes. In pastures cleared of cattle new molehills appear, and the gate bottoms become muddy again.

Once the ground is well soaked the becks fill up, and fat-bellied trout run upstream to mate. The herons await them with spear-point beaks, and stand replete in fell-side fields. Tits and robins return to our gardens, hedgehogs disappear from the roadsides, and the last few flowers smile bravely out from the hedgerows.

Before the month ends we will see the first falls of snow. The log-shed smells of sawdust and the kitchen of cake as our preparations for Winter gather pace. Despite cold misty mornings and dull grey days, we are gripped by a sense of excitement that will see us through to Christmas.

November 1st – 7th

The ritual burning of an effigy of Guy Fawkes has survived for almost four hundred Novembers. It is not that the British people are particularly given to sadism or religious bigotry, and not that we are excessively fond of politicians. Rather it is simply that if Bonfire Night did not exist we would have to invent it, as a way of getting shot of old rubbish.

Leaves are especially troublesome. Although they are useful as hen litter or garden compost, there is a primaeval delight in setting fire to a pile. Throughout October it seemed that whatever amount we raked up one day, there would be twice as many fallen the next. But the first week of November sees winds and rain that denude the trees in a few score hours. Colours that were weeks in the making, lights that were like living fire, are now just dead things on the ground, swept into corners by the fitful breeze.

Away from our yards and gardens the discarded leaves rot where they gather, putting goodness back into the soil.

Birds love to fossick amongst them in search of hibernating invertebrates and fallen seeds. Beneath beech trees the first bramblings appear, turning over the leaves to look for beech-mast. Bramblings are very closely related to chaffinches, but much less common. They often travel together in mixed flocks in Winter, but in the Dales, where beechmast is more husk than seed, there may be fifty chaffinches for every brambling. On the ground the two birds resemble each other, though the visitor has a darker head and shoulders. But on the wing the brambling's white rump patch and fast erratic flight draw attention to its presence. Viewed at close quarters the cock is a handsome bird. It is a pity that we see him here only in Winter, and then only rarely, for his summer colours are even better.

Much the same is true of the siskin. We do see siskins even in Summer nowadays, but they are non-breeding individuals which have not developed full plumage. If you go looking for siskins during their nesting season in Scotland, you will barely credit that they are the same species we have here. Winter siskins are arriving now, and can best be found amongst alders where little wooded gills run down to the river. They may be difficult to positively identify in bare branches against the sky, though their habit of repeatedly flying out in a wide circle to return to the same tree will distinguish them from all other finches except the redpoll. Where there are mixed flocks of siskins and redpolls, as sometimes happens, they are not easily told apart unless their colours can be seen. In good light the redpoll looks streaky pink and the siskin streaky green, and even in poor light the siskin's yellow wing bars can be seen.

The same alders that attract these two winter finches are also being visited by tits. The large mingled flocks of mid-Winter have not yet teamed up, though families of long-tailed tits have merged into parties of a dozen or two. Other small birds tag along with these parties, including recently-arrived migrant goldcrests. Seeing these tiny orange-capped featherweights flitting from branch to branch, it is almost impossible to believe that a few days ago they flew non-stop across the North Sea, two or three hundred miles in a single night.

But we have no problem believing it of our woodcock. There can be few birds better suited to sustained and steady flight. We can picture them high in the darkness, flying straight and fast with lazy wing-beats, heads held high, beaks dipped, all-seeing eyes gleaming in the moonlight.

There are woodcock with us all year, of course, many more than we might imagine. Their nerves are so strong and their camouflage so effective that we detect them not, and pass them by. But these arrivals from the North are flighty at first, so that as we approach they take to the wing. On a ramble through wet open woodland I see five in as many minutes. Each one springs up when I am still several yards away, and rises steeply off through the trees. What truly admirable birds they are, and what a delight to see them!

So far this week we have concentrated on long-range migrants, but there are local movements too. Now that much of the flatland is ploughed, we begin to see large flocks of woodpigeons. They have lived well on the farmer's corn, but now scour the countryside for more natural fare, acorns and berries, leaves and seeds. There are off-comed flocks of starlings too, not the huge swarms of mid-Winter but roving bands of a few dozen birds. They also spent Summer round the stackyards, but are roosting now on town hall ledges. They feed on grubs just below the surface, and find our newly-wet pastures infinitely more rewarding than the upside-down soil of the downland.

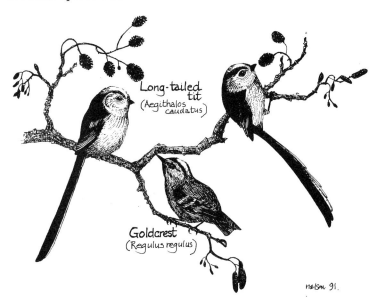

Long-tailed tit (*Aegithalos caudatus*)

Goldcrest (*Regulus regulus*)

nelson 91.

We can see some stirrings even from our kitchen windows, for a house is the best hide of all when the weather is cold and wet. Robins are re-establishing themselves as cocks of the lawn, wrens and hedge sparrows are creeping quietly in from the waysides, and tits both blue and great hang from the proffered nuts. The sparrowhawk takes note, and is increasingly seen in hamlet and village, now flapping and gliding in almost ungainly reconnaissance, now flashing and twisting in deadly pursuit.

Nor is it only birds which are on the move. In the empty meadows moles are at work, clearing out their shafts and tunnels and pushing great black heaps above ground. Wood mice clamber up the house-wall ivy and wriggle in under the roof slates, clumping about the under-drawings at night like rats with clogs on. And rats themselves invade our farmyards, only to perish for their presumption.

The increasingly cold weather affects plant growth most directly, and the grass all but ceases to grow. Fungal reproduction tails away, and there are few new toadstools to be found. The meek grey slug senses his end, and commits himself to one last act of daring. Casting caution aside he climbs a tree-trunk, to meet with a like-minded mate. And high above the ground, swinging on a mucoid trapeze, they indulge in a frenzied hermaphrodite sex session lasting for several hours. As the first grey light touches the sky, they lower themselves to the grass and go their separate ways. If a late hedgehog does not pounce their genes are secure, for each will now lay eggs in some well-protected place. And those eggs in Spring will hatch into tiny sluglets, to carry on the race.

The hedgehog, by comparison, must make provision for protecting itself, for it cannot procreate through resistant eggs, yet it can no longer find its fill. With simple stoicism it digs out a nest chamber on a wooded bank, well protected between tree roots or beneath a tangle of thorns. This it lines with grass and dead leaves until it makes a snug tight fit. Then, closing its door with a final armful, it curls up inside its insulating layers of leaf and prickle and fat. Its pulse rate slows, its breathing becomes imperceptible, a smile spreads to its soul, and the troubles of the world float away. Hibernation is a sort of almost-death, but with none of the pain or dread.

November 8th – 15th

This week sees the beginning of one of the year's cold spots. During the next fortnight we can expect the first hard frosts and the first covering of snow. As the week opens, most of the remaining flowers and fungi have but a few days left to live. We should enjoy them while we can.

There may still be occasional mushrooms afoot, but they are scarcely worth taking home. Various other toadstools are appearing in the fields, but few have English names. One pretty but inedible exception, growing in little clusters on rough pasture, is the green and yellow parrot toadstool. We may also find several different types that fall into the category of fairy ring fungi.

All toadstools seem to have been associated with the supernatural in ancient times, perhaps because some were known to be hallucinogenic and because they appeared overnight as if by magic. Thus we have names like pixy cap, dryad's saddle, fairies' bonnets, witches' butter, elf cup, and now fairy ring fungi. As youngsters we were seriously divided as to whether standing in a fairy ring would bring bad luck or ensure secret wishes granted.

To the more prosaic there is nothing magical about fairy rings. The fungus establishes itself beneath the surface, and its mycelium spreads out through the soil in all directions. When the ground cools it makes preparation for Winter by producing resistant spores. To do any good these have to be spread, and so spore-bearing toadstools are pushed up from the most actively growing zone around the periphery. The fungal network remains underground, and if it survives till Spring it will continue to spread. Next year's fairy ring will therefore be larger. In milder parts of the country there are fairy rings which have appeared at the same site for decades, increasing their circumference each year.

Many genera of toadstools produce fairy rings, and some of them are edible. Best known of all are blewits, which have come up during the last few days in damp grassland near to oak trees. They taste rather like mushrooms, but have the advantage of a firmer texture. They therefore do not bruise or crumble in your bag or pocket, and are still in good condition when they arrive on the kitchen table. With their clay-brown caps and pale lilac gills there are few fungi that look better when trimmed and ready for cooking.

During your brief reversion to hunter-gatherer you can also pick some cress. Now that its flowering season has ended, the plant is making leafy masses again in trickling upland streams. Because it is usually eaten raw, there is a risk, albeit it extremely small, of catching liver fluke from watercress. If this concerns you then stick to the supermarket stuff, which is grown under controlled conditions. There can be few streams in the Dales that are devoid of the sheep and the snails that the parasite needs. Even if there are no sheep there will be rabbits, which serve the fluke equally well.

Though watercress has long since ceased to flower, there are still a few brave plants in bloom. Shepherd's purse, a close relative of watercress, makes dots of white by the wayside, as do common chickweed and lesser stitchwort. The yellow composite flowers of dandelion, sowthistle, hawkweed, cat's ear, ragwort and groundsel are still to be found on waysides and damp grassy slopes. Rayless mayweed and common daisy continue their struggle in our yards and gardens respectively, having faced hoof, boot, wheel and mower, and weathered the lot. There are even some showier species, though they show as retreating stragglers instead of massed battalions: a few single specimens of harebell, betony, knapweed and red deadnettle; a foxglove spike by a sunny wallside; the odd yarrow or buttercup in the corner of a pasture; ivy-leaved toadflax on the sheltered side of an old stone building; and in open woodland the occasional red campion or herb Robert, a tattered bramble flower amongst the thorny vines, and a tangle of climbing corydalis. Seek them all out and bid them fond farewell, for the weather will show them no pity.

But there are plants that will not succumb to any November frost. Gorse, of course, will flower in any month, and ivy seems to actually prefer the cold. The house-wall ivy blossomed back in September, when butterflies were still on the wing, but truly wild ivy is only now in flower. In this last brief mild spell before the frost we see that the more accessible ivy, along hedges and wall-tops, is alive with late season insects, particularly of the bluebottle type.

Most of the bluebottles on the ivy nectar will be males, for the females have less Arcadian tastes. We find an avid cluster on a decaying trout by a riverside pond, and marvel at the senses that drew them there from afar. Trout are in breeding condition at this time of year, and are congregating near the mouths of the streams in which they were born. In the inevitable jostling for position the weakest perish, and their bodies turn up in the ponds left after each high river about now.

The herons know that trout are gathering, and fly in to the Dales from miles around. Where decent-sized becks run through fields and open woodland, we may see a heron on watch every few hundred yards. The trout will not run until after the next big rains, and the waiting herons may pass the

Goosander
(Mergus merganser)

time voling. We see them stalking across rushy fields, sometimes several together like a line of police, combing the
ground for clues. They stride slowly, bodies horizontal,
heads held low, poised for a darting kill.

Around the mouths of their spawning streams the trout
keep to deeper water, thinking to be safe from herons. But
they reckon without the arrival of diving goosanders, which
until recently did not pose a threat. Goosanders return to
the Dales this week, and head for beck-ends to wreak havoc.
A shoal of fish in water a yard deep is very heaven to these
gluttons, and they have a rare old time. It must break the
heart of a fisherman, but I love the sight of them at work.
They hunt cooperatively, lining out to drive the fish into a
corner, and then closing in for the dashing splashing climax.
Most trout escape, of course, and the population as a whole
is healthier for the loss of the weakest.

Most of the goosanders we see now are females and
adolescents, collectively known as brown-heads. The adult
drakes cannot bear to be seen here in eclipse plumage, and
have spent Summer in the Baltic. But their long moult is
nearing its end, and they will soon be back, to join the
youngsters which were eggs when they left.

The arrival of brown-head goosanders is a sure sign of
impending frost, and the weather stays true to form. A white
hoar puts glitter on the landscape, the trough in the yard is
glazed with ice, fallen leaves crunch as we walk, and kids

play dragons with exhaled clouds of vapour. As ponds freeze our reservoirs fill with birds; mallard and coot, of course, but also the odd pair of pochard or wigeon. Tufted ducks fly in from northern lands to join our resident few. Young Canada geese, back from Beauly Firth, join breeding flocks in waterside pastures. These flocks of geese will be increasingly mobile over the next few weeks, flying past at dusk making lines in the sky. As we see and hear the first in the ice-blue above, we are left in no doubt that Jack Frost is back.

November 16th – 23rd

The crisp weather continues for a couple of days. Hoar-rimed flowers and grass stalks glisten with crystal light. Toadstools freeze solid, and break like wafers when picked. Spring-born birds get a fore-taste of Winter, and re-consider their options.

Many small birds begin to see the attractions of garden life, and to examine the pros and cons. Instinct tells them to keep well away from these islands of unnatural vegetation. Experience tells them that fearsome people lurk there, and probably cats and hawks. But their eyes tell them that robins, tits and sparrows seem to thrive there with impunity, and that there is food enough for all when the weather is hard.

Now is the time, then, to re-stock our nut-hoppers and be liberal with our bird-table provisions. Even city centre gardens should be able to attract starlings, house sparrows and blue tits, and most will draw in the odd great tit, black-bird or robin. Many people would prefer that starlings did not visit bird-tables, for in urban areas they arrive by the dozen and clear every scrap within minutes. Away from the towns and larger villages this is less commonly a problem. And the few starlings that do arrive will more than earn their keep by singing medleys from the roof whilst awaiting their breakfast.

It is still too early in the season for bird-tables to attract the more spectacular species, such as pheasants, jays and great spotted woodpeckers. But in wooded valleys the first nuthatches are being tempted in, particularly where there are loose nuts which they can carry away and hide. Nuthatches extended their range greatly during the 1960s, thanks almost exclusively to the fashion for bird-tables which caught hold about then. I remember seeing my first one, climbing head-first down a riverside sycamore, in 1959.

Ten years later they were so common that there would be three or four at once in our garden up by the moorside. When my mother saw the first pioneer round the house, she described it to us as looking like a fat chaffinch. It was an odd description but it stuck, and each November thereafter she would tell us that her fat chaffinch was back. Even now, years after her death, I still think of her description when I see a nuthatch on a bird table.

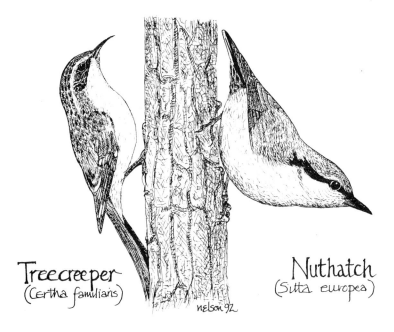

Treecreeper
(Certha familiaris)

Nuthatch
(Sitta europea)

nelson 92

Since their population explosion in the Sixties, nuthatches have fallen back somewhat, and now tend to remain on lower ground throughout the year. The chaffinch itself, by contrast, remains the commonest of British birds, particularly when winter immigrants from mainland Europe are included in the count. Like most highly successful species, the chaffinch adapts readily to many different habits and lifestyles. Some forage the flatlands in flocks of several hundred, some roam in smaller groups between scattered stands of beech, some move into gardens to take their place at the table, and some tag onto tit parties to pick through beckside woodland.

These mixed parties of tits are a common feature now, adding welcome spice to many a dull day's walk. In leafless woodland we hear the 'si-si-si-si" of long-tailed tits from a hundred yards away, and watch them flit through the twigs towards us like fairy feather dusters. Most flocks around here now comprise about a dozen long-tails, a dozen blue tits and a dozen assorted others. The others include coal and great tits, treecreepers, goldcrests and chaffinches, as well as the occasional rarity. In our steep-sided valleys we cannot usually keep up with a flock for long, but each makes a thrilling encounter and there may be several in any one wood.

Long-tailed tits rarely descend to ground level, but the three other tits are quite at home there. They especially love to prospect amongst fallen oak leaves, and on these frosty mornings they can be seen vigorously tossing aside rejects in their search for invertebrate treasure. Beneath crab-apple trees it is not the leaves which provide the interest, but the sour little apples themselves. Redwings are remarkably fond of fallen crabs, and when the ground is frozen they congregate there to pick at the rotting fruit. I suspect that they also uncover a goodly crop of slugs and similar fare half-hidden beneath the apples, for they are fond of animal protein when they can find it.

Mistle thrushes also like their bit of meat, though adults can survive for long periods on berries alone. Scandinavian mistle thrushes, which came in with the fieldfares, have a special liking for yew berries, perhaps because the yew reminds them of the conifers whence they came. There have been berries on yew trees since early August, but our resident birds have been spoilt for choice. Now, quite suddenly, every yew seems to have a dozen mistle thrushes gorging on its berries, churring and rattling at each other and scolding the odd roosting owl. These unruly mobs will soon go on to join the nomadic flocks of fieldfares and starlings which swarm across mid-Winter fields. A few residents will remain, to stake a claim on berry banks and defend them against all comers.

Towards mid-week the frost loosens its grip, the skies fill with heavy clouds, and the first snow of the season comes floating down. My wife, who had not seen snow until she was in her twenties, leaves her work to sit by an open window. For a short delightful interlude there is the most picturesque of snowfalls, and the baffled landscape is silent. As the light fades there is a good covering, but during the night the snow turns to rain, and by morning the magic is gone.

The spate that results from rain on snow is locally known as a snow-broth. The trout mistrust it, and restively bide their time. But the rain continues long after the snow is all gone, and the water is soon to their taste. Finally, exhilarated by the torrent's force, they crowd into the side-streams and start their marathon race. The journey to their spawning grounds will be fraught with danger, and only the fittest will make it. There are falls to be jumped, rocks to be avoided, rapids to be negotiated, and a gauntlet of predators to be run. Herons find easy pickings in the pools that trout use to rest, and mink follow beck-sides sure of a feast. It is a lucky mink that can catch a healthy trout in the river, but in these smaller becks it becomes quite literally child's play.

One morning towards the end of the week I take my own children down to watch the trout jumping. As each fish surges from the foaming water, wriggles through the air, and splashes into the head of the fall, it makes a wonderfully inspiring sight. We may see trout leaping upstream at any time between late October and early January, but the peak is now if the rain is right. There are several jumping each minute at dawn today, with sometimes two or three in the air at once. I tickle a couple out alive and gently massage their bellies to show my kids the cloudy milt and golden pearls of spawn.

Until recent times the beck-watcher on the local estate milked dozens of trout like this, mixing the yield from cock and hen trout to fertilize the eggs. In spawning streams you will still see the cobbled slopes ending in foot-high falls which were built to delay the trout and make catching easy. Trout would either be netted in the pool at the bottom, or caught between the cobbles by hand. After being milked they were returned to the water to resume their uphill struggle. The harvest of several thousand fertilized eggs was then kept in hatcheries over Winter, to be released as fry in Spring. Properly conducted this reduced natural wastage, but it was a process which required gentle skill and daily dedication. Now the beck-watcher is dead, the fish-house is derelict, and the estate has a trout farm instead.

November 24th – 30th

Last week gave us frost, snow, sleet and rain in rapid succession. It left most of the trees completely leafless, and the fields looking bleached and drab. Having flexed its muscles and made its point, Winter now dozes off again. This week the weather can best be summarized as dull:

sometimes mild, sometimes raw, often drizzly, but most often simply dull.

The flooded becks subside a little, but remain full enough for the trout to keep running. Those fittest fish, that have passed each successive peril, finally reach the quieter gravelly stretches to stake their claims. Each then defends its chosen patch against rivals, and works at attracting a mate. The mating pair make ready a shallow depression in the sandy gravel, and begin a ritualized underwater dance. This culminates in a frenzied display, with the two repeatedly rubbing against each other. Finally the hen releases her eggs, the cock covers them with milt, and the mixed deposit is buried with a few strokes of their well-muscled tails. Many eggs will be washed away by later floods, many will be disturbed or even eaten by other trout, some will be damaged by stones rolling along the stream-bed, and a few will provide food for dippers and crayfish. Those that survive will lie forgotten through Winter's reign, to hatch in the following Spring. When the first frogs spawn, when the first lapwings cry on the fell, transparent little alevins will wriggle up through the sand to start on their own life's journey.

The recent cold weather has served to concentrate the minds of many small creatures. A few hares have come down from the moor tops over the last few days, and can be seen in open woodland, wild and long-legged. Worms have moved deeper into the soil to avoid the surface frost, and moles have moved there after them. More and more mole-hills appear, making dot-to-dot traces across bare grassland. If you are lucky, or patient, you may see a heap stir as the soil is pushed up. If so, pause awhile in case the mowdy pokes out his little red whiskery snout. And as you wait, consider the strength in his little body, which can push several inches of loose soil up a vertical shaft with enough force to lift the surface of a mole-hill.

Sometimes when a mole is busy near a hedge or garden, a robin will visit his works. Worms, on feeling the soil vibrations made by a mole's tunnelling, will quite often bolt above ground to escape. You can achieve a similar effect by sticking a garden fork into your lawn and shaking the shaft. The robin has probably never seen a mole, and poor purblind moley knows nothing of the robin, but the bird recognizes fresh mole-hills as happy hunting grounds, and is not equipped to wonder why. How many of us, after all, have seen a banana palm, a milking parlour, or the inside workings of an abattoir?

Both moles and worms are important items in the diet of badgers. As they move deeper into the soil, so the badger loses easy access to yet another source of food. Already most berries have been eaten, fungi have ceased to appear, and there is a dearth of wasp and rabbit nests to raid. Provided that there is no great over-population or parasitic infection no badger will starve: there are still bulbs, carrion, hibernating hedgehogs and the like. But Winter's warning signal cannot be ignored. Brock senses that it is time to curtail his nightly walks, spend longer periods curled up asleep, and live off his layers of Autumn-stored fat.

Most mice, voles and shrews cannot store enough fat for hibernation, a notable exception being the southern counties' dormouse. We have already discussed the way that moles and shrews briefly store worms, by disabling their anterior segments to stop them crawling away. And we have mentioned that wood mice hoard acorns in holes protected beneath stones. But another favourite place for both wood mice and bank voles to make stores of nuts, seeds and berries is in the abandoned nests of hedgerow birds. These nests are easily visible now in the newly-bare hedgerows. Some bird-watchers like to dislodge them to avoid confusion with new nests in Spring. This is ecologically unsound, since not only are the rodents' winter larders unnecessarily laid waste, but also the presence of old nests encourages birds to build there again.

Probably the best known example of this is the rook. There are some trees in which rooks have nested for as long as our oldest folk can remember. Now that the branches are bare we can see and count all the rookery nests, and take note of the rooks that loiter there. It is odd that rooks spend so much time around their old nests during Winter. Perhaps they sometimes store food in them, for they will defend the site against other rooks. I have often seen rooks carrying acorns in Autumn, but have never seen them bury any food in the ground. I do not propose to climb up there to find out, but doubtless some intrepid wildlife film-maker will eventually show us the answer.

Rooks are also becoming more noticeable in the fields, as the resident population is supplemented by in-comers. These latter are attracted partly by the muddy state of the fields, which facilitates their feeding technique, and partly by the muck which is now being spread on the land. Large mixed flocks of rooks, jackdaws, gulls and even mallard congregate where muck has been spread, to guddle about in it for larval invertebrates and undigested corn. These mixed flocks of larger birds provide ideal hunting for peregrines, so it comes as no surprise when one turns up. I see it near dusk roosting on a rocky outcrop overlooking the valley, and next morning find the tell-tale scattered feathers where it has killed a gull in the fields below. On the same day I chance upon a buzzard, roosting in a Scots pine. It appears to be either an escaped captive or a sick bird, for it allows me to approach within 20 yards before flying away.

The sighting of these two large and quite scarce raptors within a few hours of each other makes it an exciting day. For me, however, the most interesting and heartening item of the week is not something rare or impressive. Rather it is a species which I see every day, but which now starts to do something joyous. One dull grey morning as I walk along a wooded bank, a song cuts through the mist and stops me in my tracks. "T-toodle-tee-ooo, t-toodle-tee-oo," sings the stormcock, warming up to a song that will cheer our Winter days. To the optimist at least, these few clear notes are the first bars of next May's dawn chorus. Now Winter has come, can Spring be far behind?

12 December

December sees the year come full circle, ready to start anew.

The month opens to increasing cold and cloud, with misty nights and murky days. Large nomadic flocks wander hungrily about the landscape, flying off low as we approach. Excessively fat squirrels scavenge fussily around their territories looking for acorns to tidy up. A week goes by without an hour of sunshine, and we come back from walks with notebooks unopened, glumly shaking our heads.

But by the month-end the mood has changed. Proper winter weather has taken over, with some sharp overnight frosts and brisk bright mornings. The days are beginning to draw out again, and the sun is rising higher. Dippers along the riverside have teamed up into pairs. Hazel catkins have swollen to the brink of bursting open. And on the lifeless-looking honeysuckle vines deep in the woods, the terminal leaf buds are about to unfold.

December 1st – 7th

It is easy to dismiss December as a depressing month. Were it not for Christmas it would be dull and dark indeed. But Nature loves to tease and test us, and if she sends us extra darkness we should turn it to our gain. Wild animals come alive at night more by choice than because of any well-founded fear of persecution. Indeed some of the most persecuted – rabbits, hares and deer – are amongst the more diurnal of mammals. Daylight tends to dazzle the others, but in the quieter cooler hours their acute senses of smell and hearing actually work better than by day.

So far as intelligence, communication and daylight vision are concerned, our own senses are highly refined. It is therefore a salutary experience to go out at night without a torch, and see what use we can make of the rest of our brain. We may surprise ourselves. I remember the satisfaction I felt as a teenager when I walked diagonally across a large rough pasture on a pitch black night, put my hand on the wall at the far side, and lifted my foot onto exactly the same stone that I used for climbing that wall by day.

I have had similar experiences often since then, but I must stress that you should not go wandering about fields at night unless you know them intimately. Apart from the risk of spraining an ankle, or worse, you are likely to fall foul of vigilante patrols. At this time of year in particular, farmers, keepers and foresters are all on the look-out for stock rustlers, pheasant poachers, and holly or Christmas tree thieves.

You may still attract their attention if you park beside one of the quieter country lanes after dark. But so long as it is a public highway you have a perfect right to be there, and it does no harm now and then to deflate the officious. If you can manage to find a deserted lay-by on a little-used back road, switch off the lights, walk away from the vehicle, and let your eyes and ears attune.

While you are waiting, practise sniffing, at whatever comes to hand. When Man first reared up on his back legs and took his nose away from the ground, he chose vision instead of smell as his dominant sense. But our nose goes on recording whether we like it or not, storing tens of thousands of odour images deep within our psyche. An unknown woman puts on a single drop of scent, and hours later as she passes us in the street she evokes memories of a girl who once smelt the same. A connoisseur who noses a wine can discover almost as much about it as a dog nosing a bitch, even though it may not be so vitally interesting.

And so as our eyes adjust to the darkness and our ears to the quiet, we pick out the smell of old bedding muck spread on the fields, of wood smoke, of pine resin, and of wet decaying leaves. Imagine then the world of the fox. His nose works like our ears at a noisy party, recording dozens of sensations at once and selecting those of most interest. It notices not only where a rabbit's foot briefly touched the ground, but is able to ascertain how long ago, what was the sex of the rabbit, and whether it was healthy or sick. Or imagine the world of the owl. Not only can it hear the rustle of a vole in the grass, but it can pin-point the source of the noise to within a couple of inches from dozens of yards away.

It is foxes and owls that we are most likely to hear on these still December nights. Tawny owls will call with gradually increasing gusto throughout Winter, reaching a crescendo in late February when they mate. It has been suggested that one sex calls tu-whit and the other tu-whoo, but I have often heard a single bird call both, as in Shakespeare's merry note. Usually there is a series of kewicks, or tu-whits, with only the occasional hoo-oooo, or tu-whoo.

The little owl is also calling very actively now, mainly at dusk. Like the tawny owl, it is putting up the auditory equivalent of 'Keep Out' signs around its intended breeding territory. Unfortunately many little owls will perish before Spring arrives, especially if there are prolonged frosts. Instead of intensifying, therefore, the characteristically plaintive "piu-piu-piu-piu-piu-piu" calls will progressively diminish as the few survivors are spread ever more thinly through the Dales.

The other call that you can listen for on a December night is the yipping bark of a fox. It is too early yet for foxes to be mating up here, but the dog foxes are marking their boundaries. Keepers will take advantage of this over the next few weeks by using artificial vixen calls to attract dog foxes by night, and then picking them out with spotlights to be shot with rifles. It is a dubious practice, which owes nothing to old-fashioned keepering values. But times must change, and those same traditional values included gin traps, badger tongs, and a bounty on every raptor.

Red
Fox
(Vulpes vulpes)

Foxes use scent as well as sound to make their presence known. If you know the right places to sniff, you can detect the tom-catty whiff of their anal glands and urine. More obviously, if you walk about by day, you will find their dark grey droppings by pathsides. These resemble the faeces of a large cat or small dog, but usually have a distinct tail on the end and almost always contain fur and bones. It is fasci-

nating to study these fox droppings to see what the animal
has been eating, for many items are still identifiable after
passing through the intestine. One deposit which I examine
this week contains part of the skin from a pheasant's leg,
together with bits of feather shaft; separate halves of a
field vole mandible; a single seed from a yew berry; the
remains of some fallen pears from a nearby garden; much
fur, most of it apparently from voles; and several coarse
strands of grass.

Tawny owl pellets yield similarly interesting results, and
can be easily found under evergreen trees throughout most
of Winter. The large numbers of mice, vole and shrew bones
in tawny owl pellets do not necessarily mean that these are
the main items in the diet. If the owl kills a rat or a rabbit,
it will eat only selected soft tissues which leave no residue
in the pellet.

The remains of pheasant in the fox dung probably came
from carrion, for after every weekend the countryside is
littered with unrecovered dying birds. I find one dead, and
take the opportunity to examine its crop. It contains a rich
mixture, with hawthorn berries being the basic ingredient.
A few berries are whole, but many have separated into seeds
and pulp, with the pulp fermenting slightly. Acorns, some
split, some whole, and some still with cup attached, form
the next most common item. And then there are several
of what appear to be very small bluebell bulbs, some roots
and leaves of bulbous buttercup, pignuts, a couple of grey
grubs, and a fat green caterpillar. Where it found the last
is a mystery to me, for I have not seen one for weeks. Even
the foolish pheasant has senses beyond our ken.

The study of pheasant crops, owl pellets and fox dung
allows us to indulge our curiosity on these days when there
is little else to see. We may sometimes learn things that
direct observation would never have taught us. I would
never have suspected that foxes eat yew berries or that
there are green caterpillars to be found in December, were
it not for casual sleuthing on a quiet day.

If you cannot find any pellets or dung, or if you feel that
the expelled contents of another creature's gut hold no
delights for you, there are other diversions you can follow.
Try identifying all the trees that you encounter, now that
there are no leaves or flowers to help you. Or lift a few
stones and fallen logs, albeit ever so carefully, to see what
you can find beneath. If there is not much there, scoop out
a fist-sized hollow and fill it with dead grass. Drop in a few

peanuts before you replace the cover, and you may find an occupant next time.

Nature showered us with gifts when her store-rooms were full. Now that her cupboard is very nearly bare, she expects us to use our initiative and find out things for ourselves.

December 8th – 15th

After ten dull days we long for a change. When old man Winter finally does rear up and bite, it comes almost as welcome relief. It may be suddenly colder, but at least it is clean and bright. And after the fourth or fifth night of freezing fog, it is also incredibly lovely.

The early mornings are best of all. There are pools of fog in the valley, but the air in the hills is sharp and clear. The sun rises through a soft white blanket, not shining but glowing, a perfect circle of fiery red. Every wall top, every blade of grass, every twiglet on every tree, wears a frosted crystal coat. Only the ice-cold river looks black, making a stark and savage contrast with the white lace trees and the ruby sun.

Despite several days and nights of frost, there are some surprising birds to be seen. It is almost as if they are surveying the countryside whilst they are still well-fed, taking note of the soft spots for later. Flocks of two or three dozen lapwings drift over, low and unhurried, going in no particular direction. A grey wagtail flies up the length of a little beck, lingers briefly by its spring, and flies away back down again. Two adult dabchicks turn up on a slow-moving stretch of river, and spend a couple of days diving for crayfish and bullheads. A flock of black-headed gulls, white as ghosts amongst the mist and hoar, roost each night on riverside fence-posts and go off to forage by day.

At the beginning of the week there are fieldfares aplenty, but as the frost bites deeper they become ever more restless. They long since stripped the rowans and the best of the hawthorn berries, but there are haws in abundance on the flatlands still. Gradually the fieldfares begin to separate out from the mixed flocks of winter thrushes and starlings. They gather in the trees as if awaiting a sign, looking marvellously colourful in the slanting sunlight. Then one night they slip away, navigating by starlight over the gathering banks of fog.

Rather surprisingly, the little redwings stay on after most of the fieldfares have gone, though they split up into small bands of a dozen or so. They seem to be able to cope better with holly berries than fieldfares can, despite being almost constantly harried by mistle thrushes as they flit from one stand of hollies to another. Each stormcock spots their intrusion into his domain within a minute or two, and so pesters them with his angry rattling that they grab what they can and move on.

Many other birds are moving away from the Dales now that Winter has truly begun. During an ordinary day's ramble we see barely twenty species. If we take away the half-tame pheasants and mallard, the four common crows, the garden birds around the house, and the mixed parties based on tits, there are precious few others to be seen. There may be little parties of two or four bullfinches on overgrown banks, or wandering bands of greenfinches round riverside gardens. There will be noisy jays in hillside oaks, and the odd kingfisher patrolling the river. There will even be snatches of bird song when the sun breaks through; robins and stormcocks singing simple phrases; starlings pretending to be curlews; and a great tit practising a brief repetitive call-note before closing down for Winter.

Our hardy black rooks are more conspicuous than ever, in fields that are white with hoar. There are flatlands within commuting distance, as the crow flies, if our Dales fields set too hard. But this same hard-frozen ground brings tractors and muck-spreaders out, and there is much in muck that rooks enjoy. Some of the older adults know that if there is a south-facing slope at the foot of a wall, its surface will thaw each day. When other rooks are far away, or when they are pecking at frozen muck in the open field, you will see these wise old birds working alone on these sunny banks, warm and well-fed and perhaps a trifle smug.

The sunny side of a tree trunk is also worth inspection, though there are few birds that can handle the task. To the great spotted woodpecker, however, it is as easy as falling off a log. Live trees are just as welcome as dead ones, for many invertebrates have sought shelter beneath scraps of bark over the last couple of months. The woodpecker simply rips off the scraps to get at its prey, tossing aside the unwanted debris and moving ever upwards. The south sides of large old sycamores show red-brown pathways winding up their trunks, where dusty green flakes have been pulled away to expose the living bark beneath.

Now is also a good time for seeing lesser spotted wood-peckers, which have been hidden by the leaves since Spring.

This week I quite unexpectedly disturb one in the under-growth. It flies onto a birch trunk a few feet away, and we get a good look at one another before it flees to the tree-tops. The pattern of black and white is much finer and closer than in the plumage of its larger cousin, so that it appears rather dull and ordinary to the casual glance.

Although birds can fly away when cold weather strikes, most mammals cannot. Those that could if they wished have chosen to hibernate instead. Fortunately the long nights give the other ones many hours in which to find their food, helping to compensate for the seasonal shortage. Badgers simply stay at home when the ground is frozen, though they come up to the surface to scratch, stretch, and use their latrines. This helps us to check if a sett is occupied, for the presence of considerable deposits in the latrine pits suggests permanent residents rather than passing visitors. We can also look for badger highways. Now that there is no vegetation growing, these paths have become well-worn and obvious, especially near occupied setts.

Badgers do not hibernate for long periods, and rarely stay below ground for more than a few days at a time. Even then they make use of underground latrines as required, and often change their sleeping quarters. Grey squirrels hiber-nate even less than badgers, and will leave their winter dreys within hours of the end of a blizzard. Their ratty footprints are amongst the first to appear on fallen snow. They can be distinguished either by their position – for example along a wall top – or by the brushmarks of the trailing tail.

We see no snow during this present cold spell, though the crusty hoar gives a snow-like effect. Rabbits, many already in pairs again, show up against the white from half a mile away. Red-coated hares would be even more obvious, though there are few to be seen as yet. Except during the hardest of weather, they tend to keep close to cover during daylight in early Winter. Many will still be lying up amongst heather and rushes on the high moor tops, and those that have come down are sheltering in grassy woodland.

In those same deciduous woods the roe deer are becom-ing apparent once more, for their winter pelage is dark olive grey and the cover is sparse and pale. Instead of cutting back behind us through the undergrowth, they now keep well ahead. If you want to be sure of seeing them, you should hide downwind and let a friend walk the wood towards you.

The same longer nights that give nocturnal animals time to feed mean shorter days for the rest of us. By two in the afternoon the sun is already sinking into the haze. The whole western horizon glows with a grey-tinged pink. Flocks of rooks come home to roost; two herons flap slowly across the sky; and a V of geese goes honking past, en route to the Solway Firth. In the garden cock robin picks the last crumbs from the bird table, and thickens his insulation by fluffing out his feathers. It is in this red round form that his lurid image will begin to arrive through the post towards the end of this week. For the shortest day is but a week away, and Christmas is not far behind.

December 16th – 23rd

The weather-glass drops overnight from the 'R' of fair to the 'H' of change. Stone flags that have been frozen for days turn wet with condensation. It begins to drizzle, and a wind picks up. The drizzle turns to steady rain, then sleet, then snow. For a day and a night the ground is white over, but the wind warms up and more rain falls.

Warm rain falling after snow has its usual effect on the river. The water comes roaring down the valley carrying fallen branches and trunks of dead alder. It climbs the steps of bankside cottages but stops just short of their doors. Valley bottom fields are flooded, and hundreds of mallard come flying in to guddle. The thick grassy cover of the river's edge, the sand banks and hidey holes, disappear beneath swirling waters. The entire riparian ecosystem is disrupted, and refugees fall back into the fields and woods.

To chubby little chocolate-brown water voles this is almost routine, and they have safe-houses waiting on higher ground. Waterhens simply move into the nearest patches of rough wet grass, though they cleverly remember to run away from the river instead of towards it when disturbed. Many dippers move up the smaller side streams, but the brightest and best remain by the river. They seem to find easy pickings amongst the flotsam at the high water mark, and take time off to sing their own praises, cock-sure and full of vim. Most of these dippers are already betrothed, and have been left behind to hold the fort whilst their mates seek food up the becks.

Gradually the rain eases and the river subsides, leaving the landscape looking clean and well-scoured. Several pairs of wigeon turn up on the river, mixing with goosander and mallard. Waxwings are reported on ornamental berry bushes in urban gardens. Little flocks of titlarks wander over bleak moor tops, picking tiny pupae from beds of crowberry. And a great northern diver drops in onto an upland reservoir, but is scared off by fishermen during its first weekend.

There are always unusual sightings at this time of year, but in 1990 I encountered a unique combination. A small group of red deer had moved into the area a few days before, and I went up the moor to look for them. It was a misty morning, with a residue of melting snowdrifts making white patterns against the heather and white lines down wall-sides. I settled down with my back against a grouse butt, and scrutinised the opposite slope through the wraiths of clearing mist. Finally I spotted a young stag, seated amongst thick heather, with only his head and antlers showing. Once I had found him it was easier to pick out the others, a brocket and five young hinds, all hidden in coarse ling beneath a scattered stand of rowans.

As I watched the deer, two raptors wheeled into sight over the skyline about a mile away. They worked their way over the moor towards me, long-tailed, long-winged and low-flying, immediately recognizable as harriers. As soon as they moved down into the little valley in front of me I could see their markings. The grey-brown plumage and broad white rump patch confirmed them as hen harriers, either female or juvenile. I had not seen one for years, and had never before seen two together. But even as I thrilled to their performance, quartering that very part of the moor where the deer lay, a much larger raptor drifted into view from the direction whence they had come. I was familiar with black kites in the Tropics, so that the characteristic outline and flight pattern left me in no doubt that this was a red kite, which I had never seen before. As it came closer I could pick out the pale head, bold wing markings, reddish underparts, and broadly-spread tilting tail. It was only when the kite made a pass about 30 yards in front of me that I spotted the identification tags on the leading edge of each wing and the tiny transmitter aerial protruding from its back.

The fact that this was a released introduced bird rather than a stray from Wales was a disappointment, but it was still a memorable sighting. To have hen harriers, red deer and a red kite all in view at once, in the heart of the Yorkshire Dales, is the sort of experience that keeps up our hopes on the least promising of walks.

The deer may have been wanderers from further north, but they were more likely escapees from some flatland deerpark. I was later able to stalk them to within a hundred yards, but when they finally saw me they did not linger. They seemed wonderfully at home bounding away across the heather, and in fact both they and the red kite stayed on for several months. Red deer would thrive in the Dales if poachers would let them, but they can be a nuisance and I am not sure we want them. The same applies to sika deer, which also pass through from time to time. They make a lovely surprise when met by chance – a shaggy-necked red stag looming over a moorland ridge, or a dark little sika grazing amongst sheep by the house at dawn. But like vets, whisky and Santa Claus, they are best received in well-spaced doses.

Towards the end of the week the barometer arm swings right again, the temperature drops, and the skies clear. The rasping calls of partridge cut through the stillness of dawn. A lone and hardy winter moth flutters past the outside light as I chop kindling in the yard. A blue tit calls to the rising sun, "TIT-tuder,TIT-tuder, TIT-tuder,TIT", his last simple song of the year, and possibly the last of his life.

Above the rocky bank below the house, a kestrel hovers. Does he see the flower buds on the gorse as he scowls at the scurrying vole? Certainly the vole is his chief interest, and he drops a few feet for a closer look. But a passing crow has caught him unawares, and he shears away with the carrion in pursuit. Crows have nothing to fear from a kestrel, but they seem to find it diverting to mob any hawk on their patch. Kestrels are particularly noticeable at this time of year, and take the brunt of the aggression. But carrion crows will chase off a peregrine, which is more than their match if it turns, and a carrion mobbed my kite and harriers as I watched them that day on the moor.

All members of the crow family seem to have accepted a policing role, and are always ready to tackle intruders. In this same week in 1989 I watched a sparrowhawk being mobbed in an oak near four jays. The jays at first paid it no attention. The hawk seemed offended by this and launched an attack, splitting them up and driving them off. The jays escaped easily, almost playfully, but quickly re-grouped and returned. They then proceeded to surround the hawk and molest it with little darting attacks. Surprisingly for such raucous birds, they remained silent throughout this onslaught. The only noise came from a kestrel, which spotted the disturbance and circled above the tree on fluttering wings, calling shrilly. It took several minutes before the jays felt that their honour had been restored, and they then let the hawk slip away.

One of the delights of loving Nature is that she can be simultaneously reliable and capricious. We know, for instance, that the first swallows will arrive in the third week of April or that the honeysuckle will open near Midsummer's day. In the pages of this book I have tried to depict the natural cycle as it occurs, in regular predictable sequence. But even when we know what to expect, we do not expect a sighting like the kite flying with harriers or the sparrowhawk mobbed by jays. When I set off for a walk today I wonder if I will match this week's sightings of the previous two years. In the event I see nothing spectacular, for the shortest day is also the dullest, and there is precious little astir.

Ahead of us now is the worst that Winter can send, but from this week onwards the days are growing longer, and hope is growing with them. In ten weeks time the tewits will be back, and we will feel our sap rise with each lift of the wings.

December 24th – 31st

The week begins with typical Christmas weather – cold, wet and windy – and ends with a pinch of frost and a flurry of snow. For many of us this festive break is the first chance we have had for weekday walking since the clocks went back in October. It is wonderful therapy for both body and mind to once again stride out at sunrise. We should grab the chance while we can.

There really is no finer hobby than a study of Nature. Young or old, rich or poor, able bodied or disabled, you can always find something to enjoy. You do not need to be especially fit, for there is a wealth of life in roadside hedges. You do not need lots of fancy equipment, though I have mentioned in this book the bits that I carry. And you do not need to have land of your own, for the wildlife belongs to no man.

Much of the Dales landscape is owned by hand-me-down brass, and has been since the Norman conquest. We live at the mercy of landed nobles, ideally both benevolent and absent. To possess a piece of the land we love, the land we have helped to shape, would be to realise an ancestral ambition. But if bits of these estates ever came up for sale, they would not stay long with dalesfolk. Urban name-your-pricers would buy them as retirement toys, and the 'Keep Out' signs would be up within days.

As things are, a few friendly farmers and tolerant game-keepers put up with me traipsing about where they would not want crowds to wander. This gives me a slight advantage over the casual visitor, though most of my rambles follow well-worn rights of way. Four of the seven badger setts on my home patch are within a few dozen yards of public paths, though I doubt if one walker in a hundred notices what they are. Half of the woods have trails running through them, the river has footpaths along one or both banks for most of its length, and much of the moor is a public access area.

There are not many places in the Dales that are more than a mile or two from a right of way. All the habitat types and ecological niches can somewhere be reached by a path. And at this time of year, when the trees are bare and the under-growth has died back, our eyes can wander even where our feet may not tread.

Thus as we pass through thick woodland, we are no longer hemmed in by a tangle of bracken and bramble. Now we can not only spot the roe deer as they bob away between the trees, but still see them when they pause to turn. Within the next few days the increase in day length will register on the pineal body in the base of the doe's brain, and set off a chain reaction that will start the development of her dormant embryonic twins. The new life will take root on the day that the new year opens, but will not emerge from the womb until there are bluebells and garlic on this bare floor, and sun-dappled verdure above.

The stoat is another animal which uses delayed implan-tation to carry a promise through Winter. The gap between mating and birth in stoats may be as long as nine months, though the actual developmental period is less than one. It is when the vegetation is low and bare, as now, that we have the best chance of seeing a stoat hunting. If we are lucky it may even be a white stoat, or at least a parti-coloured one. In Scotland most turn white for Winter – except for their black tail tips – and in southern England few do. Here in the Dales about half make some change in most years, though it is unusual to get an unblemished ermine.

Today I see no stoat, but I do find evidence of his passing. Near the wood gate there is a dead rabbit, with most of the meat trimmed neatly off its bones, and with its brains eaten out through a hole behind its ear. It is popularly supposed that a rabbit freezes petrified when pursued by a stoat, but in fact that is only the final stage of the hunt. A stoat will chase a running rabbit across open ground, moving with a surprising turn of speed. If it loses sight of its prey, it will follow it by scent like a dog. Eventually the rabbit crouches exhausted, unable to hide and yet fearing to be trapped below ground. In the final seconds it screams in terror, but the end is mercifully swift. If you disturb a stoat at a fresh kill, you will find that the neck is dislocated, and that the bite mark behind the ear penetrates through the skull and into the brain. The site of these bite marks beside the carotid artery has given rise to the story that stoats suck blood, which is not strictly true.

Although the want of cover in woodland helps us to spot wildlife between the trees, the same baldness in grassland means that there are few animals to be found there. Virtually the only cover in our pastures now is along the hedge sides and on the slopes that run down to streams. At this time of year it pays to go from wood to wood following becks and rivers, for the moors and fields yield little.

Watercourses have a rich and varied wildlife at any time, but are particularly rewarding now when cover is sparse. The riverside ponds left by last week's floods have bullheads and minnows, and egg-bearing crayfish. Many trout are up side-streams breeding, leaving grayling to frolic in their vacated domains. Grayling and trout are both members of the salmon family, and compete with each other for food. When the river was stocked with larger farm-bred trout, the grayling began to decline. But anglers changed to larger hooks to catch these larger trout, and the smaller-mouthed grayling would not take these lures. Thus fewer were caught and the population rose again, in one of those cycles so typical of Nature. I much prefer to see a grayling than a trout. In the water it appears the paler of the two, with more clearly marked scales and large red fins. In the hand it has a lovely silvery sheen, and a faint fishy smell of wild thyme.

The breeding trout are no longer congregated around the beck-ends, and the goosanders have dispersed along the river. Adult males began to arrive a few days ago, and are busy looking for mates. As they whizz up and down the river showing themselves off, their plumage looks smartly pied, more white than black. It is only when seen through binoculars on a sunny day that their true pinks and greens become apparent.

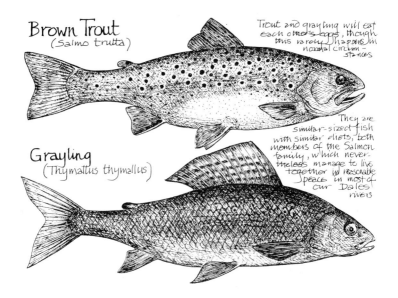

Brown Trout
(Salmo trutta)

Trout and grayling will eat each other's eggs, though this rarely happens in normal circumstances

Grayling
(Thymallus thymallus)

They are similar-sized fish with similar diets, both members of the Salmon family, which nevertheless manage to live together in reasonable peace in most of our Dales rivers

Goosanders and fish are predictable enough sightings on our winter walks by the river, but we can expect surprises too. In the stand of alder and willow where Kexbeck meets the river, I find two willow tits in a mixed flock. Under the patronage of hardier members they have followed the flock upstream from their usual haunts, though they will run back down at the first hint of frost. Nearby I catch a tantalizing glimpse of a little black water shrew, as it crosses a drift of bare sand into the base of some tussocky grass. I pause to see if it will pop back out, but am greeted instead by that feather-mouse, the wren.

Wrens flock to riversides in Winter, and look strangely at home on the water's edge. Although both water shrews and wrens feel at ease beside water, they are by no means constrained to that medium. Wrens may be found on the highest moorland, even in December, and in the hardest weather they will sleep each night in cowsheds. Water shrews will also enter farm buildings, and my mother once caught one in a mousetrap in her flag-floored kitchen, apparently in search of dripping.

Although water shrews – and wrens – will take cheese, they will both eat anything they can overpower in the wild. I have a photograph of a Guyanese house wren with a lizard in its beak, and Konrad Lorenz once fed a live water shrew to a snake, only to find it eating the snake when he returned. However both species are mainly insectivorous, and it is because there are so few insects about now that they tend to gather round buildings. The dung beetle, digging in deeper for Winter, is one of the few insects still active, though we may see gnats dance on mild calm days.

Yet even as most animals are addressing themselves to the prospect of hard weather, we can see the first heralds of Spring's sweet smile. In the fields, scattered tufts of white fur show where hares and rabbits have begun fighting for mates. Beside rabbit scrats and badger latrines in the woods, the unearthed bluebell bulbs have shoot tips already growing. Wood-edge hazels are hung with plump heavy catkins, and the honeysuckle vines that twist up their trunks have buds that are showing green.

And as this old year prepares to cede its crown to the new, we once again set our own foundations for Winter. There are cheering rites and Rabelaisian consumption, all trimmed about with tradition. The cake and mince pies home-baked with love; the holly picked within sight of our house; the Christmas tree and pheasants from local woods; the beer brewed near Leeds and the venison raised near Sheffield; carols on tape from the Huddersfield Choral Society: all these make for a really Great Yorkshire Christmas.

There is a fine line between patriotism and bigotry. But if you are able to be as proud of your own customs as you are tolerant of others', then it is grand to be Yorkshire, and a dalesman at that.

Index